Free Negro Labor and Property Holding in Virginia, 1830-1860

LUTHER PORTER JACKSON

Southern Historical Press, Inc.
Greenville, South Carolina

This volume was reproduced from
a personal copy located in the
Publisher's private Library

All rights reserved. No part of this publication may be reproduced,
stored in a retrieval system, transmitted in any form, posted
on to the web in any form or by any means without
the prior written permission of the publisher.

Please direct all correspondence and orders to:
www.southernhistoricalpress.com
or
**SOUTHERN HISTORICAL PRESS, Inc.
PO Box 1267
375 West Broad Street
Greenville, SC   29601**
southernhistoricalpress@gmail.com

Originally published: 1942
Copyright 1942 by The American Historical Assoc.
ISBN #0-89308-859-5
All rights Reserved.
Printed in the United States of America

TO

MY DEAR WIFE

JOHNNELLA FRAZER JACKSON

PREFACE

For aid in the preparation of this volume the author wishes to extend thanks especially to the Social Science Research Council for a grant of three hundred dollars and to Mr. Morgan P. Robinson, archivist of the Virginia State Library, and his staff of assistants. Without the ready assistance and spirit of helpfulness exhibited by these persons this study would not have been possible. Special acknowledgement is also due the many city and county clerks of Virginia whose local archives were freely opened to the author, and to Mrs. Elizabeth H. Buck of Washington, D. C., whose editorial suggestions have been extremely helpful.

I wish also to thank Dean James Hugo Johnston, Miss Felicia D. Anderson, Mrs. Otelia S. Howard, and Mrs. Helen E. Baker of the Virginia State College, Petersburg, for their willing assistance, and Miss Theresa D. Hodges, librarian, McKenney Library, Petersburg, for the use of the newspaper collection at that library.

LUTHER P. JACKSON

Virginia State College
Petersburg, Virginia

Introduction

The free Negro in Virginia before the Civil War was a by-product of slavery. During one period he was granted certain civil rights and had many economic opportunities; at another period these rights were withdrawn and the opportunities were diminished. The span of time in which the free Negro is thought to have suffered the most severe restrictions is that treated in this study, from 1830 to 1860. During this period limitations were many, but they were largely legal and political. Favorable economic conditions mitigated the force of the law and enabled the free Negroes to advance along with the general upward movement in the state. The advancement made by the free Negro, in spite of the law, is the theme of this study.

In 1830 there were 47,348 free Negroes in Virginia; by 1860 there were 58,042 such persons, the majority of whom were descendants of Negroes manumitted during the liberal period of the American Revolution.[1] Sixty per cent of the state's 58,042 free Negroes were classified by the United States census as black; the remaining 40 per cent were classified as mulatto. Females constituted practically 52 per cent of the group, and the free Negro element amounted to 12 per cent of the black population and 3.6 per cent of the total population.

The free Negro element in Virginia was always relatively large. In 1790 and 1800 Virginia led all the states in number of free Negroes; in 1830 and again in 1860 it held second place. At this last date the number of free Negroes in Virginia

---

[1] The term *Virginia* as used in this study is restricted to the limits of present-day Virginia. The 2,764 free Negroes in the region that is now West Virginia are not included. The free Negro population of Virginia in 1860 for the purposes of this study, then, is considered to be 55,278 rather than 58,042.

was almost as great as the entire number of blacks in New York and New England combined. In fact, one-eighth of all the free Negroes in the nation lived in Virginia. The only state which exceeded the Old Dominion in number of free Negroes was Maryland. This numerical superiority in free Negroes makes Virginia an ideal state in which to investigate the facts of labor and property among the members of this class. Findings for Virginia, by reason of its size, may furnish an index to what the free Negro was doing all over the South and perhaps throughout the nation.

Free Negroes lived in each of the ninety-seven counties and the ten or more cities of Virginia, with the largest number in the Tidewater and a lesser number in the West. They were most numerous in the Tidewater counties of Prince George, Sussex, Surry, Nansemond, Southampton, Norfolk, Accomac, and Northampton. In 1860 these last two counties, on the Eastern Shore, contained 4,380—about 7.5 per cent of the entire free Negro population of the state. Another large block lived in the five counties of the Northern Neck and still another in five counties of northern Virginia: Fairfax, Prince William, Fauquier, Loudon, and Frederick. Although free Negroes were numerous in certain counties, the urban regions, with 20 per cent of the total free Negro population, were the places of greatest concentration. The 3,244 free Negroes living in Petersburg in 1860 constituted more than 5 per cent of the whole number in the state.

Study of the labor of free Negroes presents no unusual difficulties; contemporary printed materials and accessible manuscript data yield sufficient information. To investigate the Negroes' ownership of property, however, involves racial identification and the resort to many different by-paths in an effort to arrive at the facts.

The basic data on the ownership of property by free Negroes are found in two sources, the original returns of the United States census at Washington, and the tax books of each of the counties and cities of Virginia in the state archives at Richmond. The tax books are divided into two large collections, which are frequently called "Land" and "Personal Property." In the state archives also are the original agricultural census returns of each of the counties and the many manuscript petitions to the legislature, on behalf of free Negroes, from counties and cities all over the state.[2] Unlike the other sources named, the petitions give information on property holding only incidentally. At each of the offices of the county and city clerks there are certain collateral sources —numerous deed books, will books, order books, and registers of free Negroes and mulattoes—which contain a type of information not found in the material in the state archives.

Sources of information concerning property ownership are thus reasonably abundant, but identification of the free Negro owners in a long list of owners presents a problem. Despite this difficulty, the validity of any discussion of the subject depends on the proper identification of race, so that no white person may inadvertently be classified as a free Negro. The several sources named above must be evaluated with reference to the extent to which they indicate race and to which their data on property ownership is accurate.

The original census returns are excellent for the determination of race but unsatisfactory with respect to property. They are, however, indispensable in this study because of the several different types of information to be found in them. These census returns present the names of all heads of families and all members of each family, with a statement of the race, age, color, sex, and occupation of each of these persons.[3] Such ma-

---

[2] The personal property books and the petitions give useful information concerning labor as well as property. In the years 1815 and 1851 the commissioner of revenue in each city or county was required by law to submit for his district a list of all free Negroes over the age of twelve, with a statement of the occupation of each. This was done in most cases, and with a fair degree of completeness.

[3] The 1830 census is less detailed than the 1860 census. It gives the number of persons in each family but the names only of heads of families. Furthermore it gives no information on property ownership. Carter G. Woodson's *Free Negro Heads of Families in 1830*, a compilation from this census, is very useful in checking names with other sources.

terial is very useful for checking other sources. The unsatisfactory character of these records appears in the two columns given to ownership of property, real and personal. In many cases persons are listed as having real estate of a certain value when actually they owned no real estate whatever. On the other hand, the names of persons who did own real property are sometimes not included in these records. Also, in the many instances in which property ownership is shown, the valuation of such property by the census enumerator is at variance with that made by state and local officials. This discrepancy is common to the records of all cities and counties. New Kent County furnishes a good example of variation, as the following table indicates.

State and Federal Valuation of Property, New Kent County

Name	Real Estate—State Value	Real Estate—Federal Value
Robert Burgoine	$200	$300
Nancy Bailey	176	—
John Baker	295	500
William B. Dixon	—	500
W. H. Dixon	—	960
Beverly Dixon	178	—
Patty Granger	140	—
James Jennings	—	250
Janett Johnson	358	—
Carter Lewis	457	1200
William Lewis	378	—
Thomas Meekins	—	400
William Osborne	—	700
William H. Patterson	147	1500
Thomas Pearman	800	500

In this incomplete list of fifteen persons, five are shown as owning property according to the federal enumeration, but not by the state; five are shown as owning according to the state, but not by the federal returns. The remaining five are rated by both as having property, but the value varies widely. In four instances the federal valuation is greater than the state's; in one instance the state valuation is greater than the federal. In this conflict the state authorities are probably more reliable than the federal, because the enumeration of property ownership in the land books was an annual duty imposed upon each of the local subdivisions of the state with the object of determining the amount of taxes to be paid by each property owner. The federal record of property ownership, on the other hand, was perhaps based on a hurried interview and the acceptance of any statement made by the person interviewed. The state and local records should be more accurate, also, because local officials checked upon one another's statements, and the state auditor at Richmond made still further investigations. He regularly issued instructions and criticized the land reports of the local officials.[4]

On the whole the state land books give a reliable record of property, yet the classification of property owners by race in these volumes is haphazard. Before 1891 in Virginia the use of racial labels was optional with state and local officials: some indicated race; some did not.[5] The failure to indicate race consistently in this set of records is partially offset, however, by the indication of race in the personal property books. Complete lists of the free Negroes living in a given county or

[4] The manuscript collection, Letters of the Commissioners of Revenue to the State Auditor, in the Virginia State Library, contains much correspondence on the subject of accuracy in the reporting of land ownership.

The inaccuracy of federal census statements on the ownership and value of property is revealed also by the deed books at the clerks' offices. In every instance in which the federal census lists as a property owner a person whose name is not given in the state land books, the writer has found no such person recorded in the deed books as owning the real estate in question. On the other hand, in practically all cases, the state enumeration in the land books can be quickly traced in the deed books or will books of the proper county or city. The writer has examined hundreds of such cases scattered over forty or more counties and cities.

[5] The mandatory listing of land ownership according to race was begun in the state of Georgia in 1871. Up to the present time Virginia and Georgia are the only states that list white and Negro land owners separately.

city are frequently found in the personal property records, for the capitation tax, for personal property, or merely for occupation.

The deficiency of the land books in reference to race is further offset by various other sources. The "Register of Free Negroes and Mulattoes" found in certain clerks' offices not only indicates race but furnishes some genealogical data as well. Order books regularly indicate race; deeds and wills frequently do likewise. In sum, then, racial identity can be determined eventually in almost all cases. For about fifteen counties, recourse to these by-paths is unnecessary, for the land books use the racial label consistently, with such symbols as "F.N." (free Negro), "F.C." (free colored), "F.B." (free black), or simply "Negro," "colored," "mulatto," and "black." Many other local units outside of these fifteen counties occasionally indicated race in their land books.

The term "property" as used in this study includes only those items that were subject to state taxation. In rural property the principal items of real estate were acres of land and buildings; in town property the principal items were houses and lots. Taxable personal property in 1860 included the following: slaves; horses, mules, asses, and jennets; cattle, sheep, and hogs; pleasure carriages, stage coaches, jersey wagons, carryalls, buggies, gigs; gold watches, silver and other metallic watches, metallic clocks, other clocks; pianos and harps; plate; household and kitchen furniture; other articles of personal property; solvent bonds; and capital invested in a manufacturing or other unlicensed trade or business.

This study presents a complete and accurate statement of real estate holdings only, and for two years only, 1830 and 1860. The aim throughout is to note what progress free Negroes made in property holding and what gains they made in the field of labor in the state. If they found opportunities in labor they would presumably show this good fortune in the acquisition of property. On this account, labor and property are treated together in this study.

Free Negroes held property in Virginia even as early as the seventeenth century. During the decade of 1650, for example, three free Negroes came into possession of land through the head right system: Anthony Johnson of Northhampton County acquired 250 acres of land for the transportation of five persons into the colony; Richard Johnson of the same county acquired a hundred acres for the transportation of two persons; and Benjamin Doll of Surry County gained three hundred acres for the transportation of six persons.[6] Other instances of this kind may have occurred throughout this century and on through the eighteenth, but it was not until the nineteenth century that property holding by free Negroes assumed appreciable proportions. This study rests on the theory that the total property held in 1830, however small, was at least as great as that in any preceding year in the history of the free Negro in Virginia. The year 1830, then, may well serve as the base line for a discussion of the thirty years which follow.

[6] Land Office, State Capitol, Patents (ms.), 1643-1651, no. 2, p. 326; 1652-1655, no. 3, p. 294; no. 4, p. 47.

Contents

	PAGE
PREFACE	vii
INTRODUCTION	ix

CHAPTER
I.	THE FREE NEGRO IN A PROSLAVERY SOCIETY	3
II.	THE ECONOMIC REVIVAL AND THE ELEMENT OF LABOR	34
III.	THE FREE NEGRO AT WORK	70
IV.	THE FREE NEGRO FARMER AND PROPERTY OWNER	102
V.	THE CITY PROPERTY OWNER	137
VI.	FROM SLAVERY TO FREEDOM IN URBAN VIRGINIA	171
VII.	PROPERTY IN SLAVES	200

BIBLIOGRAPHY	230
APPENDIX I. Free Negro Owners of Property, Petersburg, 1860	239
APPENDIX II. Free Negro Owners of 100 or More Acres	247
INDEX	253

Tables

		PAGE
	State and Federal Valuation of Property, New Kent County	xii
I.	Slaves in Richmond Factories, 1846	55
II.	Employers of Free Negroes and Slaves, Loudon County, 1851	75
III.	Occupations of Free Negroes in Prince Edward County, 1851	78
IV.	Occupations of Free Negroes in Mecklenburg County, 1851	82
V.	Percentage Distribution of Sexes in Certain Cities in 1860	92
VI.	Occupations of Free Negro Heads of Families in Petersburg, 1860	98
VII.	Petitions for Certain Industrious Free Negroes	100
VIII.	Types of the Farm Population	106
IX.	Acquisition of Property, Sussex County	117
X.	Free Negro Ownership of Town Lots	138
XI.	Property Owners, Petersburg, 1830	139
XII.	Manumission in Cities	174
XIII.	Slaves Who Purchased Themselves	184
XIV.	Manumission of Slave Relatives by Free Negroes of Richmond	188
XV.	Free Negro Slaveholders in Counties in 1830	205

Free Negro Labor
and Property Holding in Virginia,
1830-1860

CHAPTER I

THE FREE NEGRO IN A PROSLAVERY SOCIETY

A STANDING problem with the free Negro before the Civil War was the fact that he lived in a society intended for two classes only—free whites and Negro slaves. The slaves created one problem for the whites; the free Negroes another. There were at times certain objections to slavery: slaves were too numerous, work for them was insufficient, or the slave system did not fit into the economy of a particular region. If, however, public opinion in Virginia was occasionally critical of slavery, it was always hostile to the free Negro.[1] With the course of years this adverse sentiment became increasingly apparent. During the generation preceding the Civil War the drive against the free Negro was at its height and became so intense that he was branded as the pariah of society.[2]

This hostility toward the free Negro in Virginia was expressed in law, in politics, in literature, and in action by organized groups. The state legislature and the local units of government heaped up laws to restrain him, and candidates for office, governors, mayors, and other officials condemned him. Similarly, the proslavery writers vilified free Negroes, and the American Colonization Society made every effort to get them out of Virginia into Africa.

The laws concerning the free Negro touched many aspects of his life. First there were those that established his rela-

---

[1] Early L. Fox, *The American Colonization Society, 1817-1840*, ch. 1.
[2] Ulrich B. Phillips, *Life and Labor in the Old South*, p. 171; James C. Ballagh, *A History of Slavery in Virginia*, p. 146.

tionship with the government. He might not vote, hold office, sit on juries, bear witness against a white man, nor, after 1832, enjoy trial by jury. In punishment for some crimes the law inflicted upon him a heavier sentence than upon a white man and afforded him less protection than it gave to a slave. Another law required that the free Negro establish or prove his free status. Since all Negroes were presumably slaves, he was compelled to register with the court periodically and keep in his possession at all times a duplicate copy of his register. Failure to carry out this regulation involved a jail sentence and the imposing of a fine toward the payment of jail fees. If any offender was unable to pay the jail fees he was hired out to some employer at the minimum wage of ten cents a day.[3] Free Negroes who came into a community without written evidence of their freedom were also frequently given jail sentences.[4]

In addition to the state laws restricting free Negroes, municipalities imposed their own regulations. For example, Petersburg enacted the following ordinances: anyone employing a free Negro without his register should be fined $5 for each offense; any free Negro not having his register should also be fined $5 for each offense; and any free Negro who came into the city and resided more than two months without making application for his register should be treated as a vagrant.[5]

One of the most severe restrictions on members of this group was the law forbidding them to move from place to place freely. Under this system a free Negro might not go from one county or town to another seeking employment without having a copy of his register made especially for

[3] The minute books and order books in county and city clerks' offices show many such cases. See, for example, Minute Book, Hustings Court, Petersburg, 1853-1856, pp. 17, 307, 349. In one of these cases James Valentine was hired out by the jailer to pay his jail fees of $3.10.

[4] A typical experience was that of a Negro sailor from New York on the occasion of his arrival in Petersburg, as reported in *Niles Register,* Sept. 2, 1826.

[5] *Charter and Laws of the City of Petersburg,* pp. 76-77.

the county to which he was going.[6] At a later period free Negroes were denied altogether the right to change their residence unless given previous permission by the authorities of the county or corporation in which they were seeking residence.[7] Finally, for a brief period they were forbidden to go from one county to the next even though they had their "free papers." A good example of the effect of these handicaps is furnished by the case of Henry Mason, a highly skilled bricklayer of Petersburg. Because there existed a much greater demand for his trade in Richmond than in Petersburg, he went to the capital and secured regular employment. In accordance with the law, however, Mason was ordered to leave Richmond and return to Petersburg.[8] In all probability there were many similar cases.

In the nineteenth century the prevailing attitude toward the free Negroes in Virginia was that either they should be expelled or their number should be kept as small as possible. In common with the rest of the nation, Virginia during the Revolutionary period had embraced the doctrine of the rights of man. The acceptance of this doctrine had led in turn to a wholesale manumission of slaves and to the admission of free Negroes into Virginia from other states. By 1790, how-

[6] Register of Free Negroes and Mulattoes (ms.), Hustings Court, Petersburg. Several volumes. These registers show hundreds of cases in which free Negroes were allowed to take up residence in Petersburg, but in each case the statement is made that the free Negro in question has been duly registered in the court of some particular county or town.

[7] On the whole, the cities of Virginia were liberal in permitting free Negroes to come in, but there were periods when such permission was sharply restricted. An example is an order of the Petersburg court that the delegate from that city to the legislature seek to procure the passage of an act enabling the local court to refuse to register free Negroes and mulattoes unless such persons had been born within the limits of the town. Minute Book, 1848-1851, p. 102. Three years later, however, this same court ordered about a hundred free Negroes from other districts to be registered. In each instance the court was "satisfied by certificate of registry from other courts in the State, or by other satisfactory evidence." Minute Book, 1851-1853, p. 31.

[8] Virginia State Library, Legislative Petitions (mss.), Henrico County, Dec. 22, 1847. In subsequent footnotes, petitions to the state legislature are listed by county and date, omitting reference to Virginia State Library, Legislative Petitions.

ever, a reaction had developed, which soon led to a reversal of this humanitarian policy. In 1793 legislative action made it unlawful for free Negroes to come into Virginia and instituted the system of requiring the registration of the many already in the state.

The most severe attempt to check the increase in the Virginia free Negro population consequent on manumission was the well-known law of 1806: "Any slave hereafter emancipated who shall remain within the commonwealth more than twelve months shall forfeit all such right, and may be apprehended and sold by the overseers of the poor of any county or corporation in which he shall be found for the benefit of the poor of such county or corporation." [9] This statute, with some modification, remained in force until 1865. Its later modification brought about a system whereby manumitted slaves might get special permission from the local court to stay in Virginia if they had performed some act of "extraordinary merit," or if they were persons of "good character, sober, peaceable, orderly, and industrious." This banishment law afforded a continuous battleground between those who advocated its non-enforcement in particular cases and those who stood for its execution regardless of the circumstances. Its operation is of great significance in this study in that the demand for labor and the ownership of property by free Negroes often stood as barriers to its enforcement. Practically all the statutes and points of view noted above were in operation before 1830. After this time the attitude of the dominant race became still more hostile. The underlying spirit of the new day led to a demand for the enforcement of all the old laws and for the making of other laws as well.

The new conditions faced by the free Negro were closely related to the still larger problem of the Negro slave. Generally speaking, despite the existence of antislavery views here and there, the South ranks in history as a region that was

[9] *Virginia Statutes-at-Large,* new series, 3:252 (1803-1808).

always proslavery. The intensity of this proslavery feeling, however, varied from time to time. The latest studies of the subject indicate that the period from 1790 to 1820 may be called the period of quiescence, a time when this region, although proslavery, was rather passively so. The Missouri Compromise, however, awakened a militant attitude toward slavery; and from the time of its adoption until the Civil War, Southern leaders embarked upon what amounted to a literary crusade in defense of their "peculiar institution." In these later years slavery became to them a positive good.[10]

After a short delay, Virginia swung over into the proslavery ranks about 1830 and, like the rest of the South, pronounced the institution a blessing to all concerned. The commonwealth had previously been especially quiescent; its western half, and occasionally even its eastern half, had shown some antislavery tendencies. Virginia had faced all of the positive and negative arguments on the slave question; her final proslavery decision emerged with two epochal events of the years from 1829 to 1832: the constitutional convention of 1829-1830 and the legislative session of 1831-1832. At this time, among the various political and constitutional problems that faced the state, slavery loomed so large that the four-year period in question has become known as the period of slavery agitation in Virginia history.[11]

In the minds of the men of western Virginia, the possible abolition of slavery was a leading reason for calling the constitutional convention; yet the institution remained intact, for the westerners were shown that slavery might very soon come to their section and bring with it profit.[12] The subject of slavery arose again in the following year, however, because of the Nat Turner slave insurrection in Southampton

---

[10] William S. Jenkins, *Pro-Slavery Thought in the Old South*, pp. 48 ff.; William B. Hesseltine, "Some New Aspects of the Pro-Slavery Argument," in *Journal of Negro History*, 21: 1-14 (Jan., 1936).

[11] Cf. Theodore M. Whitfield, *Slavery Agitation in Virginia, 1829-1832*.

[12] Hesseltine, "Aspects of the Pro-Slavery Argument," in *Journal of Negro History*, 21: 13, citing Charles H. Ambler, *History of West Virginia*, pp. 221 ff.

County, and was passed on to the legislature of 1831–1832, this time in its most virulent form.

Brought face to face with the Southampton massacre, the governing authorities took quick action. Governor Floyd attributed the uprising to the influence of "unrestricted fanatics" from neighboring states and to the work of Negro preachers. To solve the problem he recommended three measures: silencing the Negro preachers, enacting laws to keep the slaves in greater subordination, and removing from the commonwealth the free people of color.[13] In the midst of this excitement the people deluged the legislature with petitions and memorials, which one student of Virginia history classifies under three heads: those asking for the removal of the free Negroes from the state, those asking an amendment to the federal constitution to give Congress power to appropriate funds for purchasing Negro slaves and transporting the colored population from the United States, and those urging the state to devise some scheme for gradual emancipation.[14]

The first class of these petitions—those asking for the removal of the free Negroes from the state—is of chief concern in this work. These petitions represent the views of those Virginians who firmly advocated slavery and the promotion of a program to make slavery secure. Such documents came only from the counties of the Tidewater and the Piedmont, the proslavery sections of the state. The petitions of the second and third class, on the other hand, came largely from the people of the Valley and of the Piedmont foothills.[15]

Among these petitions for abolition and gradual emancipation may be mentioned those from Augusta, Loudon, and Caroline counties. The Augusta petition, which was signed

[13] *Journal of House of Delegates,* 1831–1832, pp. 5–14.
[14] Charles H. Ambler, *Sectionalism in Virginia from 1776 to 1861,* p. 189.
[15] *Ibid.* Ambler states that only two petitions—from Caroline and Charles City—from the Tidewater favored emancipation. The Charles City petition came from the Quakers.

by 343 women, asked for the immediate abolition of slavery. The Loudon petition declared that a continuation of slavery was "forbidden by the true policy of Virginia; repugnant to her political theory and Christian profession; and an opprobrium to our ancient and renowned Dominion"; the petitioners therefore favored a gradual emancipation and removal of the slaves.[16] The main argument of the Caroline petition was that in the territory east of the Blue Ridge the blacks were gaining on the whites and that in consequence many of the commonwealth's "most industrious and enterprising people" were seeking new homes in distant states. In view of this fact the Caroline antislavery group recommended that the state should at least remove the annual increase of the 4,189 slaves and should also provide for the removal of the free blacks.[17]

Though many Virginians thus stood for the abolition of slavery at the time of the constitutional convention, the legislature of 1831–1832 failed to act to this end, mainly because slaves were property and slavery was so closely integrated with the economic system of the state. A further obstacle to abolition was the inability of the legislators to agree on what to do with the slaves after emancipation.

Slavery came through unscathed, yet the opposition to it was so strong that, to silence the antislavery forces, something more than mere legislative action was necessary: a campaign of proslavery education and the formulation of a proslavery philosophy. This teaching emerged at once from Thomas R. Dew of William and Mary College, and in due time from George Fitzhugh, Alfred Bledsoe, Thornton Stringfellow, and Edmund Ruffin—all Virginians. In common with the proslavery thought of the entire South, the arguments of these men attempted a justification of slavery on moral, scriptural, and ethnological grounds and were supported by reference to history—ancient, medieval, and

[16] *Ibid.*, citing *Washington and Lee Historical Papers*, no. 5, p. 84.
[17] Petition, Caroline, Jan. 20, 1832.

modern—and to the Constitution of the United States.

The proslavery leaders contended that the slave of the South was in far better case than the hireling of the North, that slave labor was superior to free labor, and finally, above all else, that slavery was justified in view of the depraved condition of the slave's racial brother, the free Negro. Slavery, not freedom, was the normal condition for the Negro. Further to prove that freedom for the Negro was undesirable, they pointed to the results of abolition in the West Indies.[18] Among all these writers, it is safe to say that Dew in his *Review of the Debate in the Virginia Legislature of 1831 and 1832* did most to lead opinion in Virginia to the proslavery view already accepted in the lower South.[19] Speaking of the free blacks, he said:

> Taken as a whole class . . . they must be considered the most worthless and indolent of the citizens of the United States. It is well known that throughout the whole extent of our union they are looked upon as the very drones and pests of society.[20]

The proslavery forces were intensely hostile to the free Negro; indeed, the more that Virginians were won over to the proslavery view, the more did the opposition to the free Negro increase. After the long and bitter legislative debate in the memorable session of 1831–1832, the general concensus of opinion was that the real menace in Virginia was not the slave but the free Negro. In this connection Dew reported that "some looked to the removal of the free people of color by the efforts of the Colonization Society" as the one great cure for all their "ills."[21] Many of the legislators wholeheartedly supported the effort to banish this undesirable element.[22] The proslavery forces won the legislative contest partly because the cost of abolishing slavery would be

---

[18] Jenkins, *Pro-Slavery Thought*, p. 105.
[19] William E. Dodd, *The Cotton Kingdom*, pp. 49–53.
[20] Thomas R. Dew, *Review of the Debate on the Abolition of Slavery in the Virginia Legislature of 1831 and 1832*, pp. 88–95, 246.
[21] *Ibid.*, p. 6.   [22] Whitfield, *Slavery Agitation*, p. 82.

very great, whereas the cost of disposing of the free Negro would be small. The cost in his case would be only that of removal; to free the slaves, on the other hand, would involve not only the cost of removal but also the reimbursement of their owners at about $400 for each slave.

The shift of legislative attention from slaves to free Negroes appeared all the more inviting since it was felt that the free Negroes would be only too glad to leave the state and that they would otherwise "tax the capacity of the system." [23] One member of the legislature advanced the view that "we will not force the free Negroes to go but they will go." He felt that when the means of their removal were provided they would "be expelled by that mighty influence, public opinion, and that without cruelty and injustice." [24] This change of emphasis from one class to the other was grounded on the belief that slavery was the natural lot of the Negro and that in order to impress him with this fact a dreadful example must be made of the free Negro. The free element of the black race must now become the scapegoat. Cotton culture in the lower South and the arguments of the proslavery leaders had guaranteed the existence of slavery, but this very fact made the position of the free blacks almost untenable.

The crystallizing of public opinion concerning the free Negro in Virginia serves to give the period from 1830 to 1860 a setting distinct from any previously known. Restraining laws had been heaped upon the free Negro before, but now there were to be more of them; the people had talked expulsion of the whole group before, but now they were to put the legislative wheels in motion toward that end; the Colonization Society had succeeded in transporting a few free Negroes before, but now it was to redouble its efforts. In sum, the free Negro in Virginia was doomed to adversity.[25]

Virginia hostility to the free Negro may be indicated by further reference to the many petitions with which the peo-

[23] *Ibid.,* p. 95.   [24] *Ibid.,* p. 101.
[25] Carter G. Woodson, *The Negro in Our History* (6th ed.), p. 279.

ple flooded the legislature, especially in the session of 1831–1832, urging the removal of free Negroes from the state. Naturally the Virginia branch of the American Colonization Society took the lead in this effort and stood ready to advance the programs of all other petitioning groups in so far as its funds would allow. Relief was sought either in financial aid from the state to the Colonization Society or in independent action by the state itself. The colonizationists felt that the state was obligated to do something, since the law of 1806 had merely directed recently emancipated slaves to leave Virginia without providing for them any definite destination. Further, the colonizationists argued that the state government should assist them because the legislature during the decade of 1820 had officially approved their organization.

Colonization as an organized movement had been in existence for ten or more years prior to 1831. During the decade ending in 1830 the society had sent from Virginia only 575 emigrants,[26] but now it felt that the number might be greatly increased. On this subject one member of the legislature of 1831 wrote: "The horrible affair of Southampton has given rise to new and decided feeling in the breast of Virginians from every part of the State in regard to the black population, and the friends of colonization may now find willing and anxious agents to push to the utmost practicable extent their philanthropic wishes." [27]

The many advocates of the removal of the free Negroes predicted that the "horrible" Southampton affair would act in another direction, to bring about the actual enforcement of the law of 1806 requiring banishment for emancipated slaves twelve months after they received their freedom. This law had lain inoperative for years.[28] These expectations were

[26] American Colonization Society, *Annual Report*, Jan., 1852, p. 49.
[27] C. S. Carter to American Colonization Society, Dec. 22, 1831, in Letters of American Colonization Society (mss.), quoted in Fox, *American Colonization Society*, p. 26.
[28] D. J. Burr of Richmond to Gurley, June 23, 1831, *Ibid*.

fulfilled at least by legislation, in that additional force was given the law of 1806 by the supplementary measure of 1831. Under this act emancipated slaves convicted of exceeding the residence period of twelve months were to be sold by the sheriff or city sergeant rather than by the overseers of the poor. In addition, the commissioners of revenue were to present to grand juries once each year a list of all free Negroes who had remained in the county contrary to law.[29]

The Eastern Shore of Virginia, embracing the counties of Northampton and Accomac, was one of the main centers of hostility toward the free Negro. Cut off from the rest of the state by Chesapeake Bay, this section felt a greater sense of insecurity with respect to its Negroes than did other parts of the state. With this fear as kindling, the Nat Turner affair set the Eastern Shore ablaze. In a series of meetings held in Northampton County the citizens expressed the view that the free Negroes were "a most prolific source of evil" to their community in that they might combine with slaves to make trouble. The citizens, 180 in number, demanded action. They planned, with the consent of the legislature, to send all of the free Negroes to Liberia, and for this purpose they authorized a committee to borrow a sum not exceeding $15,000. In the meantime they agreed not to employ or have any dealings with free Negroes, nor to rent them any houses or land. Those Negroes who were already employed were to be notified that they should have no further employment after the following June.

These drastic measures, the people of the Eastern Shore contended, were justified because of the alien character of the free Negro. They expressed their estimate of this group in a petition as follows: "Degraded by the stain which attaches to their color, excluded from many civil privileges which the humblest white man enjoys, and denied all participation in the government, it would be wholly absurd to expect from them any attachment to our laws and institutions, or any

[29] *Virginia Acts of Assembly*, 1830–1831, p. 107.

sympathy with our people." [30] The plan of raising a sum not exceeding $15,000 to remove the free Negroes of Northampton was approved by the legislature shortly after it received this petition.[31]

Among other petitions to the legislature of 1831 urging the removal of free Negroes was one signed by 189 citizens of Westmoreland County. The free Negroes, said this petition, were of necessity "degraded, profligate, vicious, turbulent, and discontented." They were "a burden on the community," pursued "no course of regular business," and were "negligent of economy and husbandry." "Their locomotive habits," these citizens asserted, "fit them for a dangerous agency in schemes, wild and visionary." Free Negroes could never have in Virginia the respect that is essential to happiness, "but in other lands they may become an orderly, sober, industrious, moral, enlightened, and Christian community." [32]

The legislation urged by such petitions for the removal of free Negroes came up in the form of a bill in February, 1832. This measure compelled removal from the state, not for all free Negroes, but for that numerous class who had remained within the state contrary to the law of 1806. The bill included an appropriation of $35,000 for 1832, and $90,000 for 1833, which was to be used by a central board to send free Negroes to some place outside of the United States. The House of Delegates passed the bill by a vote of seventy-nine to forty-one, but one month later the Senate rejected it, by eighteen to fourteen.[33] Thus the attempt to rid the state of

---

[30] Petition, Northampton, Dec. 6, 1831.

[31] *Virginia Acts of Assembly*, 1831-1832, p. 23.

[32] Petition, Westmoreland, Dec. 8, 1831. Petitions from other counties recited similar charges. Thus to large numbers of citizens in Isle of Wight, Powhatan, James City, Surry, and Northumberland counties, free Negroes were "altogether a burden on the community," and were also of necessity "degraded, and profligate." *Ibid.*, Isle of Wight, Dec. 7, 1831; Powhatan, Dec. 26, 1831; James City, Dec. 27, 1831; Surry, Jan. 11, 1832; Northumberland, Jan. 23, 1832.

[33] *Niles Weekly Register*, Feb. 25, March 31, 1832.

the free Negroes by legislative action failed, just as the abolition of slavery failed at the same time and in the same session.

The Virginia citizens concerned were not, however, discouraged by this action of the legislature; they proceeded to bombard the General Assembly further on this subject. At the very next session, in 1833, citizens of Norfolk County indicated to the lawmakers that, although they had failed to pass an expulsion bill in the past session, they should try again. "That the State ought to do something" was an expression, they said, which was upon every tongue. The Norfolk County citizens asserted that action on this matter was especially necessary to their section because the census of 1830 had reported that 10,783 of the 47,349 free Negroes in the state were concentrated in the counties of Accomac, Northampton, Princess Anne, Norfolk, Nansemond, Isle of Wight, and Southampton, and in the borough of Norfolk.[34]

A few years later 180 Gloucester County citizens attacked the free Negro as a menace to slavery. They contended that the slaves were becoming more and more unmanageable, all because the free Negroes were an easy prey to Northern fanatics. Following the example of the citizens of Northampton, the Gloucester group held a meeting and appointed a committee to borrow $15,000 for removing the free blacks. Since the legislature had already done something for Northampton County, the Gloucester citizens asked that the same relief be extended to them and that this be done at once, to check the efforts of Northern fanatics who were then flooding the post office with incendiary literature.[35]

---

[34] Petitions, Norfolk, Jan. 5, Feb. 2, 1833. Nansemond citizens advanced similar arguments and also suggested greater assistance for the Colonization Society. In line with the general trend, citizens of Elizabeth City County and the town of Hampton urged the legislature to make an appropriation for the Colonization Society, since the enterprise was too costly for individuals to undertake. Such action was essential, they reasoned, because despite legislative enactments and individual exertion the number of free Negroes was increasing. *Ibid.*, Hampton and Elizabeth City, Feb. 12, 1832.

[35] *Ibid.*, Gloucester, Jan. 3, 1836.

Two years after the Gloucester County appeal, members of the Colonization Society in Northumberland, Lancaster, and Dinwiddie gave drastic expression to their views on this subject. The Northumberland branch said in condemnation of the free Negro: "We can cordially bear testimony to the oft-repeated fact that free persons of color among us are the most degraded as well as the most wretched class of our population; and we believe nothing short of colonizing them in Africa, could be done to ameliorate effectually this condition." In the neighboring county of Lancaster in the Northern Neck the colonizationists maintained that the free Negroes subsisted either by their own predatory habits "or by acting as factors for the reception and disposal of goods stolen by slaves." Since the free Negroes exerted "a malign influence" upon the slaves, these petitioners attempted to secure a more liberal use of the funds appropriated by the state for the removal of this group. The Dinwiddie branch expressed practically the same feeling; to them the free black population was "highly injurious," and its increase brought an "intolerable burthen." [36]

Closely related to these petitions of colonization societies were the utterances of individual colonization leaders. One prominent Virginia worker in this cause remarked that "emancipation must be followed by emigration" since it was impossible for the two races to live together. Any attempt to live together, he asserted, would lead to extermination; and the blacks would of course be the group exterminated.[37] A Virginia churchman and member of the Society said, "Every year only rivets the conviction more deeply in my mind, that to do them real good they must be separated from those of a different color." [38]

In addition to requests for the complete removal of free

---

[36] *Ibid.*, Northumberland, Jan. 2, 1838; Lancaster, Jan. 23, 1838; Dinwiddie, Jan. 9, 1838.

[37] Library of Congress, Letters to American Colonization Society (mss.), Atkinson to Gurley, Nov. 10, 1831.

[38] William Meade, quoted in Whitfield, *Slavery Agitation*, p. 8.

Negroes, the legislature of Virginia was confronted by petitions relating to other aspects of the problem. Having failed, in the decade of the thirties, to bring about the emigration of the free Negro by legislative action, the people of Virginia turned their attention to asking for various types of restriction on the Negro. One demand was for the more stringent enforcement of the banishment law of 1806, so that if the free Negroes could not be removed collectively, their number should be restricted to the lowest possible quota.

During the decade of 1840, citizens of Loudon County showed great concern about this particular question. As a step towards better enforcement of the law of 1806, the Loudon residents on one occasion proposed that any person be authorized to inform against a free Negro who had maintained residence beyond the twelve months' period, and that such a person might cause a warrant to be issued for the arrest of any suspected Negro of this group. If it were proved that the free Negro in question had remained in Virginia longer than twelve months, he should be sold as a slave for life, "one half of the proceeds to go to the informer and the residue as heretofore." Five years later citizens of this county again complained that the removal laws were not being enforced and that prosecutions of offenders were rare. "The legislature must do something," they said, since the free Negroes were "increasing in number all of the time." [39]

Citizens of Rockingham County demanded even more rigid laws. They recommended that the time allowed for free Negroes to leave the state after emancipation be reduced from twelve months to one month, because such persons might do "a lot of damage in twelve months"; they might, for instance, entice slaves to go off to the mountains. The petitioners felt that the change suggested was necessary because of the activity of the abolitionists.[40]

Many Virginians who desired primarily the quick removal

[39] Petitions, Loudon, Dec. 7, 1842; Dec. 10, 1847.
[40] *Ibid.*, Rockingham, Jan. 30, 1849.

of all free Negroes were ready with other suggestions to curtail the Negroes' freedom of action if removal could not be accomplished. They expressed their fears that the free Negroes might corrupt the slaves, not only by stirring up insurrection but also by interfering with slave discipline. For example, free Negroes might convey them liquor, or might act as receivers of goods stolen by slaves. On these subjects as on others, Virginians freely expressed themselves in petitions.

In 1831 Charles City and New Kent residents complained to the legislature that their slaves who worked as millers were a "link in a chain" with free Negroes. They asserted that while the slaves were engaged in milling, squads of free Negroes stood about to secure flour for their own use, and that as a result the slave millers were compelled to cheat their regular customers in the amount of flour they should receive. The petition demanded that this nuisance be suppressed.[41]

Six years later Northumberland and Powhatan citizens, expressing doubt that the commodities sold by free Negroes were products of their own labor, suggested that a free Negro should be allowed to sell grain or other provisions only when licensed or certified by two or more respectable white persons. Such restriction was necessary, they asserted, because the free Negroes were "characterized by everything opposite to honesty and industry." Still later, in 1843, Richmond County citizens petitioned the legislature on similar grounds. They complained that at least seven-tenths of the grain and other articles sold by free Negroes was in excess of what they could produce by their own industry and that therefore most of what they sold must have come from slaves. About the same time citizens of Accomac County advanced a similar claim. Many country stores, they said, received grain from free Negroes. Since in most cases free Negroes did not raise such products, they should be required to have licenses before they might sell goods. These petitioners also de-

[41] *Ibid.*, Charles City and New Kent, Dec. 27, 1831.

manded a law forbidding merchants to sell liquor to free Negroes. Such a law was in effect for slaves, but this measure was alleged to be useless so long as free Negroes might get liquor and pass it on to the slave group.[42]

Such petitions as these, reflecting the opinion of the great mass of Virginia people, clearly indicate that in a proslavery society, such as Virginia developed after 1830, free Negroes were in an anomalous position. They were not, however, entirely friendless; occasionally groups of people petitioned in their behalf. At one time, for example, the Henrico County Quakers protested the injustice of the law that sent a free Negro to jail because he was without his "free papers." They held that this law should be modified, for in some cases free Negroes had been kept in jail from one to fifty years, or had been sent out of the state, simply because they either had lost their "free papers" or had not registered.[43]

The many petitions against the free Negro, however, led to further restrictive legislation. Perhaps the most important of many such measures was the act of 1831 which made it unlawful to teach free Negroes to read and write. "Colonization" and "removal" were the watchwords of the day, to which practically all Virginia citizens subscribed. But if removal did not materialize, the denial of instruction in letters would tend to make the free Negro harmless, or at least his illiteracy would prevent his reading the abolitionist, incendiary literature which perhaps gave rise to this restrictive measure.[44] The law prohibiting the instruction of free Negroes or mulattoes ran as follows: "All meetings of free Negroes or mulattoes, at any school house, church meeting house, or any other place for teaching them reading and writing, either in the day or night, under whatsoever pretext,

[42] *Ibid.*, Northumberland, Feb. 27, 1837; Powhatan, Mar. 10, 1838; Richmond, Feb. 18, 1843; Accomac, Mar. 2, 1848.
[43] *Ibid.*, Henrico, Dec. 31, 1844.
[44] Fox, *American Colonization Society*, pp. 27 ff. The most fiery pamphlet of the time was *Walker's Appeal to the Colored Citizens of the World*, which the mayor of Richmond discovered in the house of a deceased free Negro. Richmond *Enquirer*, Jan. 28, 1830.

shall be deemed and considered an unlawful assembly." Any violation of this measure by free Negroes involved dispersal of the meeting and corporal punishment not to exceed twenty lashes. If any white persons assembled with free Negroes for this purpose they were to be fined not more than fifty dollars or to be imprisoned not more than two months.[45]

This law was effective in preventing the education of free Negroes in Virginia. Before 1830 they had, through their beneficial societies, instituted formal schooling in all of the towns of the state, but the law of 1831 brought all these efforts to an end.[46] Suffering under this law, a group of well-to-do free Negroes of Fredericksburg petitioned the legislature in 1838 for permission to operate a school, because of the great expense involved in sending their children North. One of their very significant contentions was: "Knowledge now has become so diffused that persons who are uneducated are cut off from the ordinary means of self-advancement and find the greatest difficulty in gaining an honest livelihood by consequence of these conditions and prohibitory statutes of Virginia." Their request was refused, and their problem was made still more difficult by another statute passed in the same year, providing that free Negroes who went North to be educated, as Fredericksburg free Negroes had been doing, should not be allowed to return to the state.[47]

---

[45] *Virginia Acts of Assembly*, 1830–1831, p. 107.

[46] Carter G. Woodson, *The Education of the Negro Prior to 1861*, ch. 7. One of these schools was operated in Petersburg by John T. Raymond, a free Negro of unusual learning for that day. He said of his pupils in 1820: "School has afforded instruction to hundreds and contributed greatly to preserve order on the Sabbath Day." Petersburg *Republican*, Oct. 17, 1820.

Despite the law a certain amount of clandestine instruction was given after 1831. Mrs. Eliza Elebeck, late citizen of Petersburg, once informed the writer that there were at least three free Negroes of Petersburg who taught secretly. A more open attempt at giving instruction was made in Norfolk by Mrs. Margaret Douglass, a white woman. Her school was eventually closed by the authorities. This teacher related that in 1853 she was imprisoned for one month in the common jail of this town "for the crime of teaching free colored children to read." Margaret Douglass, *Educational Laws of Virginia*.

[47] Petition, Spottsylvania, Mar. 16, 1838; *Acts of Assembly*, 1838, p. 76.

This law was only a part of the larger movement to keep free Negroes out of the state. Four years earlier, the legislature had provided that "any free person who shall bring a free Negro into this State, shall be confined in jail not more than six months and fined not exceeding five hundred dollars." To strengthen this restriction, the legislature later enacted the corollary prohibition that no free Negro might migrate into the state alone.[48]

The ban on the education of free Negroes was followed the next year by a similar measure dealing with preaching. Under this law no slave or free Negro might conduct a meeting for religious or other purposes in the day or in the night, nor might any slave or free Negro attend a meeting conducted by one of his race or by a white minister, without written permission. The punishment for violation of the act was stripes not to exceed thirty-nine lashes.[49] This law against preaching followed closely upon the Nat Turner insurrection and was grounded on the belief advanced by Governor Floyd that Turner had been misled by Negro preachers.

The prohibition of preaching had the desired effect of completely removing Negro preachers as pastors of churches or ministrants at religious ceremonies. The law worked so much hardship on free Negroes in such matters as the burial of the dead, baptism, and marriage that "sundry free persons of color" of Richmond in 1834 sought to relieve their condition by petition. They observed that "many colored human beings are interred like brutes" and that frequently white ministers of Richmond were unavailable for burial services. Five years later 142 white persons of Petersburg made the same complaint, but on the grounds of the inability of free

---

This law, forbidding the return of free Negroes who had left the state to be educated, appears to have been enforced. At any rate, James Campbell of Staunton experienced difficulty in being allowed to remain in Virginia because he had previously spent two years in Philadelphia for purposes of education. Petition, Augusta, Jan. 16, 1847.

[48] *Code of Virginia*, 1849, pp. 746, 747.
[49] *Ibid.*, 1831-1832, pp. 20-21.

Negroes to pay for the services of white ministers. Both of these petitions failed.[50]

The hostile legislature of 1831-1832 trained still other guns against the free Negroes. In criminal trials prior to 1832 free Negroes were on the same footing with white men, but from this year on they were denied the right of trial by jury except for offenses punishable by death. In all other cases they were to be tried by courts of oyer and terminer, which had been in use since 1692 for the "speedy prosecution of slaves without the sollemnitie of jury." [51]

By an act of 1806 free Negroes had been forbidden to "keep or carry any firelock of any kind, any military weapon or any powder or lead" unless they obtained a license from the county or corporation court. By an act of 1832 they were forbidden to have firearms under any circumstances. If the experience of the Giles County free Negroes, Thomas Beasley and James and Joseph Viney, was typical, this ruling operated as a serious handicap upon free Negro farmers. Beasley complained to the legislature that so many wild beasts roamed the mountainous country in which he lived that persons of his class without firearms had no means of protecting their domestic animals and crops. In spite of this remonstrance the law remained in force until the Civil War.[52]

The legislature of 1831-1832 dealt still another blow to the free Negro class. Ever since the seventeenth century this group had had the right to acquire, own, and alienate slaves; until 1670 free Negroes even had the right to own indentured white servants. Prior to 1806 slave ownership by free Negroes was frequently the opening wedge to manumission of slave members of their families, but after this date free Negroes kept their slaves because under the new law manumission must lead to banishment and the breaking of family

[50] Gillfield Baptist Church (Petersburg), Record Book (ms.); Petitions: Henrico, Dec. 17, 1834; Dinwiddie, Jan. 8, 1839.
[51] Quoted in John H. Russell, *The Free Negro in Virginia*, p. 104.
[52] *Virginia Acts of Assembly*, 1831-1832, p. 20; Petitions, Giles, Dec. 24, 1840; Dec. 18, 1841.

ties. After 1832 even this privilege was curtailed, for an act passed in that year made it unlawful for a free Negro to acquire property in slaves, except by inheritance, other than husband, wife, parent, or descendant of such free Negro. Finally, toward the close of this stormy period, still another law provided that "no free Negro shall be capable of acquiring, except by descent, any slave [whatsoever]." As expressed by a judge of that day, the probable intent of this law was to keep the slaves entirely under the control of white men.[53]

Legislative enactments are only one phase of the expression of public opinion. Often in more stringent, extra-legal action a community expresses its feelings regardless of public law. Thus, in addition to urging the passage of the restrictive measures discussed above, the Virginia people took action in their private capacity. In some communities they instituted a reign of terror that foreshadowed the Ku Klux Klan of a later day. Desirable and undesirable free Negroes were physically apprehended and either beaten or driven out of the state. The operation of this extra-legal system was openly discussed in the legislature of 1831–1832. General Broadnax explained the procedure as follows:

> Who does not know that when a free Negro, by crime or otherwise, has rendered himself obnoxious to a neighborhood, how easy it is for a party to visit him one night, take him from his bed and family, and apply to him the gentle admonition of a severe flagellation, to induce him to go away. In a few nights the dose can be repeated, perhaps increased, until, in the language of the physicians, quantum suff has been administered . . . and the fellow becomes perfectly willing to go away.[54]

Realizing the cruelty of this procedure, another member of the legislature argued in favor of a compulsory colonization scheme as a protection for free Negroes.[55]

[53] *Code of Virginia*, 1849, p. 458; 1860, p. 510; Russell, *Free Negro*, p. 94.
[54] Richmond *Enquirer*, Feb. 14, 1832.
[55] *Ibid*. Russell, who made his study of the free Negro about 1910, fre-

One of the most blatant examples of community lawlessness occurred on the Eastern Shore of Virginia. In a number of meetings held there between 1825 and 1834 the citizens of Accomac and Northampton planned and waged a campaign to drive free Negroes from the state. In reviewing their nine-year record, the people of Accomac County observed in 1834 that they had succeeded in driving out several hundred free Negroes.[56] At the same time, Northampton was sending out so many that in 1840 its free Negro population was only half the number of 1830. Many of the best element of the Northampton free Negroes, compelled to seek homes elsewhere, went to Philadelphia, where they found a safe place as efficient cooks, caterers, and operators of shops of various kinds.[57]

The decade of 1830 was marked in Virginia by a relative decline in population. Whereas the gain in population was 13½ per cent from 1820 to 1830, this figure dropped to about 3 per cent from 1830 to 1840. During this decade the slaves declined from about 469,000 to about 448,000. The free Negro element likewise declined in thirty-six of the eighty-eight counties of the state. The percentage of decrease ranged from 1 per cent in Chesterfield County to 66 per cent in Elizabeth City County. Northampton County had 1,133 free Negroes in 1830 but only 754 in 1840. Princess Anne and Prince George counties likewise suffered a decline.[58] But the heavy loss in these counties did not prevent a slight increase in the free Negro population of the state as a whole.

It is well known that slaves from Virginia were absorbed

---

quently interviewed Negroes who were free men during the generation preceding 1865. One of these, William Miles Cuffee of Norfolk County, stated that in 1859 the whites assembled in bands to intimidate the free Negroes of his community. Cuffee remained hidden in the woods for about three days and nights while the raids were being conducted against his people. Russell, *Free Negro*, p. 173.

[56] Petition, Accomac, Dec. 31, 1834.

[57] Booker T. Washington, *The Negro in Business*, p. 47.

[58] *Documents Containing Statistics of Virginia*, 1850–1851. Table showing free white, free colored, and slave population.

by the states of the lower South, but this was not true of the free Negroes. A small group of less than 500 freeborn Negroes joined the colonization movement to Liberia between 1830 and 1840, but the bulk of the migrating free blacks went to the North and the Northwest. Jackson and Ross counties in Ohio received a large number of Virginia Negro exiles.

The period of greatest migration of free Negroes from Virginia was in the 1830 decade, especially between 1830 and 1835,[59] but the movement continued until the Civil War. The decline in the free Negro population of Northampton County was later paralleled in other counties. Northumberland, for instance, dropped from 519 in 1850 to 222 in 1860, so great a loss that it attracted the attention of the county authorities. The hostility toward free Negroes expressed in petitions from this county would indicate that the free blacks found conditions in Northumberland unbearable.[60]

Other places likewise became unbearable. After the flat refusal of the legislature to permit them to operate the school for which they petitioned in 1838, the progressive free Negroes of Fredericksburg immediately undertook a trek to Michigan.[61] Another stream of free Negroes poured from Loudon County. In this instance a group of citizens complained that the laws against free Negroes had served to rid that county and the state of a valuable supply of free labor, the kind of labor which many persons from conscientious motives preferred to employ. To them it seemed unfair to expel anyone whose labor might be useful.[62] Another stream poured from Alexandria immediately after the retrocession of this city to Virginia in 1846. In migrating because Vir-

---

[59] Carter G. Woodson, *Free Negro Heads of Families in the United States in 1830*, Foreword, p. iii.

[60] Clerk's Office, Northumberland County, "Order Book" (ms.); Petitions, Northumberland, Jan. 23, 1832; Feb. 27, 1837.

[61] W. B. Hartgrove, "The Story of Maria Louise Moore and Fannie M. Richards," in *Journal of Negro History*, 1:23-33 (Jan., 1916).

[62] Petition, Loudon, Jan. 24, 1843.

ginia's laws were "very obnoctious to them," [63] the free Negroes simply went over into the District of Columbia.

Free Negroes also moved from Virginia into North Carolina, although in much smaller numbers than into Ohio. The attraction of North Carolina was that its laws were more lenient than the laws of Virginia. One of these free blacks who went to North Carolina was the industrious Archer Carey of Lynchburg. Although he had been expelled from Virginia, the North Carolina officials agreed not to enforce the laws of their state against him.[64]

The hostility to the free Negro did not stop with the decades of 1830 and 1840; it continued until the Civil War. Private citizens, public officials, and the press, while they continued to sing the praises of the Negro slave, continued also to condemn the free Negro and to urge his removal from the state.

On the contrast between the slaves and the free people of color, the press of Virginia was especially outspoken. The Richmond *Enquirer* expressed the view that slavery would endure because it represented the "best condition of the black race in this country." According to this paper, there was "not a more worthless or dissolute set of men than free Negroes." [65] The Richmond *Examiner* declared that the South would never abandon its peculiar institution because this region could not do without slavery, which "belongs to southern society" as "inherently, intricately, and durably as the white race itself." [66] The Petersburg *South-Side Democrat* advanced similar views. Slavery was the proper condition of the Negro, and the slaves had fared well, but the free Negroes were a nuisance everywhere: they lived in dirt and filth and committed more crimes than did any other group. The

---

[63] Virginia State Library, "Letters to the Auditor" (mss.), Deputy Sheriff to State Auditor, May 12, 1851.

[64] John S. Bassett, *Slavery in the State of North Carolina*, p. 42; Petition, Amherst, Dec. 23, 1833.

[65] Richmond *Enquirer*, Sept. 6, 1855, quoted in Frederick L. Olmsted, *A Journey in the Seaboard Slave States, with Remarks on Their Economy*, p. 334.

[66] Richmond *Examiner*, 1854, quoted *Ibid.*, p. 334.

position Providence intended for the Negro, therefore, was not freedom but slavery; and in Virginia "all of her memories, [and] bright hopes" were inseparably interwoven with "that humane and heaven directed institution." [67]

Though some newspapers of the period may be discounted as organs of yellow journalism, the books by proslavery writers such as Thomas R. Dew were hardly less violent in their denunciation of the free blacks. Worthy successors of Dew appeared fifteen years later in such writers as Edmund Ruffin and George Fitzhugh. Ruffin remarked, "If there is any existing institution of divine origin, and manifestly designed and used by the all wise and all-good creator to forward his beneficent purposes, slavery and especially African domestic slavery, is such an institution." [68] His high regard for slavery was accompanied by a haughty contempt for free Negroes.

This group of writers so strongly influenced George Fitzhugh that he wrote a pamphlet, *What Shall Be Done with the Free Negroes?* The free black was to him "an intolerable pest and nuisance to society." Since the condition of the free Negroes was "getting worse" all the time, Fitzhugh recommended that for the time being they enter a form of peonage by binding themselves to white men. Ultimately, he said, the state should endeavor to get rid of them entirely, because the Anglo-Saxons were the only people in America fit for freedom.[69]

The condemnation of the free Negro by the proslavery writers was accompanied by a corresponding condemnation of the Colonization Society, whose purpose was to make slaves free men. From the beginning of its existence this nation-wide body had met with the opposition of some Virginians. Noteworthy among its opponents was Governor Giles, who criticized the society even to the point of defend-

[67] Petersburg *South-Side Democrat*, July 20, 1854; March 11, 1857.
[68] Edmund Ruffin, *Address to the Virginia State Agriculture Society, Dec. 16, 1852*, p. 18.
[69] George Fitzhugh, *What Shall Be Done with the Free Negroes*, pp. 1-6.

ing the free Negro. He said that this class of the population was by no means "so vicious, degraded and demoralized as represented by their prejudiced friends and voluntary benefactors." He felt that all the evils attributed to this group by the colonizationists were vastly magnified and exaggerated.[70] Because of such opposition the Colonization Society by 1850 had lost most of its influence throughout the country.[71] Attacks by Garrisonian abolitionists on the one hand and by Southern proslavery leaders on the other were sufficient to dissipate whatever antislavery force the body ever possessed.

The unfortunate position of the free Negro in a proslavery society is further revealed by the statements of Virginia governors. Governor Giles felt that this class was not so bad as its enemies indicated; Governor Floyd, on the other hand, led the attack against it because of the Southampton massacre. In the late forties Governor Smith characterized the free Negroes as "a race of idlers, thriftless, and unproductive." "They labor," he said, "only from necessity, are content to put up with only a meager supply of wants, prowl at dead of night and filch the labor of others." [72] Other governors of Virginia shared Smith's views because of the apparent disproportion of crimes among the free Negro group. Governors Floyd, Smith, Johnson, Wise, and others repeatedly submitted this matter to the attention of the legislature.[73]

The governors' statements and the continuous pressure by citizens from all parts of the state finally were reflected in further legislation restricting the free Negroes. Among these measures was the law of 1843 prohibiting any free Negro from selling or offering to sell any agricultural products without having a written certificate from a respectable white

---

[70] William B. Giles, *Political Miscellanies, American Colonization Society*, p. 9.
[71] Fox, *American Colonization Society*, p. 178.
[72] *Journal of House of Delegates*, 1846–1847, p. 9.
[73] Robert R. Howison, *A History of Virginia, from Its Discovery and Settlement by Europeans to the Present Time*, 2:458; Russell, *Free Negro*, p. 166.

citizen indicating that the Negro had raised the products in question. Because this particular measure had been demanded only by citizens of Richmond and Accomac counties, the legislature made it operative in these two counties only but provided that any other county might have the same system if its courts so ordered. Sussex County, and probably many others, adopted this regulation.[74] Another restriction of business opportunity was the legislative provision of 1853 that free Negroes might not be licensed to keep ordinaries or to retail ardent spirits. This measure was buttressed by similar local restrictions, some of which had been in operation even before the blanket ruling of the state. In 1844, for example, Goochland County revoked the license of Jacob Sampson, who operated a tavern in the county. His appeal to the legislature for a reversal of the local order was refused.[75]

The general reconstruction of the laws of Virginia by the constitutional convention of 1851 was the occasion for further action in the continuing drive against the free Negroes. Their removal had been attempted in 1832 through an act of the legislature, and another attempt had been made in 1849. Three years later the policy received constitutional sanction in the following provision: "The General Assembly may pass laws for the relief of the Commonwealth from the free Negro population, by removal or otherwise." Following up this permissive provision, a member of the lower house of the legislature of 1853–1854 introduced a bill to expel the 54,000 free Negroes from the state. The bill passed the lower house, as in 1832, but it apparently was defeated in the Senate.[76]

One strong supporter of the removal measure was John C.

[74] *Code of Virginia*, 1849, p. 748; Clerk's Office, Sussex County, Order Book, 1852-1864. John L. Wilkerson of Louisa County, grandson of a prosperous free Negro farmer of Louisa, reported that his grandfather and his great-uncle, Ned and Cyrus Wilkerson, did all their buying and selling through white men. Interview, July 20, 1936.
[75] *Code of Virginia*, 1860, p. 224; Petition, Goochland, 1844.
[76] *Ibid.*, p. 46; *Journal of the House of Delegates*, 1853-1854, p. 345.

Rutherford of Goochland County. He brought forward the usual argument that the free Negroes were "idle, ignorant, degraded and immoral," and he charged that they consumed more than they produced and therefore reduced the wealth of the state. Frankly admitting, however, that he would not advocate the removal of these people if slavery did not exist in Virginia, he said: "In the delicate relations between master and slave, they are a disturbing element." [77]

The controversy in the early fifties and the policy declared in the new constitution produced more laws affecting this "disturbing element." By an act passed in 1850 the sum of $30,000 was appropriated annually for five years for transporting free Negroes to Liberia through the Colonization Society.[78] At the same time a special poll tax of $1 was levied on male free Negroes between the ages of twenty-one and fifty-five, the income from which was to be applied exclusively toward removal. After the act of 1850 had been in effect for three years it was further strengthened and the same appropriation was made for another five years. A colonization board was created to administer the state funds, and the original poll tax of $1 was continued. After 1858, when the annual appropriation of $30,000 expired by limitation, the Colonization Society in Virginia was again thrown back on "Christian friends" for support.[79] Further action by the legislature came in 1860, when an additional poll tax of eighty cents was levied on all free male blacks over twenty-one years old. Again the income from this tax was to be applied to the removal of the free Negroes.

Discrimination colored all these measures. In the first place white males during this period paid poll taxes ranging from thirty to eighty cents only; in the second place, although the entire revenue from the tax on Negroes was to have been

[77] John C. Rutherford, *Speech of Rutherford on the Removal of the Free Colored Population*, p. 4.
[78] *Code of Virginia*, 1860, p. 520, note.
[79] *Religious Herald*, July 15, 1858.

used for colonizing free colored people in Liberia, only limited amounts were so applied. In no year between 1850 and 1858 was more than $2,100 spent for colonization from this particular fund, even though in 1852, for example, the gross sum accruing to the state from this source was $8,987; in 1859, $9,272; and in 1860, with the extra levy, $13,065.22. The difference in the amount spent on the free Negroes and the amount actually collected was held in the state treasury for general purposes.[80]

The oppressive measures heaped upon the free Negroes in the period from 1830 to 1860 reflect one conviction: that this group had no place in a state wedded to slavery. Having failed, however, to get rid of the entire mass by state legislation, the commonwealth seems to have concentrated its efforts finally on reducing these people just as near to slavery as possible. One step in this direction came in the unique statute of 1856 that provided that "it shall be lawful for any free person of color" to choose "his or her master." [81] Another measure of this nature was adopted in 1860 when the legislature provided that in criminal cases in which free Negroes were sentenced to the penitentiary they might be punished instead by sale into absolute slavery. The proceeds of such sales were to be placed in the state treasury.[82]

The foregoing review of the legal position of the Virginia free Negro tells much about what he might not do. It remains to indicate what he might do. He was divested of many rights, yet there was one that the state never took away: the right to acquire, own, and sell property. The retention of this important right served as a strong bulwark against many

[80] *Annual Report of the Auditor of Public Accounts*, 1852; 1858–1859, pp. 416–417; 1859–1860, p. 407; 1861, pp. 653, 669.
[81] At least thirty free Negroes reënslaved themselves under the provisions of this act. As the law directed, they petitioned the courts of their respective counties, their value was ascertained, and the masters whom they chose paid to the court half their valuation. June P. Guild, *Black Laws of Virginia*, pp. 119–122.
[82] *Acts of Assembly*, 1859–1860, p. 163.

of the efforts to remove the free Negroes, particularly the legislative attempt of 1832.[83] At least one effort was made in the legislature to deny the free Negro even this right, but the House of Delegates bill in question received slight consideration.[84]

The repressive measures against the free Negroes in Virginia were enacted in the reactionary period of the history of slaves and free Negroes, when, in so far as legislation was concerned, the latter were well-nigh crushed. In this connection a sympathetic Northern writer of that day compared the hardships of the free Negroes of the country to those suffered by the Jews of medieval Europe.[85]

Nevertheless, a study of the laws passed by an unfriendly government to control one element of the population furnishes only a limited view of the actual condition of that group. The real status of the free Negro in Virginia cannot be determined by the many derogatory statements of individuals and groups. Their statements deserve critical examination. Carter G. Woodson suggests that one important group, the Colonization Society, could say only that which was bad about the free Negroes in order to make a strong case for deportation; another group, the slaveholders and proslavery men, could only do likewise, since any evidence to the contrary would destroy their arguments for keeping the Negro in perpetual bondage; still another, the abolitionists, who viewed the situation only from afar, dared not point out progress among free Negroes in a land of slavery.[86]

Another error involved in accepting at face value the statements of colonizationists and the acts of the legislature is that they represent ideas about the entire group, and then only in the abstract. In attempting to discover something of the entire status of the free Negroes of Virginia, one under-

[83] Richmond *Enquirer*, Feb. 14, 1832.
[84] *House Journals*, 1841–1842, pp. 66, 114, 162.
[85] James F. Clark, *Present Condition of the Free Colored People of the United States*, p. 16.
[86] Woodson, *Free Negro Heads of Families*, p. xxxiv.

lying fact presents itself: that, despite the avalanche of laws and abuses, they stayed in the state, and they prospered.

To determine the influences that kept the free Negro in Virginia and enabled him to prosper, the investigator must turn from the political to the economic story. Virginia political history during the period under review has had extensive treatment, but only recently have economic forces been explored. These forces reveal a new interpretation with reference to the free Negro, just as they have revealed new interpretations in other aspects of the history of the state.

CHAPTER II

THE ECONOMIC REVIVAL AND THE ELEMENT OF LABOR

IN the field of economic endeavor, the position of Virginia in 1830 was dubious. Since about 1815 the economic life of the commonwealth had been, in relation to that of the states north and south of it, declining. The state of Virginia, which had been on a political pinnacle in early American history, seemed now to be declining to a second-rate position. The depletion of its soil, the emigration of its people, the deflection of its imports to other ports of the country, the decline in its land values, its lack of manufactures, its backwardness in transportation, and its surplus of slaves were among its economic handicaps.

Soil depletion and the general agricultural decline were the most frequent subjects of discussion among contemporary economic observers. One of these tells of farms exhausted by long and injudicious cultivation; of originally good soil that because of mismanagement—such as overcropping, frequent grazing, bad plowing, scanty manures, and cultivation of tobacco—had become barren; of light and poor soil; and finally of the diminished yield of tobacco due to soil exhaustion. For the state at large about 1830 the indictment ran that Virginians continued the old practice of cultivating land every year until it was exhausted and then leaving it to recover by its own resources.[1]

The exhausted soil led to a considerable migration from Virginia. Under a system of agriculture common to the whole country, large numbers of people went to the new West and

[1] Joseph Martin, *A New and Comprehensive Gazetteer of Virginia and the District of Columbia*, pp. 99, 216, 238, 264, 285.

Southwest in search of fresh lands.[2] The lure of new land offered more promise than any attempt to restore the fertility of soils at home. The census reveals the extent of emigration: from 1820 to 1830 the rate of population increase fell from 37½ to 13½ per cent, while in 1840 there were some 26,000 fewer people in the older portion of the state than in 1830. By 1850 nearly a third of Virginia-born people were to be found in the West and the Southwest. According to one historian, thousands of young people were leaving the state; only those in good circumstances or those too poor to move remained.[3]

Emigration resulted not only from exhausted soil but also from other handicaps. The old question of the high cost of goods, domestic and foreign, which Virginians had to buy, contrasted with the low returns for products they had to sell, created fundamental discontent. This disparity in prices resulted from the fact that Virginia and the South had no direct trade with European centers but only an indirect connection by way of New York. In the thirties and later the annual imports of New York City were six times greater than all the imports of the Southern states. In 1836, for example, the imports of New York City amounted to $118,253,416; those of Virginia to only $1,106,814.[4] This meant that the cities of Virginia were tributaries to New York and the North for practically their whole volume of business. "When they [the Virginia people] enjoyed the direct trade," one observer remarked, "our cities and towns and country were alike prosperous, and emigration did not desolate our land."[5] Obviously such a deflection of imports and exports wrought economic hardship for the state.

Soil exhaustion and the loss of import trade were linked

---

[2] Petition, Middlesex, Feb. 3, 1838.
[3] Avery O. Craven, *Soil Exhaustion as a Factor in the Agricultural History of Virginia and Maryland, 1606–1860*; p. 122; Thomas J. Wertenbaker, *Norfolk, Historic Southern Port*, p. 190.
[4] J. D. B. DeBow, ed., *Commercial Review*, 4:208.
[5] *Farmers' Register*, 6:114, 699–704.

with a decline in land values. In 1836 the assessed value of lands, houses, and other property in the entire state was $207,000,000—actually less than the assessed value of the real estate in New York City alone.[6] Virginia was particularly deficient in urban wealth. Whereas in the Atlantic states north of Virginia the moneyed element in cities represented one in four persons in the general population, in Virginia this proportion was about one in twenty-five. Thus Virginia found itself in economic vassalage to the North. Its leaders asked: "Who build our lines of improvements? Who export and import our goods? Who own our lines of steamers? Who are studding our water courses with manufactories? And above all, who glean the profits?" The answer was, "Not ourselves but northern men."[7]

About 1830 Virginia, largely without manufactures, depended almost completely upon the North for its manufactured goods. As early as 1827 some Virginians, highly conscious of this condition, suggested that cotton mills be established. Such establishments, a Norfolk paper remarked, "would set the idle to work, draw out hidden wealth, and revive our drooping trade." Whig newspapers and Whig leaders were especially eager for manufactures. This group asserted that the eloquence of Southerners should be expressed in the "puffing of locomotives, the busy murmur of factories, and the splashing of steam paddles" instead of in so much talking.[8]

Backwardness in internal improvements both contributed to and resulted from the economic stagnation. In 1818 a critic remarked that the state which was "the proudest and most powerful in the union, the first in war, and the first in peace" had highways that were "the meanest and most wretched in the world."[9] Indeed Virginia's chief weakness

[6] *Ibid.* [7] *Views on the Internal Improvement System of Virginia*, p. 1.
[8] *Norfolk Herald*, Oct. 29, 1827, quoted in Wertenbaker, *Norfolk*, p. 218; Arthur C. Cole, *The Whig Party in the South*, p. 208.
[9] Petersburg *Intelligencer and Commercial Advertiser*, June 23, 1818; Samuel Mordecai, *Richmond in By-Gone Days*, p. 239.

lay in the fact that the several sections of the state were unconnected by transportation facilities.

It followed that the legislature of 1831 addressed itself to the task of bringing about adequate transportation facilities. Sectional jealousies, however, frustrated this effort; the west arrayed itself against the east, and the fall line towns against the seaports. In contrast, successful programs of internal improvement in other states resulted in an increase of wealth, population, and export trade, while Virginia was letting its opportunities slip. The one great need of the time was to turn the commerce of the western section of the state from its northern direction into the area of Richmond, Petersburg, and Norfolk.[10]

The last in Virginia's economic ills in 1830 was its unwieldy slave population. The problem of slavery had always confronted the state, but about 1830 it became more pressing, both politically and economically. In the section of the state where slaveholding was most prevalent—east of the Blue Ridge—each recent census had found the blacks increasing over the whites. From a majority of 3,004 in 1800, the blacks increased to a majority of 81,077 in 1830.[11] At the same time the owners of the growing black population were faced with the problem of less employment for their slaves and a greater expense in maintaining them. John Randolph's facetious remark that if the decrease in the value of slave labor continued and the slaves did not run away from their masters, the masters would have to run away from their slaves, expressed the actual situation. Slaves were a financial drain upon their owners.

Yet, despite the low economic status of Virginia in 1830, signs of a better day were appearing. The state was in a stage of transition and readjustment. By 1840, in agriculture at least, Virginia had come out of its depression.[12] Indeed, some

[10] Wertenbaker, *Norfolk*, pp. 190, 204; *Farmers' Register*, 1:622; *Report on Internal Improvements*, 1815, p. 5.
[11] *Railroad Advocate*, Nov. 19, 1831, p. 85.
[12] Edmund Ruffin, *Slavery and Free Labor Described and Compared*, p. 23.

who in one moment gave a dreary picture of conditions, in another emphasized their improvement.

A decisive betterment in agriculture was made by the use of certain fertilizers. King and Queen County had extensive beds of marl, which by 1830 furnished "inexhaustible improvement to the once barren soil." Joseph Martin noted that in this county land which had formerly produced only six to eight bushels of corn to the acre was at that time producing twenty to twenty-five. Farms were exhausted everywhere, but Martin found that "the present use of clover and plaster authorizes the prediction that in twenty years the soil will again become fertile." In Bedford County, as in many others, the soil was worn out by excessive tobacco culture; but many farmers were turning their attention to land improvement by clover and plaster. Throughout the state there was a tendency to abandon tobacco as a crop in favor of wheat and other grain—a change sought as a measure of land improvement. Martin predicted that the growing success in clover and wheat would animate agriculture and check the tide of emigration.[13]

These signs of a better day in agriculture were accompanied by growth in manufacturing. At several points in the state cotton mills appeared. Those near Petersburg under the enterprise of John Y. Stockdell were especially notable, one of them in 1835 containing 4,000 spindles and 170 looms. Three years later there were in Petersburg four flourishing cotton factories, one iron foundry, and several flour mills and tobacco manufactories. This modest beginning was made partly because the state government wished to encourage manufacturing.[14]

Along with the changes in these basic industries came a new interest in internal improvements. The Petersburg–Roanoke Railroad, built in 1831, was one of the earliest rail-

[13] Martin, *Virginia Gazetteer*, pp. 140, 160, 200, 203, 216, 239, 280.
[14] *Farmers' Register*, 4:368; *Niles Register*, July 21, 1838, p. 323.

roads in the United States. In 1833 state aid gave new life to the James River and Kanawha Canal. All over the state similar new projects were being launched. Stimulation in one direction led to stimulation in others. Property values were also increasing. In the opinion of *Niles Register*, Petersburg and other towns had already profited by the "American System" and should continue to make progress.[15] Hope was expressed by other papers that Virginia's lost foreign trade would be restored. In 1838 the Commercial Convention held in Richmond expressed the same desire. A contemporary, writing of this convention, said that the healthful exercise of a direct trade to foreign ports would "rejuvenate the aged and declining mother of states." Although distinct changes were indeed to take place in the fields of agriculture, manufacturing, internal improvements, and slavery, the hopes of Virginia and the South for a direct trade with Europe were to remain a fond dream.[16]

During this cycle of change, Negro slavery underwent considerable modification. From a moribund condition prior to 1830, this institution developed a high degree of vitality and became a source of profit. For a time, in the opinion of some observers, slaves represented Virginia's only profitable crop. The explanation of the change was the demand for slaves in the cotton-raising Gulf states and the subsequent rise in slave prices. The Southampton massacre and the consequent action of the legislature introduced so strong a feeling of insecurity that many slave owners sold their slaves in the South or moved with them to that section. Concurrent with the Southampton massacre was the "cotton fever," which raged so intensely in the deep South in the early thirties that it drew from northern Virginia and other areas their normal supply of manual labor. Between keeping slaves for needed work in

[15] *Ibid.*, Nov. 23, 1833.
[16] Petersburg *Constellation*, June 8, 1838; John G. Van Deusen, *Economic Bases of Disunion in South Carolina*, ch. 7.

Virginia and selling them South at a profit, planters often chose the latter course.[17]

The upward turn of business in the thirties continued and grew more marked in the forties and fifties. The most notable advance was perhaps in agriculture, under the leadership of Edmund Ruffin of Prince George County, a scientific agriculturalist. Ruffin contended that the soil was not exhausted but contained too much acid, and he began research to find a remedy. At first he recommended that farmers use marl as a neutralizing base; later he suggested Peruvian guano.[18] He further suggested that gypsum, lime, and bone be applied along with these other substances. The researches and writings of Ruffin had a marked effect on the agricultural life of the state. A newspaper correspondent observed in one section improved conditions that were common to others. He wrote: "[It is] refreshing to see what a change for the better has been wrought by guano on the poor and gullied hillsides of Hanover and Louisa. Instead of fields of pine the traveler now is relieved by frequent exchanges of fresh looking fields of wheat." [19] The rise of small-scale farming, the introduction of grain-growing, fruit-growing, and market gardening, and the use of new machinery were some of the reforms set in motion by Ruffin and others. The new methods of agriculture resulted in higher prices, greater yield per acre, a more careful selection of slaves, and an expanding market. During the forties and fifties this happy turn of events within the state was aided by the reopening of the West Indies market, the abolition of the corn laws in England, and the Crimean War.

Virginia agriculture was especially prosperous in the fifties. Contemporary observers asserted that the farms of Virginia in the years immediately preceding the Civil War were quite as well managed as any other farms in the United

---

[17] *Southern Planter*, 13:23 (1853); Dew, *Review of Debate on Abolition*, p. 50; *Farmers' Register*, 6:458 (1836); Frederick L. Olmsted, *The Cotton Kingdom*, 2:111–112.

[18] Petersburg *South-Side Democrat*, Oct. 25, 1855.

[19] Fredericksburg *Weekly Advertiser*, Jan. 29, 1859.

States. Farmers had turned to book farming with the result that more agriculture literature was read in Virginia than in any other state in the union. In like manner the soil of the state was being improved in productivity more rapidly and more extensively, perhaps, than was the soil of any other section of the country.[20]

Improved production led to higher land values. In the Norfolk area, for example, small farms that before 1850 had sold for a few hundred dollars sold readily for thousands in later years. One farm that before 1850 was sold for $1,400 brought $5,000 in 1854. In the whole state the concentrated manures, guano, and other preparations improved two million acres at the rate of $4.50 an acre. According to agricultural assessments in 1850 and in 1856, the state and local enumeration showed that the increase in land values ranged from 5 per cent in Accomac County to 48 per cent in Fairfax and Westmoreland.[21]

Naturally the revival in agriculture affected the entire social and industrial life of the state. From 1840 to 1850 population increased 12.79 per cent, whereas the increase during the previous decade had been only 2.29 per cent.[22] Emigration decreased and immigration increased. Immigration occurred principally in the northern counties, where some pronounced changes in crops, methods, and labor system took place. Fairfax County in particular underwent striking changes at the hands of northern farmers.[23] The preëminence of Virginia in agriculture even caused some of its leaders to feel that the state was "too agricultural." Agriculture alone, they argued, cannot furnish the basis for wealth and power. Instead, they contended, it is the combination of

---

[20] Richmond *Enquirer*, Sept. 21, 1854, quoting Washington *Star; DeBow's Review*, 26: 613: Craven, *Soil Exhaustion*, p. 159.
[21] Richmond *Enquirer*, May 10, June 27, 1854; *Wealth, Resources, and Hopes of the State of Virginia*, p. 9; *DeBow's Review*, 23: 58; *Southern Planter*, 17: 486 (1857).
[22] Editorial in Petersburg *South-Side Democrat*, Oct. 25, 1855.
[23] *Southern Planter*, 5: 244–245 (1845); Richmond *Enquirer*, Sept. 21, 1854.

agriculture, manufacturing, and commerce that makes a thriving and prosperous economy.[24]

Though demand for manufacturing in Virginia and the South came as early as 1830, it was not until the decade of 1850, after long preachment from certain groups in the state as well as from some Northerners, that manufacturing became important. "The duty of Virginians is to manufacture." This was the slogan of the day, a slogan motivated by desire to throw off the state's economic vassalage to the North. The real basis of political independence for the South, certain leaders maintained, was economic independence. Southern manufactures must be spurred toward this goal. Hence to Southern buyers, interested promoters gave this advice: "Purchase as little of Northern manufactures as possible"; "We have factories for the manufacturing of coarse articles springing up among us"; "We have the material"; "We have the labor." Finally these promoters demanded that Virginia manufacturing should be general: "Open manufactories of cotton in all its branches; of iron, in all its branches; of wool and of wood, including clocks." This action, they contended, would furnish the only safe basis for the maintenance of Southern rights, since it would keep within the limits of the state the wealth that had been flowing into Northern coffers. In this scheme of things, Richmond and Alexandria would supersede Philadelphia and New York in Virginia patronage.[25]

The cry for manufacturing as a basis for Southern independence met a full response in Virginia. In the late fifties, although New York, Pennsylvania, Ohio, and Massachusetts led the nation in number of manufacturing establishments, Virginia, with 4,841 establishments, stood fifth among the states and first in the South.[26] Among the Southern states,

[24] Editorial in Petersburg *South-Side Democrat*, July 9, 1854.
[25] Richmond *Enquirer*, June 20, 1854; Sept. 27, 1854, quoting the Staunton *Vindicator*; Howison, *History of Virginia*, 2: 502.
[26] *DeBow's Review*, 24: 555–559.

Virginia ranked first in number of woolen mills, first in pig iron, first in tobacco, and fourth in number of cotton mills. In the manufacture of tobacco Virginia led the nation. In 1860 there were in Richmond alone some fifty-two factories with a combined capital of four or five million dollars. In this city more tobacco was inspected and sold than in any other place in the United States. According to one contemporary, the road to wealth for many citizens of Richmond was paved with tobacco.[27]

The progress noted here stamped Virginia as both an agricultural and an industrial state. This dualism of development was not, however, confined to Virginia. Since all over the South similar changes had taken place, one recent student of this subject believes that this region no longer deemed industrialism its arch enemy, that a strong minority had surrendered to industry, with the proviso that the industry must be Southern.[28] It is not surprising, then, that the progress of Richmond in tobacco manufacturing was hardly greater than its progress in iron production. In 1860 the city had seventy-seven iron-working establishments, valued at three and a half million dollars. The most celebrated iron foundry of Richmond, and indeed the most celebrated of the entire South, was the Tredegar Iron Works. In 1852 this establishment was furnishing locomotives for Virginia railroads, so that the management no longer had to buy locomotives and other equipment in the North. Channing estimates that the iron works and other manufacturing establishments of Richmond in 1860 had a value of twenty-five million dollars.[29]

There were also in Richmond seven or more flour mills, the oldest of which was the Haxall Mill. The rise of the flour industry resulted from a relative decline in tobacco

---
[27] *Ibid.;* Mordecai, *Richmond,* p. 333.
[28] Kathleen Bruce, *Virginia Iron Manufacture in the Slave Era,* pp. 275–276.
[29] Richmond *Dispatch,* Aug. 23, 1852; Edward Channing, *A History of the United States,* 6: 29.

raising and a steady rise in the wheat crop, which increased from six million bushels in 1830 to twenty million in 1837.[30] In flour milling as in tobacco manufacturing princely fortunes were built up. In the generation preceding the Civil War, Virginia flour attained nation-wide celebrity.

The industrial advance in Richmond was paralleled in all Virginia cities and towns. The Richmond *Enquirer* sketched the picture thus: "In agriculture, manufactures, and the mechanic arts and internal improvements, Virginia now presents a glorifying spectacle. Virginia cities have . . . increased in wealth, population, and resources and the country has been tied to the town." [31] One of the leading cities to receive new life was Norfolk, which about 1840, after remaining stationary for nearly half a century, began to advance in population. Many new buildings were erected, gas was introduced, and new branches of manufacturing were begun.[32] The manufactories included a flour mill, an iron foundry, an establishment for the manufacture of lubricating oils from rosin, plow factories, and furniture factories. The furniture made in Norfolk was considered unexcelled in workmanship. The building of the railroad to Petersburg and the West was vital to Norfolk's development, for this road gave Norfolk its first connection with the Virginia railway system.

Petersburg stood next to Richmond as a manufacturing center of tobacco, flour, and woolens; in cotton goods it stood first in the state. Both of these cities flourished; one recent investigator writes that in 1860 they were the industrial centers of the entire South. Richmond ranked twenty-fifth in size among the cities of the country but thirteenth in the value of its manufactures. Charleston, South Carolina, on the other hand, which ranked twenty-second in size, was eighty-fifth in manufactures. Similar disparities prevailed

---

[30] *DeBow's Review*, 25: 582.
[31] Richmond *Enquirer*, Oct. 1, 1853, quoting the Alexandria *Gazette*.
[32] *Ibid.*, July 14, Aug. 27, 1853.

as between Richmond and Petersburg and other Southern cities.[33]

The importance of Petersburg as a manufacturing center, like that of the other towns, is indicated by its growth. The contrast between 1830 and 1860, as well as between 1840 and 1860, is striking. A contemporary made certain comparisons between the Petersburg of 1843 and the city of 1859. He stated that in 1859 Petersburg was about twice as large as in 1843, that real estate was worth about twice as much, and that the population had almost tripled. Sugar, coffee, bacon, and all the necessities of life, according to this observer, cost twice as much in 1859 as in 1843. Cotton at the earlier date had sold at from six to eight cents a pound and wheat at from sixty to ninety cents a bushel. This writer ascribed the difference to the fact that in 1843 there were no extortionate prices for Negroes, no guano, none of the new machinery and general farm improvements to make labor easier and farm products more expensive.[34]

Petersburg, like Richmond, was advancing in the iron industry. In 1854 the president of the Petersburg–Roanoke Railroad stated that of the $150,000 spent in the previous four years for engines, cars, and other equipment, at least $125,000 had been spent at home. Most of the locomotives used on the Richmond–Petersburg Railroad were made at Petersburg. With eight or ten tobacco factories in full operation in the late fifties and with an increasing quantity of cotton from North Carolina coming in for manufacture, Petersburg was prosperous at the end of the 1850 decade. Real estate values had risen from $4,250,214 in 1855 to $6,478,460 in 1859.[35]

Fredericksburg experienced a somewhat similar boom. Here in 1859 there were in operation various factories—including one for the manufacture of wheat fans, known all

[33] Robert R. Russel, *Economic Aspects of Southern Sectionalism*, 2:229.
[34] Petersburg *Daily Express*, Oct. 31, 1859.
[35] Petersburg *South-Side Democrat*, May 6, 1859; Olmsted, *Seaboard Slave States*, pp. 57–58; Petersburg *Daily Express*, April 10, 1857; Dec. 31, 1859

over the state; another for all kinds of farm machinery; and one for the manufacture of carriages. Besides these a woolen mill, a paper mill, and a tobacco factory had only recently been put into operation. These various establishments employed many hands.[36]

Alexandria too felt the industrial awakening. Fostering the progress of this town was the Chesapeake and Ohio Canal, which, beginning in the fifties, poured into the locality the riches of the Cumberland coal region and an extensive and expanding flour and grain trade. Between 1850 and 1852 the population of the city increased by 2,000, and its average real estate value increased 100 per cent. According to one observer, the success of Alexandria was due to the fact that in 1847 the town had been retroceded to Virginia and consequently could make headway under "old mother Virginia." [37]

Much of the progress noted here resulted from the ideal of Southern independence. "The North by its fanaticism," one paper remarked, "is forcing us on to prosperity." Throughout the state many persons were urging Virginia buyers to patronize their own cities and towns and encourage their own factories. Richmond and Fredericksburg, some asserted, manufactured the best cotton yarn in the world; yet their merchants were going north to purchase an inferior article. The manufacturers of these towns boldly declared that their products were as good as Northern products; that, for example, furniture made in Richmond was cheaper than that made in the North; and that consequently purchasers should buy Virginia-made articles.[38]

The progress of the 1850 decade in agriculture and manufacturing was, of course, accompanied by a similar rapid development of internal improvements. As a matter of fact,

[36] Fredericksburg *Weekly Advertiser*, Jan. 22, 1859.

[37] *DeBow's Review*, 13:310 (1852); Richmond *Enquirer*, Sept. 26, 1853, quoting Martinsburg *Gazette*.

[38] Richmond *Enquirer*, Sept. 6, 1853, quoting Staunton *Messenger;* Petersburg *South-Side Democrat*, Nov. 18, 1853; Richmond *Whig*, March 13, 1854; Fredericksburg *News*, July 2, 1853; Fredericksburg *Weekly Advertiser*, Feb. 18, March 10, 1860.

agricultural reform and internal improvements were a twofold program. By 1839 the James River and Kanawha Canal was finished to Lynchburg, with the result that the products of the West flowed into Richmond. The two or three railroads of 1832 had increased to twenty-three or more by 1860. In 1855, of a total projected mileage of 2,263½ miles for these railroads, 1,328¾ miles had been completed, and 637¼ miles were still in progress. The longest of these railroads in Virginia were the Covington and Ohio, the Virginia and Tennessee, and the Virginia Central. During the early fifties Virginia also had about 872 miles "of the most spacious and substantially constructed canals in the union." [39]

Despite the notable advances in these several fields, Virginia never succeeded in making Norfolk a great seaport, although it was one of the best natural harbors on the Atlantic seaboard. This failure Virginia leaders constantly bewailed, especially during the fifties. They looked at Boston, with a hinterland far less extensive than Norfolk's, and in like manner at other ports with fewer natural advantages than Norfolk, only to find that this city and Virginia lagged far behind. They noted also that Baltimore had swallowed up much of the commerce of western Virginia and Ohio, which they claimed rightfully belonged to Norfolk. Everyone recognized that phenomenal progress had been made in agriculture and that a commendable beginning had been made in manufacturing, but that in commerce Virginia had accomplished little.[40] The old dream of direct trade with Europe still remained unfulfilled.

This rapid survey of economic progress in Virginia is sufficient to prove that the state did not maintain until 1860 the "worn out," "run down" condition of 1830 and earlier. Contemporary material fairly teems with indications to the contrary and has been used by recent scholars to show that Vir-

[39] *Thirty-ninth Annual Report of the Board of Public Works*, 1855, p. xxiii; *DeBow's Review*, 13: 87 (1852).
[40] *Wealth, Resources, and Hopes of Virginia*, p. 29; Petersburg *Daily Express*, Nov. 3, 1859; Petersburg *South-Side Democrat*, March 1, 1854.

ginia, before the disaster of 1861–1865, was making distinct progress.[41] The state fully shared in the general upward economic trend experienced by the whole country during the decade of 1850.

This economic revival in Virginia was accompanied by some changes in the labor system of the state. Fundamental changes in agriculture, manufacturing, and internal improvements were bound to effect a reorganization in the field of labor. Indeed, the main theories of this study have their roots in this larger economic change which overtook Virginia society. Without these changes, free Negro labor and property holding might have taken another turn. The political and legal attacks on the free Negro during this era might have had a far greater success if these economic elements had not entered into the situation.

The developments that took place in the field of labor in Virginia between 1830 and 1860 may be summarized as follows: (1) a greater attachment to Negro slave labor, (2) a diminishing importance of slave labor in the new agriculture, (3) an increasing demand for slave labor in manufacturing and internal improvements, (4) the prevalence of white labor in spite of the demand for Negro labor, and (5) the demand and the opportunity for free labor, white and Negro, by reason of the diversion and high cost of slave labor.

The greater attachment to Negro slave labor was grounded upon certain other factors. Among these were the proslavery reaction to the attacks made by Northern abolitionists, the superior economic advantages—real or imaginary—of Negro slave labor over free white labor, and the rising prices of slaves.

The policies of Southerners toward their Negro population cannot be separated from the conflict between the antislavery men of the North and the slaveholders. The greater

---

[41] Cf. Craven, *Soil Exhaustion*, 160–161; Bruce, *Virginia Iron Manufacture*, pp. 80–85.

the criticism leveled by Northerners at Southern institutions, the more determined were the Southerners to perpetuate and redefine these same institutions and practices. The remark of a Southern Methodist in the field of religion may be said to have applied to all aspects of the life of the Negro. In reaction to "northern meddling," he said:

> As the abolition movement waxed fiercer, the zeal for Negro missions waxed warmer. As abolition societies multiplied at the North, missions among the slaves multiplied at the South; as plans and measures for the final extirpation of slavery were growing into gradual proportions at the North, plans and measures for the salvation of the slaves were rapidly enlarging at the south.[42]

The same reaction prevailed with respect to labor. In proportion as Northerners cast reflections on the Southern Negro labor system, so did Southern men extol this system.

In the previous chapter it has been noted that to the Southerners the slave labor system seemed in every way superior to the hireling system of the North and of Europe. Edmund Ruffin was certain of this. In the fifties he took the position that all the Virginia antislavery notions of 1830 had passed away and that slave labor was more profitable to the employers than any other type of labor. He assumed that this idea prevailed not only in Virginia but throughout the other Southern states as well. At the same time he buttressed his arguments for slave labor by saying that free Negro labor was utterly worthless.[43]

The views of men on any public question are greatly affected by financial considerations. The swing to Negro slavery by Virginians beginning in 1830 was influenced by the

---

[42] *Methodist Quarterly Review*, 18:431, quoted in Luther P. Jackson, "Religious Instruction of Negroes, 1830 to 1860," in *Journal of Negro History*, 15:78 (Jan., 1930).

[43] Ruffin, *Address to Virginia State Agriculture Society*, p. 16. Ruffin operated plantations in Prince George and Hanover counties. He owned and employed a large number of slaves for these plantations, but, according to the tax books of these counties, he never employed a free Negro from the many in Prince George and the surrounding territory.

rising value of their slave property occasioned by the opening of new cotton land in the far South. Virginia slave owners, hoping to reap profits not from slave labor within the state but from the Southern demand for this labor, were impelled by economic considerations to take up the proslavery position. Once before, in the early eighteenth century, Virginia and the South had taken such a position because of the paying quality of slave labor.

After 1830, though Virginians were more than ever attached to slavery, they faced the fact that the new agriculture made smaller demands for this type of labor. The shift to grain production, truck gardening, fruit growing, and dairying introduced branches of agriculture for which slave labor was essentially unfitted.[44] Leaders of thought in agriculture, including men of the most decided proslavery views, advised that farmers rid themselves of some of their slaves in order to make more intelligent use of the rest. This procedure was advised in the belief that slaves in moderate numbers were just as capable of fitting into the new agriculture as free labor.[45] This advice was followed, yet slaveholding on a large scale was still found profitable on large river plantations and on tobacco plantations. After 1840 tobacco was grown on a scale equal to that of colonial days.[46]

The situation in agriculture gave to Virginia slavery in the new period three prominent features: the raising of slaves more as a marketable and money-returning commodity than for their productive labor for the owner, the excessive hiring of slaves, and the greater development of the domestic slave trade.

All of these characteristics resulted from the demand for labor in the cotton states along the Gulf. The growing de-

[44] Henry Howe, *Historical Collections of Virginia*, p. 160.
[45] Craven, *Soil Exhaustion*, p. 140; *DeBow's Review*, 20:459.
[46] Some of the largest river plantations in Virginia were in Essex County along the Rappahannock. William B. Beverly, Richard Baylor, W. L. Waring, M. H. Garrett, Thomas R. Waring, Lewis Warner, Henry W. Leland, and Robert M. T. Hunter held seventy-five or more slaves apiece. Richard Baylor exceeded all others with 335. U. S. Census Bureau, *Slave Inhabitants*, 1860.

mand there, with the resultant rise in price, gave Virginia slaves high rank as marketable commodities. Because of their great cost, slaves then became unremunerative units in Virginia agriculture proper. On this subject one Virginia planter remarked in 1860: "I look upon it as murder to lay out money in Negroes to work in Virginia." [47] Unlike the situation in the cotton states, the prices of agricultural products raised in Virginia had no effect on the price of Virginia slaves. Prices of cotton and sugar, commodities produced outside of Virginia, determined the prices of slaves within the state. As one Virginia farmer stated the case, prospective buyers had always to pay more than the real value for slaves because they had to bid against the slave traders.[48] Hence slaves in Virginia, like American farm land at other times and in other places, possessed little productive value yet did represent a good investment.

Since high-priced slaves must be employed in raising low-priced farm products and since the overstocked slaveholder now more than ever must reduce his holdings, the practice of hiring out slaves assumed large proportions. Fortunately for the owners, at this time Virginia slaves were in demand for lumbering, mining, steam-boating, dock labor, railway and canal building, and other public works.[49] Slave hiring served as an accommodation in two directions: it gave slaveholders, whether with many or few slaves, the opportunity to hire out all or some of them, and it gave non-slaveholders the opportunity of securing slave labor. This was the situation of a certain New Jersey farmer living then in the neighborhood of Richmond, who said that he used Negro labor because it was difficult to get any other type but that in hiring slaves only the poorer ones could be secured. In his case first-class hands

---

[47] Quoted in Phillips, *Life and Labor in the Old South*, p. 246; *Southern Planter*, 12: 56 (1852).

[48] *Farmers' Register*, 2:763.

[49] Lewis C. Gray, *History of Agriculture in the Southern United States to 1860*, 1:566; *Farmers' Register*, 3:207–208; Howard D. Dozier, *History of the Atlantic Coast Line Railroad*, pp. 89–90.

were hard to obtain.⁵⁰ Hiring out was widely practiced by those who had inherited large numbers of slaves and had bought or sold none. Often the working force on a large plantation would actually be only a third of the whole number, while all the rest of its slave population would be hired out.

The cities of Virginia were the great slave-hiring centers. In Richmond, Lynchburg, and Petersburg a large number of slave boys drawn from the country were regularly hired in the tobacco factories.⁵¹ Large numbers were also placed in the iron works of these same cities. It has been estimated that during the fifties some 5,000 slaves were hired out annually in Richmond alone and that in all Virginia the number was at least 15,000. Hiring thus played an important part in the shifting economic organization of Virginia during the years under discussion. It enabled the manufacturers of the cities to get the labor they needed and at the same time it relieved the overstocked slaveholders of the countryside. In addition, slave hiring had one other very important result; it frequently led to manumission, a subject to be discussed in a later chapter.

The non-productiveness of slaves in Virginia agriculture finally led to a sudden rise in the domestic slave trade. The number of slaves sold from Virginia and the upper South has never been accurately determined; but according to contemporary statements it was enormous. A great many masters would not sell their slaves to the Southern market, but there were others who made the breeding of slaves for this market a regular branch of their business.⁵²

The slave trade saved the financial situation for many Virginia farmers. One observer found the farmers out of debt because they had recently sold their Negroes at the late high prices. Olmsted reported that Virginia slave laborers

---
⁵⁰ John T. Trowbridge, *The South*, p. 181.
⁵¹ Frederic Bancroft, *Slave Trading in the Old South*, pp. 153, 404.
⁵² Richmond *Whig*, July 25, 1845.

were constantly being sent away. He declared during the fifties that he had not been on a train nor seen one that did not carry a considerable number of the best class of Negro laborers. Because of the hundreds of slaves who successively passed through Petersburg on their way south, it was predicted that in ten or twenty years Virginia would be completely cleared of that part of its population. During three months in 1858–1859, 2,312 passed through this town; and from Weldon, North Carolina, came the information that about 2,000 passed there during the month of January, 1859, alone. One recent estimate is that the number of slaves sold south from Virginia between 1830 and 1860 averaged annually 9,371.[53]

The slave population of Virginia, sometimes in company with slave owners, thus was being transferred to the cotton South; but economic interests outside the field of agriculture soon arose to counteract the southern drift. The growing manufactures and internal improvements began to attract slave labor. The manufacturing interests of the state, although severely hampered in instituting some phases of their operations, had no difficulty in finding labor. The industrialists could appeal to the agriculturists for their slave labor which was otherwise unproductive. The owners of slaves thus found at last a number of opportunities for the productive employment of their property.

The introduction of slaves into capitalistic manufacturing, however, like all new movements, necessitated a campaign of education. One strong advocate of the employment of slaves in the rising factories of the South was the Southern Commercial Convention. This convention of cotton planters, which met in Augusta in 1851, passed resolutions encouraging the employment of slave labor in industry.[54] The argument that the South was "too agricultural" had its implica-

---

[53] *Farmers' Register*, 7:210; Olmsted, *Cotton Kingdom*, 1:112; Howison, *Virginia*, 2:520; Petersburg *Daily Express*, March 9, 1857; Feb. 3, March 10, 1859; Bancroft, *Slave Trading*, p. 386.
[54] *Harpers Magazine*, 4:121 (1851–52).

tion in the field of labor as well as in the general economy of the region.

The usual arguments employed to show the need for a greater diversification ran thus: the South should have a division of labor; the slave population was being doubled so that in time the increasing numbers could not profitably be absorbed by agriculture; the Negroes could learn manufacturing inasmuch as they had learned blacksmithing, carpentry, boot and shoemaking, and all handicrafts with as much facility as white men; they should be taught when young; slave labor could be used especially in iron manufacture, since the demand in this industry was constantly increasing; and application of labor to one staple and the neglect of manufacturing meant the loss of billions of dollars. The final admonition was that Southerners should stop investing in land and slaves and should put their money into manufacturing, that instead of sending slaves to the fields they should send them to the cotton mills to be instructed as operatives.[55]

The call for slave labor in cotton factories was not general in Virginia, but in the iron and tobacco manufactures Negro labor both slave and free was in great demand. Slaves had gained a firm footing in iron manufacturing in the twenty years or more before 1860. By 1840 the iron masters of the South and particularly Joseph Anderson of the Tredegar Iron Works in Richmond took the position that slave labor was indispensable. In support of his contention Anderson reasoned that slave labor was cheaper than Northern white labor and that if a sufficient number of skilled white technicians from the North could be employed to teach the large number of slave operatives, the cost of operation would still be comparatively low and Tredegar would be able to compete with other iron works throughout the country.[56]

[55] *DeBow's Review*, 3: 187–215.
[56] Bruce, *Virginia Iron Manufacture*, p. 244.

Some indication of the success of the drive to bring slaves into factories may be seen in the numbers employed in certain Richmond establishments in the year 1846.[57] The factories and mills represented in the following list include tobacco, cotton, iron, flour, and other enterprises. In many instances the slaves represented were hired rather than owned by the head of the business.

TABLE I
Slaves in Richmond Factories, 1846

Manufacturer	Number of Slaves	Manufacturer	Number of Slaves
Joseph R. Anderson	40	Thomas Hardgrove	78
William Barrett	49	Samuel Myers & Co.	148
E. B. Bartley	79	Joseph Mosby	35
Beasley & Quarles	70	P. Robinson	100
John Enders	99	Sanders & Luckie	58
James H. Grant	100	James Thomas	62

In all these and other establishments, as the years passed, the number of slaves steadily increased. Whereas the total number of slaves over twelve years old in Richmond factories was 5,667 in 1846, the number ten years later was 6,326.[58]

In like manner internal improvements throughout the state created a demand for slaves quite as heavy as that made by manufacturing. In this field slaves hired out by overstocked farmers figured conspicuously. The growing demand for slave labor may be shown in the calls made by the railroads in newspaper advertisements during the period. The Norfolk and Petersburg Railroad one year wished to hire 100 Negroes; the Wilmington and Weldon sought 100;

---

[57] Virginia State Library, Tax Books, Personal Property, Richmond, 1846. Hereafter the citation "Virginia State Library, Tax Books" will be omitted and the tax books will be identified by "Personal Property" or by "Land," with the county and date.

[58] *Ibid.*, 1846–1856.

the South-Side called for 150; the Virginia and Tennessee wanted 300 to work on repairs during 1860.[59]

Manufacturing and internal improvements, it may be remarked, seemed attractive to some Virginia leaders for still other reasons. The Richmond *Enquirer* advanced the view that Virginia must enter the manufacturing field in order to check the current that annually swept away many slaves from the state. The rise of internal improvements had brought some increase in the value of slaves and tended to check emigration. The use of slaves in manufacturing would stop the southern movement altogether.[60] The demands for slaves in the far South and in Virginia enterprises were numerous. Though Virginia farmers, mill owners, tobacconists, cotton manufacturers, iron manufacturers, steamboat owners, contractors, carpenters, railroad companies, and canal boat owners needed slaves, nevertheless slaves were constantly being drawn from the state. The need for laborers in Virginia was great, but apparently that in the cotton raising states was still greater.[61]

In this general picture of labor, of course, white labor also appeared. The view once expressed that the white man displayed no inclination for manual toil in a slave society is a misrepresentation of the facts. A better interpretation is that the white man as a hired laborer was averse to employment with the slave and the free Negro but that he did not object to engaging in the type of labor performed by Negroes provided that he labored in company with persons of his own race.[62] The yeoman farmer and owner of a few slaves, on the other hand, worked side by side with slaves. As between urban and rural districts, in the cities of Virginia and

[59] Petersburg *South-Side Democrat*, Dec. 21, 1853; Sept. 9, 1854; Petersburg *Daily Express*, Dec. 28, 1859.
[60] Richmond *Enquirer*, May 19, 1854.
[61] Olmsted, *Cotton Kingdom*, 2: 111–112.
[62] Alfred H. Stone, "Free Contract Labor in the Ante-Bellum South," in *The South in the Building of the Nation*, James C. Ballagh, ed., 5: 143; *DeBow's Review*, 20: 467; Petition, Dinwiddie, Dec. 20, 1831; Olmsted, *Seaboard Slave States*, p. 211.

the South numerous white artisans found an opportunity for work, but in the country they fared harder because the rich planter owned slaves trained for the mechanic arts.[63]

White labor of all kinds flourished in the non-slaveholding regions of western Virginia, particularly in the Shenandoah Valley, where there were many German settlers, and in parts of northern Virginia, where in some instances a county was divided between a slaveholding section and a free labor section. This division was strikingly manifest in Loudon County.[64] In such sections, since slave labor was rare or had never existed, manual toil could have no stigma attached to it. White labor, in fact, existed to some extent throughout Virginia, even in the entirely rural counties with a heavy slave population. In Sussex County, for example, in 1860 there were whites engaged as carpenters, seamstresses, cabinet makers, coach makers, bootmakers, lumberers, common laborers, harness makers, wheelwrights, weavers, hucksters, painters, tanners, and tailors.[65] In Mathews County in the same year almost all of the many ship carpenters and seamen were white.

In the villages throughout Virginia white mechanics were numerous. In 1830 Orange Court House, with 503 inhabitants, was typical. About this time there were in this village two cabinet makers, one silversmith and jeweler, three blacksmiths, one boot and shoe manufacturer, one house and sign painter, two bricklayers, three house carpenters, one wagon maker, two tailors, one coach maker, one saddle and harness maker, and one turner, most of whom were white. In the adjoining county of Louisa the village of Mechanicsville actually derived its name from the many white mechanics there.[66]

Of the cities of Virginia in 1860, Norfolk stood first in

---

[63] D. R. Hundley, *Social Relations in Our Southern States*, pp. 194, 197; *Farmers' Register*, 1: 37.
[64] Martin, *Virginia Gazetteer*, p. 210.
[65] U. S. Census Bureau, Free Inhabitants (ms.), 1860.
[66] Martin, *Virginia Gazetteer*, p. 255.

the number of white mechanics as against free Negro mechanics. Among the free artisans at this place, the whites did all the blacksmithing and virtually all the bricklaying. They even invaded the barber business, in which there were at least six white barbers as against five among the free Negroes.[67] This situation in Norfolk resulted from an increasing white population and a declining Negro population, slave and free. This population trend showed itself somewhat in Petersburg, Richmond, and other cities; but in none of them was it so marked as in Norfolk. From 1840 to 1850 in Norfolk the urban white population increased by 46½ per cent; the slaves increased by 15⅔ per cent; but the number of free Negroes decreased by about 6⅔ per cent. In the next decade the whites gained 13½ per cent, the free Negroes stood practically still, and the slaves declined 23 per cent.[68]

Over the entire state the whites engaged not only in the mechanic arts but also in various forms of heavy manual labor. Their work in this field reached its peak in the decade of 1850. In Culpeper County in 1850 a gang of 175 Irish laborers worked in railroad building; in Dinwiddie County about the same time there was another large group of Irishmen employed by the railroads; in Fairfax still another; in Chesterfield County natives of England and Ireland worked in coal mines and at other hard manual labor.[69] White labor, like free Negro labor, frequently found a place in the economy of Virginia from 1830 to 1860 because of the high cost of hired slaves. Such, at least, was the position taken by the newly arrived New Jersey farmers in Fairfax County.[70]

Although white labor held a sure place, especially in northern Virginia, such labor was not always satisfactory. The use of slaves at some previous time by employers offered

---

[67] U. S. Census Bureau, *Free Inhabitants* (ms.), 1860.
[68] These figures are based on computations from the U. S. Census.
[69] Personal Property, Culpeper, 1851; U. S. Census Bureau, *Free Inhabitants*, 1850.
[70] Olmsted, *Seaboard Slave States*, pp. 99–100.

them an opportunity to make comparison between slave labor and white labor. This was the region in which the greatest number of Germans and Irish from Pennsylvania and Maryland had settled, and it was here that the farmers spoke of the evils of white labor. White workers, some complained, charged too much; they took offense at trifles; they could not be worked to advantage with slaves; furthermore, they showed a tendency to idleness. If such laborers had so much as a horse, a second-hand cart, and $20, they would go off to Illinois or Wisconsin and there in time become independent farmers. Edmund Ruffin echoed these complaints and added that the greater cheapness and economy of Negro slave labor made it preferable to free labor.[71] This economy was practised in the iron industry of Richmond. J. R. Anderson of the Tredegar Iron Works thus hired a large number of slaves and made it clear to white men that Negro slave labor was in his establishment to stay. The effort of a white mob to oust the slaves was regarded as "a movement which the whole community would condemn." [72]

White labor held an important place in Virginia by 1860, but it faced a constant struggle. The situation of this class was especially difficult in the thirty or more counties where there was a large Negro population. White men had to compete with Negro labor, while the whites who possessed political and economic power were inclined to side with such labor against their own race. Much of the bitterness that arose between white laborers and blacks grew out of the fact that the free element of the latter class was frequently in as good circumstances as the whites, or even better. The return to white mechanics in the form of property ownership and satisfactory standards of living was in many cases no greater than that to the free Negroes. White rural mechanics in the slave

[71] Olmsted, *Cotton Kingdom*, 1:112; *Farmers' Register*, 5:743, 747; Ruffin, *Slavery and Free Labor*, p. 20.
[72] Richmond *Enquirer*, May 29, 1847.

regions acquired little property because most of the work in the trades was done by slaves who had been trained by their masters for this purpose.[73]

The low economic level and the general insecurity of white skilled labor caused protest through the press and petitions to the state legislature. A protest in a newspaper in 1845 implied that the feeling against slavery should be aroused again. The slaves, it was said, were being taught all of the trades so that white laborers were compelled to leave the state. "Thousands of our young mechanics, carpenters, blacksmiths, bricklayers and so forth annually leave Virginia and go to some of the free states of the west." Further charges made were that in the city of Richmond the carpenter shops, blacksmith shops, and shops of all kinds were crowded with Negro apprentices and workmen; that though slavery was desirable, it was dangerous to teach trades to Negroes and thus elevate them at the expense of the poor white mechanics; that the black man should be restricted to agriculture and the white man should be allowed to monopolize the mechanic arts.[74] A group of citizens of Culpeper County, themselves slaveholders, went so far as to ask that slaves be restricted to encourage white mechanics. This was to be done by prohibiting any slave, free Negro, or mulatto from learning a trade or becoming an apprentice. Like the other complainants, these citizens reported that there had been a heavy emigration of white men to the western states because the mechanic arts were "fast falling into the hands of the black population." [75]

White men had their difficulties in finding employment, and so did white women. Throughout the thirties and forties

---

[73] Sir Charles Lyell, *A Second Visit to the United States of North America*, 2:36.
[74] Richmond *Daily Whig*, Dec. 11, 1845; *DeBow's Review*, 26: 477–478; Russel, *Southern Sectionalism*, pt. 1, p. 53; pt. 2, pp. 219–220; Petitions, Dinwiddie, Dec. 20, 1831; Norfolk, Feb. 25, 1851.
[75] Petition, Culpeper, 1831.

there was constant complaint that white women had nothing to do but sew. Even this occupation was limited because of the large quantity of ready-made clothing imported from the North. The sewing done by white women in the city of Richmond brought them extremely low wages, in some instances as little as twelve and a half cents for working all day and part of the night. During the fifties cotton factories offered white women some employment, but with pay so low as to jeopardize their moral standards. Toward the end of this period white girls had some opportunities in domestic service, as newspaper advertisements testify, and they also found an opening in the tobacco factories.[76]

As free white labor managed to find a place for itself in a slave economy, so also did free Negro labor. Free Negro labor emerged and maintained itself because of several fortunate circumstances: the factor of race, the occasional dearth of slave labor, the high cost of slave labor, the availability and low cost of free Negro labor, color prejudice by white labor against certain kinds of tasks and against employment with free Negroes, and, most important of all, the business boom of the fifties. By a good turn of fortune the free Negro thus found a niche in both the industrial and the agricultural life of Virginia.

Thus far a distinction has been drawn between slave labor and free Negro labor; yet in one sense there was no sharp line of separation. From the economic point of view, as one writer indicates, slaves and free Negroes were not sharply distinguished, and socially they were still less differentiated. This attitude of white men toward free Negroes is understandable inasmuch as the two classes of blacks shared the same blood and the same standards of living. Their social identity was fostered through frequent intermarriage, and the economic position of rural free Negroes, who worked

---

[76] *Farmers' Register*, 3: 257–258, 380–381, 575; Richmond *Whig*, Nov. 22, 1845; Petersburg *Daily Express*, August 18, 1858.

under agreements for small wages, was quite like that of slaves.[77] Many contemporary references to slave labor and Negro labor embrace the free Negro as well as the slave proper. All told, his race counted in favor of the free Negro in his competition with white labor.

As has been noted, the dearth of slave labor caused by the domestic slave trade was one argument advanced in favor of establishing manufactures in Virginia to keep the slaves at home.[78] This scarcity of slave labor was more pronounced in some sections of the state than in others. It was quite notable in the decade of 1830 and evoked considerable comment. In this connection a petition of citizens of Westmoreland County in the Northern Neck is significant. According to this document, a group of people with interests in the fishing trade in the Potomac River wanted forty-eight hands, but they could not get them from the slave group "owing to the great diminution of slaves in their county, as well as in the counties generally of the Northern Neck by exportation and emigration." Since the fishing season in this case occurred at the same time when the farmers were engaged in planting their crops, hiring of slaves would be very expensive and greatly reduce the profits from fishing. Previously, hired slaves had been used for the fishing on the Virginia side of the Potomac, while on the Maryland side free Negroes had been used at smaller cost. The Maryland fishermen had thus been able to undersell those of Virginia. In view of this fact the Westmoreland fishermen petitioned the Virginia legislature for the privilege of using Maryland free Negroes, whose services could easily be procured and whose cost was less than that of slave or free white labor.[79]

The scarcity of slave labor available for the draying business in Norfolk evoked a petition on behalf of Ackey White, a free Negro drayman, who in 1836 was at the point of being

---

[77] James M. Wright, *The Free Negro in Maryland, 1634-1860*, pp. 17, 43.
[78] Richmond *Enquirer*, May 19, 1854.
[79] Petition, Westmoreland, March 9, 1838.

removed from the state within the twelve months' period following his manumission. White citizens "prayed" the legislature to allow this free man to remain in Virginia because of "the great drain in the Negro population by the South" and because the job of drayman was a "Negro job" and no white person would engage in it. This work, they said, though highly responsible, could be done by slaves; but the drain of such persons to the South had left this "very responsible" occupation without sufficient laborers.[80] Because of this strong argument, perhaps, Ackey White was allowed to remain in Norfolk the rest of his life.

In Fauquier County and in other counties of northern Virginia the removal of slaves left a void in the labor market. It was found in 1838 that although this wheat-producing section did not need as much labor as did lower Virginia, yet the supply was insufficient. Farmers in this region stated that the "cotton fever" of the early thirties had carried off not only some of the best white people but also, unfortunately, their Negroes. In this instance the demand was filled largely by white labor, but such labor was frequently found to be unsatisfactory.[81] As will be shown later, the northern counties of Frederick, Fauquier, and Loudon leaned heavily on free Negro labor—no doubt, because of the scarcity of slaves.

Employers of labor throughout Virginia during the economic revival faced the realization not only that there was a dearth of slaves but also that it was unprofitable to use even the supply available. The demand for slaves in internal improvements in Virginia, on the one hand, and the heavy southern demand, on the other, made the cost of slave labor in the late fifties well-nigh prohibitive.[82] Just as the prices of all goods were very much higher in the fifties than earlier, so was the price of slaves. Exorbitant prices of slaves meant

---

[80] Petition, Norfolk, Dec. 28, 1836.
[81] *Farmers' Register,* 5:474 (1837); 6:458.
[82] Phillips, *Life and Labor in the Old South,* p. 187.

also a rising cost of slave hire. In 1858 the cost of a year's hire of women on the Petersburg market ranged from $70 to $100; girls about fourteen years old brought from $40 to $50; girls eleven and twelve brought from $20 to $30. Healthy men brought as high as $220, although the average price was a $150. All of these prices were regarded as enormous by persons who customarily hired slaves. In 1834 slave men had been hired for only $60 to $70.[83]

The purchase price of slaves became so high that one contemporary even declared a good house servant in the late fifties was worth her weight in gold. The high cost of slaves is shown by the following figures from a sale in Petersburg in 1856: Richard, $915; James, $1,070; Charles, $930; George, $1,250; William, $990; and Carter, $1,250. These prices were regarded as approaching the highest in the history of the state, but three years later prices were still higher. In 1859 men and boys from fifteen to thirty years of age were sold in the slave market at from $1,400 to $1,600.[84]

Because of these high prices employers began to find it cheaper to pay wages to free labor, white or black, than to purchase or to hire slaves. These discoveries resulted in a definite shift of labor policy. Free Negroes and whites were employed in larger numbers in the tobacco factories of Petersburg and Richmond, and throughout the state whites were given greater opportunities in various kinds of labor. Free Negroes were introduced into the tobacco factories of Richmond for the first time during the decade of 1850.[85] In both Richmond and Petersburg white women, as has been noted, were employed beginning in 1858, at first merely as an experiment, but as one that proved successful. A be-

---

[83] Petersburg *Daily Express*, Dec. 31, 1858; Dec. 29, 1859; Raymond B. Pinchbeck, *The Virginia Negro Artisan and Tradesman*, p. 57.

[84] Petersburg *Daily Express*, Dec. 17, 1856; Sept. 13, 1859.

[85] This statement is based on the absence of free Negro tobacco factory laborers in the original enumeration of the U. S. Census of 1850 and in the Richmond city directory of 1852. On the other hand, such workers are listed in both of these sources in 1860.

lief was arising that the slave's place was in agriculture.[86]

Nevertheless the whites and free Negroes did not displace slave labor in the tobacco factories of Petersburg and Richmond. On the contrary the number of slaves in the many tobacco establishments there steadily increased.[87] The introduction of free Negroes and whites merely meant a general increase in the total number of workers.

Employers of labor in Virginia embraced a large number of non-slaveholders. In the South at large non-slaveholders constituted at least two-thirds of the white population; furthermore, in Virginia approximately one-fifth of the slaveholders held one slave only.[88] This situation thus opened large opportunities for one of three types of labor —white, hired slave, and free Negro. In the competition of these three groups for employment not only by non-slaveholders but also by employers generally, free Negroes had certain advantages. First among these was the fact that they could be hired for shorter periods and at cheaper rates than could slaves. Under such circumstances this class of labor was a distinct aid to the man of small means who could afford neither to own slaves nor to hire them for the whole year. In the free Negro such employers found a person who frequently was willing to work for almost anything he could get.[89]

Hired slaves, even when they could be secured at low rates, were not suited to small irregular jobs; and in such work again the free Negro found an opportunity. In short, there was a certain amount of labor for which the free Negro

---

[86] Petersburg *Daily Express*, March 1, 1859; Phillips, *Life and Labor in the Old South*, p. 187.

[87] Personal Property, Richmond, Petersburg, 1845-1860. Contrary to the statement of Phillips cited in note 86 that there was a substitution of white laborers for slaves, a more nearly correct view is that white laborers were employed in larger numbers. Regardless of the high cost of their labor, slaves held their own at least in tobacco manufacturing. Thomas and Samuel Hardgrove, tobacconists of Richmond, for example, employed 89 slaves in 1854, 97 in 1859, and 108 in 1860.

[88] *DeBow's Review*, 17:433.

[89] Richmond *Daily Times*, Feb. 12, 1853.

had no competitor except the white laborer. Among these small, irregular jobs on a farm into which the free Negro peculiarly fitted may be mentioned ditching and well-digging. In addition there were assigned to him those tasks that were regarded as too unhealthful or too perilous for a slave.[90]

In the list of occupations in which the free Negro competed with whites, as Russell shows, he had the advantage in two respects: his standard of living enabled him to accept lower wages than the whites could accept, and, being naturally obedient, tractable, and respectful of personal authority, he was considered to be a better servant.[91] In a choice between a white man of low station and a free Negro, the latter usually won. One newspaper editor styled the low white man "a far greater pest." [92] George Fitzhugh, however, an arch enemy of free Negroes, contended that their competition was injurious to white workers, that their few and simple wants enabled them to accept wages lower than whites could afford to take. He therefore maintained that the state should seek to elevate the position of white laborers.[93] With respect to the advantages named above, Governor Smith again testified that the free Negroes performed a thousand little services to the exclusion of the white man, that they were preferred by their employers to the detriment of the white man because of the authority and control which employers could exercise and frequently because of the ease and facility with which they could remunerate such services.[94] Free Negroes sometimes made even better "slaves" than the real slaves, since they could be discharged for incompetence whereas the latter were with the owner always.

To summarize, the free Negro had a definite place in Virginia employment. If he was efficient, he could always

[90] John H. Russell, *Free Negro*, 147; David Dodge, "The Free Negro of North Carolina," in *Atlantic Monthly*, 57:26 (Jan., 1886).
[91] John H. Russell, *Free Negro*, p. 149.
[92] Richmond *Whig*, Jan. 25, 1853; Richmond *Daily Dispatch*, Jan. 26, Feb. 15, 1853.
[93] George Fitzhugh, *What Shall Be Done with the Free Negroes*, p. 6
[94] *Journal of House of Delegates*, 1848-1849, p. 22.

find work, regardless of discriminatory statutes and white competition.⁹⁵ White laborers were also at a disadvantage in their own disinclination to engage in certain kinds of labor because such labor was performed by Negroes. Certain jobs in a Negro-white society were "Negro jobs," and white men would not degrade themselves by engaging in them. In this connection it must be repeated that white men drew no line of distinction whatever between slaves and free Negroes socially and only a very faint one economically. To them a Negro always remained a Negro.

All in all, the free Negro, like the slave, constituted a standing menace to white labor. The competition between these two groups in some localities was as serious as the competition between whites and slaves. White men emigrated to the West because of the free Negro. Concern over this situation was expressed by whites both as individuals and as groups. Citizens of Henrico County in 1825 stated: "No white laborer will seek employment near him [the free Negro]. Hence it is that in some of the richest counties east of the Blue Ridge the white population is stationary and in many others retrograde." In Culpeper, as has been noted previously, 100 or more citizens, complaining that in the mechanic trades the blacks were displacing the whites, asked the legislature to prohibit slaves, free Negroes, and mulattoes from learning the trades. Similarly, Portsmouth citizens complained some years later that Negro mechanics had retarded the prosperity, enterprise, and progress of the state by driving out native Virginians to other states where they might have remunerative employment.⁹⁶

This question was also agitated by the press and by public functionaries. A citizen writing in the Richmond *Whig* in 1845 said: "Those whose hearts are now sickened when they look into the carpenters' shops, the blacksmiths' shops and the shops of all the different trades in Richmond and see

---

⁹⁵ Stone, "Free Contract Labor," in *South in the Building of Nation*, 5: 139.
⁹⁶ Petitions, Henrico, 1825; Culpeper, 1831; Norfolk County, Feb. 25, 1851.

them crowded with Negro apprentices and Negro workmen, are ready to quit in disgust." In 1847 Governor Smith in his message to the legislature said: "I venture the opinion that a larger emigration of our white laborers is produced by our free Negroes than by the institution of slavery." Thousands of young white men left Virginia for Ohio, Indiana, and the Northwest because of Negro competition.[97]

Opportunities for free Negro employment grew as time passed; in the fifties they were greater than ever before. Better conditions in the state were ushered in on the wings of industrialism. Although Virginia never equaled the Northern and Eastern states in industry, it did manifest considerable progress in diversifying its economic life. Industrial activity in the cities serves to illustrate this fact.

Virginia's leading manufactures were flour, cotton, iron, and tobacco, but the greatest of these in relation to the free Negro was tobacco. In the fifties the tobacco business was booming, as witnessed by the Petersburg *Daily Express*: "Railroad trains arrive daily heavily laden with tobacco; dray teams block up our streets with tobacco in transition; warehouses crowded to overflowing." A few days later the same paper indicated that 104 hogsheads of tobacco had arrived at one warehouse in one day, the largest amount thus far. It continued: "Never has there been so much tobacco coming into Petersburg." Much of this tobacco was to be manufactured in Petersburg, where an immense business was being done. A Boston newspaper correspondent reported that he visited one Petersburg factory where there were no less than 230 hands, all Negroes, ranging in age from six to sixty.[98]

In Richmond, likewise, the manufacture of tobacco was constantly growing. In 1852 the Richmond *Daily Dispatch*

---

[97] Richmond *Whig*, Dec. 11, 1845; *Journal of House of Delegates*, 1847–1848, p. 20; *New York Times*, Aug. 15, 1854, cited in Charles H. Wesley, *Negro Labor in the United States, 1850–1925*, p. 70.

[98] Petersburg *Daily Express*, May 20, 26, 1856; Feb. 22, 1859. Cf. John H. Claiborne, *Seventy-five Years in Old Virginia*.

pointed out that there were five new brick establishments in process of erection and that others were projected. This increase in trade and business, the paper observed, would give employment to many slaves who might otherwise be unprofitable. A growing number of tobacco factories meant a greater employment of slaves and free Negroes; greater employment meant increased wages. Not only in the tobacco factories but also in the mechanical industries, free Negroes were finding steady work. Their chances had never been better. In this connection Olmsted advanced the opinion that at the current rate of wages any "free colored man" might accumulate property faster than any man in the North who depended solely on his labor.[99]

The general boom in the economic life of Virginia saved the day for the free Negro and made him all the more valuable to the state. The circumstances and conditions discussed above were favorable to the free Negro and gave him a safe place in the labor supply of Virginia.

[99] Richmond *Daily Dispatch*, Aug. 21, Sept. 23, 1852; Olmsted, *Seaboard Slave States*, p. 141.

CHAPTER III

THE FREE NEGRO AT WORK

THE economic revival of Virginia had opened to the free Negro the opportunity to work. A survey of the system and the conditions under which he worked, and of the actual occupations he pursued in country and town, will give a clearer picture of his place in the economic life of the state.

The extent to which free Negro labor fitted into the economy of Virginia may be inferred from statistics of population. In 1860 free Negroes constituted from 22 per cent to 34 per cent of the total black population in eight eastern counties of the state—Isle of Wight, James City, Nansemond, Surry, Southampton, Richmond, Westmoreland, and York. In Accomac County, which had the largest number of free Negroes in the state, they constituted 43 per cent, and the total of 3,418 free Negroes approached that of 4,507 slaves. In the cities of Virginia, notably Alexandria, Petersburg, Norfolk, and Richmond, the free Negro population, in comparison with the numbers of slaves, was always high. In 1860 the free Negroes in Alexandria constituted 51 per cent of the total black population; in Petersburg, 27 per cent; in Norfolk, 24 per cent; in Richmond, 18 per cent. It is obvious that free Negroes must have formed an indispensable element in the labor supply of such places.

One circumstance which contributed to the value of free Negroes as laborers was the fact that many of this group, rather than living in their own homes, lived in the homes of white families as farm hands or domestic servants. The original census of 1830 shows that in thirty-one counties, about a third of the whole number, at least 25 per cent of the free

Negroes lived in white families.[1] In eleven of these thirty-one counties the number ran as high as 40 per cent. In one of the counties, Southampton, the vast majority of the 1,745 free Negroes lived in this way. In fifteen other counties, from 15 per cent to 25 per cent of the free Negroes lived thus. Altogether there were in the state approximately 8,000 free Negroes who lived with or near white families.[2] Granting that there may be errors in the census enumeration of "families," it is certain that many free Negroes lived directly with white families in the same manner as house slaves.

This custom prevailed in 1860 as it had in 1830, although in some counties it had somewhat declined. In Sussex, for example, the number of free Negroes living in white families was 236 in 1830, but 133 in 1860. Of these 133 free Negroes, sixty lived singly in as many white families and thirty lived in fifteen such families, two to a family. In Isle of Wight County, of a total of 237 free Negroes in white families, ninety-five, or 40 per cent, lived singly in as many white families.[3] In both counties, and throughout the state, groups of three or more free Negroes lived in a smaller number of white families.

The exact situation of free Negroes is frequently shown by the records in still another way. Often the free Negro is listed under one of three captions: "at" somebody's place,

[1] Under the census classification the term "family" embraces all persons living under the same roof regardless of blood relationship.

[2] The method of arriving at these figures was to count the total number of free colored persons in a county according to Carter G. Woodson's list of families and to subtract this total from that officially given by the U. S. printed census. For example, in Woodson's enumeration there are 630 free Negroes in Surry County (*Free Negro Heads of Families*, p. 190), while the official printed census gives 866. The difference of 236 is due to the fact that Woodson's enumeration embraced only free Negro heads of families and the members of the families living with them (*Ibid.*, lviii). Many of the 236 persons unaccounted for by Woodson bore a blood relationship to the 630 persons he lists, but since they were living as servants in white families, they were classified as members of white families.

[3] U. S. Census Bureau, Free Inhabitants (ms.), 1860. The 1860 count is based on the direct use of the original census returns for various counties. This same method was applied for the 1830 tabulation as a check on Woodson's figures.

"on" somebody's place, and "on his own land" or place.⁴ The free Negro "at" somebody's place lived with a white family and usually apart from his own free Negro relatives; the person "on" somebody's place was frequently a farm tenant or a mechanic renting the land and living with his own family; the Negro "on his own place" was, of course, the owner of the land on which he lived. Free Negroes "at" a particular place were "fed, boarded, and clothed" like the slaves, and they ate and slept at the houses of their employers. In reporting on Maryland, Wright says that if the number of free Negroes was large, they lived in quarters like slaves and received the customary food allowance of so much meal, so many pounds of bacon, and other rations.⁵ The free Negro "on" somebody's place enjoyed a greater measure of self-direction than the free Negro "at" somebody's place, and the Negro land owner, insofar as the law allowed, completely directed his own operations.

The numerical proportion of these three classifications will be reviewed in a later chapter. But, in passing, the status of Fauquier County may be noted. In one section of this county in the year 1851, of 104 free Negroes, 103 are listed as "at" somebody's place; only one is classed as being "on" somebody's place. In this county many whites were similarly situated, for they too were "at" various places as laborers and servants.⁶

The free Negroes resident in white families were employed under various kinds of contracts and by various methods. One type of contract was apprenticeship, voluntary and involuntary. This system was widely used in Southampton County. The apprentice not only learned a trade, but also earned a small amount of money for himself and often for his parents. For example, William Peterson of Southampton

---

⁴ The records that use this classification are the manuscript tax books, Personal Property, in the Virginia State Library. The most complete data are for the year 1851.
⁵ Wright, *Free Negro*, p. 164.
⁶ Personal Property, Fauquier, 1851.

was bound out in 1850 to Merit Davis for the sum of $20 a year, to be paid the mother except for the last two years, when payments should go to the apprentice himself. Dinks Artis, aged seven, of this same county was apprenticed, to be paid an annual sum of $5 until he reached the age of eighteen, and $15 afterwards until he became twenty-one. In the adjoining county of Sussex, many similar contracts were made. In Culpeper County, in one instance, a still more favorable arrangement was effected. Here the free boy William, aged twelve, was ordered to be bound out to William McFarland "to learn the art or mystery of a farmer." The mother of William was to receive during her son's apprenticeship a progressive increase in pay, from $2 for the first year to $16 for the eighth year. The last year, at the age of twenty-one, William was to receive $25 for himself.[7]

Another type of contract involved no money payment whatever. This type is illustrated in the agreement drawn between Jesse Johnson, "free man of color," and Philip T. Chandler of Westmoreland County. In consideration of Johnson's services for a period of twenty years, Chandler merely agreed to feed, maintain, and clothe Johnson as hirelings were usually fed, maintained, and clothed.[8] In this county, in which more than 1,000 free Negroes constituted about 25 per cent of the black population, it is likely that many free Negroes found employment under similar terms.

The system of labor whereby persons of this class closely attached themselves to whites was no doubt most prevalent in those counties where the free black population was large and where the whites desired to keep the free Negroes under surveillance as they did the slaves. This watchful attitude was especially pronounced in Accomac, where the free black pop-

---

[7] Clerk's Office, Southampton County, Minute Book (ms.), 1848-1855, pp. 355, 421; Clerk's Office, Culpepper County, Minute Book (ms.), 22, 1848, p. 89. Cases from Sussex County are those of James, Nancy, Eliza, Benjamin, Richard, and Adeline Owen, who were bound to David Mayes with the consideration of $60 each, to be paid at the age of twenty-one. Clerk's Office, Sussex, Order Book (ms.), August court, 1854.

[8] Clerk's Office, Westmoreland County, Deed Book (ms.) 35, p. 113.

ulation was the largest in the state. In 1852 many citizens of the county petitioned the legislature to permit the binding out of all male free Negroes under the age of forty-five unless they were mechanics, sailors, or farmers, and the "hiring to service" of all female free Negroes under the age of forty unless they had children.[9]

Some free Negroes worked as the only employees of white persons, but more of them labored as extra help side by side with slaves. The combined work of free Negroes and slaves was common throughout the state. The employment of the two together was exemplified in the tobacco factories of Richmond, Petersburg, Lynchburg, and other cities. In 1831 Leslie and Brydon, tobacco manufacturers of Petersburg, for example, employed twenty-one free Negro boys with fifty-two slaves, fifteen of whom were owned by the company and the rest hired. During this year and others the company also employed about twenty free Negro women as stemmers. Some of these employees, men and women, worked by the day, while others did piece work.[10] In 1840, at Petersburg, the brick yard of Daniel Lyon gave employment to sixty slaves and twelve free Negroes; James Orr's factory employed forty-four slaves and twelve free Negroes; George Vaughan's factory employed four slaves and fifteen free Negroes; and H. D. Bird, President of the Petersburg Railroad, employed seventeen slaves and sixteen free Negroes.[11] The majority of the manufacturing establishments in Petersburg and elsewhere, however, employed slaves only.

Joint labor by free Negroes and slaves was not uncommon in the counties where free Negroes constituted a large portion of the black population. Of a group of twenty-two employers of Negro labor in Sussex County in 1842, seventeen used slaves and free Negroes jointly; the other four, who

---

[9] Petition, Accomac County, Feb. 18, 1852.

[10] Leslie & Brydon, Pay Roll Book (ms.), 1830–1833, in the possession of W. L. McGill of Petersburg, Va. This book lists the names of employees with the wages received.

[11] U. S. Census Bureau, Slave Inhabitants (ms.), 1860.

were probably non-slaveholders, used free Negroes only.
A similar arrangement existed in Southampton County, but
on a larger scale. William Bryant of this county had his four
slaves and one "free boy," O. Artis; Jacob Barnes had seven
slaves and the one "free boy," E. Powell. Mixed free and
slave labor was also common in northern Virginia. In
Loudon County, for example, the following persons employed free Negroes and slaves together.[12]

TABLE II

Employers of Free Negroes and Slaves, Loudon County, 1851

Employer	Number of Free Negroes	Number of Slaves
Francis Gulick	1	3
Lydia Chambliss	1	
Thomas Humphrey	1	2
Robert Sherley	1	1
Nancy Hatcher	1	1
Marcus Kendrick	1	1
A. M. Moore	2	6
Charles Alexander	1	1
Joseph C. Mock	1	2

To some extent, free Negroes worked in gangs. One group
of this kind was employed in the Chesterfield County coal
mines, and many free Negroes of the town of Manchester in
this county were rated as colliers. At the Blackheath Mine
in Chesterfield a British company deliberately employed 130
free Negroes rather than slaves. This particular gang preserved good discipline, and, to the astonishment of some
Virginians, white men worked with them. Proprietors of
other mines made this same satisfactory arrangement.[13]

Free Negroes in Virginia pursued many occupations and
furnished a labor supply of no small value to the state. They
occupied places as farmers, farm hands, gardeners, laborers,

[12] Personal Property, Sussex, 1842; Southampton, 1851; Loudon, 1851.
[13] Personal Property, Chesterfield, 1851; Lyell, *Second Visit*, 1:217.

ditchers, sawyers, well diggers, colliers, blacksmiths, strikers, wheelwrights, millwrights, carpenters, coopers, cabinet makers, caulkers, painters, whitewashers, brick masons, brick makers, stone masons, millers, boatmen, seamen, fishermen, fishmongers, oysterers, wagoners, draymen, hucksters, teamsters, hack drivers, hostlers, tanners, shoemakers, factory hands, bakers, butchers, laundresses, seamstresses, cooks, nurses, housemaids, spinners, weavers, confectioners, shopkeepers, merchants, barbers, porters, musicians, and proprietors of restaurants, taverns, and livery stables.[14]

In some of these fields free Negroes operated as independent owners and proprietors of land and shops. For example, there were independent farmers, blacksmiths, carpenters, millers, boatmen, fishmongers, wagoners, shoemakers, barbers, restaurant operators, grocerymen, tavern keepers, and operators of livery stables. In each of these fields free Negroes also served as employees. As between town and country there were certain differences of occupation. The draymen, hackmen, factory hands, barbers, porters, and operators of restaurants, livery stables, and shops of various kinds were found only in towns and villages. Farmers, farm laborers, ditchers, and sawyers, on the other hand, were confined exclusively to the country. Most of the other occupations such

[14] Data on occupations of free Negroes are found mainly in two sets of records: the 1851 lists of free Negroes in Personal Property, submitted by each commissioner of revenue to the state auditor, and the original returns of the U. S. census for 1850 and 1860. Classification of occupations in both of these sources shows wide variation. The enumerator in one county would call practically all persons connected with agriculture "farmers," while other enumerators went to the other extreme and classified them all as "laborers." Some drew a further distinction by using the term "farm hand" instead of "laborer." In a few cases the exact status of a farmer was indicated by the term "farm tenant." In a few other cases the term "planter" was used even to designate a man who owned only five acres of land. "Laborer" was extensively used by some officials to indicate occupations which others would style as "ditcher" or "sawyer" or even mechanic. The confusion of terms in agriculture was no worse than that in nautical employment. "Sailor," "seaman," "waterman," "boatman," "oysterer," and "fisherman" were used interchangeably. The subject is further complicated by the fact that many federal census enumerators neglected to note occupation for many persons who through other sources are known to have had employment.

as carpentry, blacksmithing, and painting were followed in either place.

A further classification of these occupations shows that some were skilled and some unskilled; some demanded managerial ability; some demanded employment of others; and some even required a small amount of capital. A few of the carpenters and masons ranked as contractors.

Although free Negroes engaged in these occupations, they did not monopolize any of them. Slaves worked in all of these fields, even as operators of shops and livery stables, but always in the name of some owner.[15] Slaves even "owned" various retail businesses, but the legal titles to such enterprises were vested in white persons. In addition to slaves and free Negroes, white persons engaged in most of these occupations. Generally speaking, however, white people avoided domestic and personal service, barbering, and driving drays or hacks. Despite the diversity of occupations noted, the great mass of free Negro workers in Virginia were engaged in agricultural pursuits as farmers, farm tenants, farm hands, and laborers.[16]

Boatmen, fishermen, and oysterers constituted another large force of workers. In the counties bordering on the rivers and bays they even outnumbered the farm laborers. The watermen were numerous because in a choice between employment on land and working on water, according to Russell, they preferred the latter; at any rate, free Negroes held an important place in the internal navigation of the state. Probably a few were employed in the merchant marine and in the naval service of the country. Boatmen were especially numerous in the counties of Campbell, Cumberland, Prince Edward, and Powhatan, on the James and Appomattox rivers, which carried shipments of tobacco and other

---

[15] With the consent of his master, a slave of Richmond, Albert Brooks, operated a well-patronized livery stable in the city for at least ten years before his emancipation. Testimony of his son, the Reverend Walter Brooks, of Washington, D. C.

[16] See the next chapter for a full discussion of free Negroes in agriculture.

products by bateaux to Richmond and Petersburg. In these counties a majority of the many boatmen, slave and free, were employed in this particular type of navigation. In 1840, about forty bateaux operated on the Appomattox River, a service which, of course, demanded a large force of these laborers.[17]

The engagement of many free Negroes as boatmen and other types of non-agricultural laborers in a particular section tended to reduce the usual large number of farm hands in that section, as is indicated in the following table of occupations of free Negroes in Prince Edward County in 1851. In this instance the enumeration includes not simply heads of families in the county, but all persons of both sexes over the age of twelve.[18]

TABLE III

Occupations of Free Negroes in Prince Edward County, 1851

Boatmen	58	Bricklayers	3
Housekeepers	39	Railroad hands	3
Tobacco factory hands	31	Foundry workers	2
Washerwomen	25	Painters	2
Seamstresses	19	Wagoners	2
Servants	11	Cooper	1
Planters	9	Farmer	1
Spinners	8	Miller	1
Shoemakers	8	Hostler	1
Ditchers	7	Washing and sewing	1
Blacksmiths	6	Tanner	1
Weavers	3		

Boatmen were likewise numerous in Petersburg and other towns. In 1850 at Petersburg there were forty or fifty such

[17] John H. Russell, *Free Negro*, p. 150; "Virginia Illustrated," in *Harper's Magazine*, 12:174 (Dec., 1855–May, 1856); Howe, *Historical Collections*, p. 432.

[18] This table is one of the most complete of the occupational lists of free Negroes sent to the state auditor at Richmond. The commissioner in this case omits the term "laborer" entirely and gives a more specific occupation.

persons among the free Negroes, some of whom were owners.[19] The boatmen, there and elsewhere, were a thrifty group of people; many of them became owners of houses and lots. Often they were fishermen who, with the help of their wives, operated stands in the city markets.[20] Oysterers were naturally most numerous in the Chesapeake Bay and tidewater region of the state. In Gloucester County in 1851 there were seventy-six free Negro oysterers, above the age of twelve, as opposed to sixty-two so-called farmers. A relatively large number of oysterers lived also in the adjoining county of York. All told, free Negroes and whites found considerable employment in oystering in this region because of the size of the business and the "large amount of capital invested." [21]

Free Negroes also entered the field of transportation on land; in the rural occupations listed there were a few wagoners. Before the coming of the railroad, the wagoner, who hauled farm products a hundred miles or more, was valuable to his community. Making the trip to Richmond or Petersburg from a distant south-side county necessitated the ownership of wagons and teams, besides the ability to defend oneself against robbers on the road. Such was the work done by Anderson Stewart of Lunenburg County, who owned six horses and for many years served the farmers of this

---

[19] One of the earliest of the Petersburg boatmen was Richard Jarratt. His memorandum book, covering the years 1800 to 1810, gives accounts of many trips between Petersburg and Norfolk. This manuscript record is in the possession of Jarratt's great-grandson, William Jarratt of Petersburg.

Another boatman of Petersburg, John Updike, between 1824 and 1862 owned such sloops and schooners as the *Jolly Sailor,* the *Two Brothers,* the *Jannett,* and the *William and Mary.* One of these vessels was built at New Bedford, Massachusetts; two others were built in Virginia, one in Mathews County and the other in Petersburg. During his career of more than thirty-five years, Updike frequently had occasion to borrow money for his business. He usually offered one of his vessels, or his real estate, as security. Clerk's Office, Petersburg, Deed Books (ms.), 7: 197, 347; 8: 325, 371; 10: 115, 308; 11: 411; 12: 366; 14: 224, 254; 22: 46, 513.

[20] Testimony of the late J. F. Jarratt, of Petersburg, a man of free negro birth and lineage.

[21] Personal Property, Gloucester County, 1851; Petition, Gloucester, Jan. 8, 1849.

county.[22] John Lipscomb of Cumberland County and William Hayes of Mecklenburg County were also wagoners.

In the skilled trades the free Negro blacksmith, carpenter, and shoemaker were outstanding. Next to farm labor these vocations absorbed more free colored persons than any others. In every county in which there were many free Negro workers, there were from one to fifteen engaged in each of these trades. Blacksmiths and shoemakers were to be found at many crossroads. In shoemaking, as Wright indicates for Maryland, some men worked in fixed places, but many went about from farm to farm, making the supply of shoes at each place from leather furnished by the master of the premises. These tradesmen, who had frequently learned their vocations as slaves, were of substantial value to their communities. In many instances they had bought their freedom and had been kept in the state by white friends, notwithstanding the law to the contrary. In some cases, as in that of James L. Smith of Northumberland County, masters taught slaves the shoemaking trade and afterwards established shops for them. This type of action sometimes paved the way for manumission.[23]

Few free Negroes in rural sections were brick masons, perhaps because of the small number of brick structures in that day. An unusual number of stone masons and stone fencers were located in Fauquier County because of the stone and rock quarries there.[24] There were fewer free Negro coopers and wheelwrights than carpenters and blacksmiths.

Free Negro rural labor went into several special occupations aside from the mechanical trades and farm labor proper. Ditchers, sawyers, wood choppers, and well diggers were numerous. In some instances free Negroes, who were roughly classed as "laborers," specialized in ditching or terracing and thus served the farmers of their neighbor-

---

[22] Land, Personal Property, Lunenburg County, 1845–1860.
[23] Wright, *Free Negro*, p. 156; *Atlantic Monthly*, 57:26 (Jan., 1886); James L. Smith, *Autobiography*, pp. 4, 25, 28.
[24] U. S. Census Bureau, Free Inhabitants (ms.) 1860.

hood. In 1851 Mecklenburg County had fifteen ditchers above the age of twelve, Gloucester had ten, Dinwiddie had six, and Greensville five. Sometimes well digging and other difficult farm tasks fell to the lot of free Negroes because such work was considered too perilous or too unhealthful for slaves. Such employment of free Negroes further indicates that their labor was regarded by slaveholders as supplementary to that of the slaves. In this way free Negroes found a useful place in the agricultural labor of the state.[25]

Aside from engaging in manual labor, skilled and unskilled, certain free Negroes in rural communities attempted to support themselves by small business enterprises. Some sold ginger cakes, watermelons, and fruits in the neighboring towns, or on Saturdays and "big" days at the crossroad stores and post offices.[26] A few operated shops, markets, confectioneries, restaurants, and grocery stores; and some even became merchants. At least one man kept a well patronized rural tavern, and here and there free Negroes operated tanneries and brick yards.

Some of these people engaged in business with considerable success. For a number of years Osborn Vick operated a grocery store at Lawrenceville and owned the store building and lot. At Fort Monroe, Stephen Allen conducted a similar business which had a value of $2,000. John Cooper at Port Royal held a merchant's license and operated his business in his own establishment, valued in 1830 at $700. Jesse Booker operated a tannery in Pittsylvania County, had funds in cash, and had a small capital invested in his manufacturing enterprise. Jacob Sampson of Goochland not only operated a tavern but also engaged in large scale farming. Sampson operated his tavern fifteen or more years and entertained many white guests; his place was one of great convenience to people taking stock to market "as well as other travelers."

[25] Personal Property, Mecklenburg, Gloucester, Dinwiddie, and Greensville counties, 1851; *Atlantic Monthly*, 57:26 (Jan., 1886); Wright, *Free Negro*, p. 153; Bassett, *Slavery in North Carolina*, pp. 42–43.
[26] *Atlantic Monthly*, 57:26 (Jan., 1886).

Fortune Thomas of Halifax once faced the danger of having her confectionery shop closed by the officers of the law. But the white women of the community interceded and said that because of the high quality of this woman's service in baking cakes and making candy, no party or wedding could well be given without her.[27]

From the personal property taxes of a typical agricultural county, Mecklenburg, an unusually complete list of the occupations of free Negroes may be made. In 1851 this south-side county had a free Negro population of approximately 900. The occupations of 162 of these, presumably the adults, were as follows: [28]

TABLE IV

Occupations of Free Negroes in Mecklenburg County, 1851

Blacksmiths	7	Musicians	3
Boatmen	3	Painters	2
Cakemakers	1	Plowboys	2
Carpenters	9	Sawyers	6
Cooks	4	Seamstresses	3
Ditchers	15	Spinners	29
Farmers	25	Strikers	3
Factory Hands	15	Shoemakers	14
Hostlers	3	Wagoners	1
Masons	1	Washers	1
Midwives	2	Weavers	8
Millers	3	Wheelwrights	3

The three leading farmers among the twenty-five listed were William H. Mitchell, Beverly Valentine, and William H. Mayo. The two painters listed were members of the Quinichett family, of mixed blood; three of the carpenters were Brandums, presumably brothers; the three musicians,

---

[27] Personal Property, Brunswick, 1851; Land, Brunswick, 1860; U. S. Census Bureau, Free Inhabitants, 1860; Personal Property, Caroline, 1830; Land, Personal Property, Pittsylvania, 1860; Petitions, Goochland, Dec. 13, 1844; Halifax, 1850.

[28] Personal Property, Mecklenburg County, 1851.

following an unusual occupation among free Negroes, were all Dunstans; the one wagoner was William H. Hayes. Most of these particular tradesmen and farmers owned land.

That many free Negroes were efficient and valuable to the agricultural and industrial life of Virginia is indicated by the hundreds of petitions sent to the legislature by white citizens concerning the industrious character of particular free Negroes, and by statements of newspaper correspondents, editors, and prominent officials. Petitions to the legislature concerning industrious free Negroes urged that they be granted special permission to remain in the State, in spite of the law of 1806 which provided that all slaves emancipated after that date must leave Virginia within twelve months of their emancipation. The granting of many such requests shows a tendency to disregard the law about as frequently as to enforce it. Though the requests began to pour in shortly after the passage of the act of 1806, the cases here cited fall within the period from 1830 to 1860.[29]

Among the petitions on behalf of free Negroes during the decade of 1830, several are of interest. In a petition pleading for Charles of Sussex County, 175 signers wished him to remain because of his intelligence, good behavior, humility, respectfulness, and "extraordinary merit." Isaac Atkins of Isle of Wight County was the subject of a petition because as a slave he had bought his freedom, and "for many long

[29] The manuscript petitions in the Virginia State Library indicate that at least as many appeals were made after 1830 as before this date. Some of the reasons given for permitting free Negroes to remain in Virginia are as follows: Godfree of Brunswick County, "extremely useful to the public"; the Dean and Floyd families of Amherst County, "generally useful and industrious mechanics"; John Charleson of Amherst, "an industrious and honest citizen"; Benjamin Hoard of Middlesex County, "a good citizen . . . very useful as a blacksmith, industrious and obliging"; Elick of Nottoway County, "a carpenter . . . saves his money"; Cousins of Nottoway, "a good shoemaker . . . the manager of a farm . . . professor of religion . . . instructor of his people"; Cousins' wife, "a fine woman, a good housekeeper and weaver"; Dungee of King William County, "waterman, knowledge of the waters of the Chesapeake bay region so great that farmers of a wide region loath to be without him"; Phil Cooler of Gloucester County, "by mutual industry he and his wife have accumulated property."

years labored assiduously for that purpose." [30] Other petitions were grounded on the need for the services of the free Negroes in question. Three such petitions came from the county of Accomac, one on behalf of John, a sawyer and a "useful citizen," whose services were "much required in his neighborhood"; another using the identical phrase in characterizing the services of Solomon, a gardener and day laborer; and a third on behalf of Isaac, a farm manager and "a man of good habits and correct deportment," whose employer was anxious to have him remain in the state.[31]

The services of blacksmiths were much in demand, and petitions for them were frequent. Powhatan County citizens asked that Abraham Depp, a smith, be allowed to remain. While he was still a slave, his master had given him special privileges and had willed his manumission. Subsequently Depp had acquired property and a fixed residence. Though his sympathizers supported that for such a person the law should be waived, their petition was not granted.[32]

Another blacksmith, who probably did more for himself than any other slave, and who therefore merited all the aid he could rally, was Arthur Lee of Alleghany County. Prior to 1835 Lee had been a slave for forty years and had passed through the hands of three masters. During the period of enslavement he had learned the blacksmith trade under one of his owners and he followed this occupation the rest of his life. Under his last master he was allowed to hire himself out until he earned for this man the sum of $1,200. After accomplishing this he was then permitted to buy himself for $500 in installments. After he had completed the purchase of his

[30] Petitions, Sussex, 1831; Isle of Wight, 1836. The petition for Daniel Warner, a barber, made almost the same plea. A large number of citizens of the town of Warrenton attested to this man's good qualities. Petitions, Fauquier, 1836.

[31] Petitions, Accomac, 1838.

[32] Petitions, Powhatan, 1831. Dennis Comer, another blacksmith, was "extremely useful," in the opinion of his white friends. He had bought his freedom, and since that time had acquired a farm of two hundred acres in Fairfax County. Comer was allowed to stay in Virginia. Petitions, Fairfax, 1837.

own freedom, he bought his wife and child for $1,250. Having spent a great part of his life in this way, in 1835 Lee was confronted with the necessity of leaving the State. In his plight 140 white sympathizers interceded in his behalf. They sent in three separate petitions to the legislature declaring that Lee was a first rate blacksmith and a very industrious and well behaved man and that consequently his expulsion would mean a loss to the county.[33] On the strength of these arguments he was allowed to remain in Virginia.

Pleas were also made on behalf of a few free Negro women. The petition of Patty of Accomac bears the signatures of twenty-two persons, one of whom was Henry A. Wise. Patty, they said, was no ordinary menial, but rather the "confident, intimate nurse, and friend of her master and mistress." The signers of the petition of Eliza Purdie indicated that she was useful in serving sick persons, "especially among the ladies." [34]

Petitions concerning the labor of certain free Negroes continued to go to the legislature in the decade of 1840. One of the strongest of these was presented by thirty-eight citizens of Essex County on behalf of Ben Goodman. His petitioners regarded him as "a very useful man in many respects." They further said "he is a good carpenter, a good cooper, a coarse shoemaker, and a good hand at almost anything that is useful to us as farmers." [35] Henry Parker of Loudon County was another worthy free Negro. Unlike most of the others mentioned here, he was not a mechanic but a day laborer. As such he was considered by white friends "a good and useful man" and one who should not be exiled. A large number of white people came to the aid of Fleming Jordan

---

[33] Petitions, Alleghany, 1835.

[34] Petitions, Accomac, 1838, Isle of Wight, 1839.

[35] Petitions, Essex, 1842. Peter Snead of Accomac stood in grave danger of being apprehended and sold by the overseers of the poor in conformity to the law of that time. His white patrons endeavored to save him on the ground that he was "a man of unexceptionable character, an industrious, honest and worthy citizen." Richard Chandler of the same county, supported by seventy-five signers, made a bid for staying in Virginia merely on the ground that he was "an honest and worthy citizen." Petitions, Accomac, 1845.

of Buckingham when there was a possibility of his removal from the State. He had acted as a body servant to his late master and in this way apparently had won the good will of many persons.[36]

Among the last of the free Negroes to petition the legislature for permission to remain in Virginia was Billy Williamson of Campbell County. The desire of the citizens of Campbell to have Williamson remain was about the strongest expressed in behalf of a free Negro. Williamson was a farmer, the owner of one hundred acres of land, and a man in prosperous circumstances. His fifty-seven white neighbors and friends rallied to him in these words:

> We are his neighbors—and all of his neighbors—and are willing and indeed desirous that the legislature pass a law permitting him to remain in the State as he is not only an honest prosperous man—but in truth a most useful and accommodating man to his neighbors, and with all with whom he has anything to do. We further certify that we know of no one in this county who is unwilling that he should remain.[37]

Edmund Kean of Winchester is a good example of the many slaves who bought themselves and afterwards labored to buy the freedom of their wives and children. By 1850 he had accomplished the task of buying himself and was well on the road to buying his wife, but at this point the possibility of deportation faced him. Because of Kean's great ambition and the fact that he was "industriously engaged in the employ of a white person," his petitioners in 1849 sought and obtained permission to have him remain in the state.[38]

In the nearby county of Loudon the next year the case of a washerwoman, Harriet Cook of Leesburg, was agitated. Almost a hundred white citizens, including seven justices of the peace, five ex-justices, sixteen merchants, six lawyers, and the postmaster, made an appeal to the legislature that

[36] Petitions, Loudon, Buckingham, 1848. [37] Petitions, Campbell, Jan. 17, 1851.
[38] Petitions, Frederick, 1849.

she should be saved to their community. They said: "It would be a serious inconvenience to a number of citizens of Leesburg to be deprived of her services as a washerwoman and in other capacities in which, in consequence of her gentility, trustworthiness, and skill she is exceedingly useful." [39]

Such frequent efforts by white persons to have certain free Negro workers remain in their neighborhood forces the conclusion that many of the free Negroes were of economic value to the state. Testimony of free Negroes who were still living about 1910 throws some light on this question. Some of this group insisted that there were two classes of free Negroes: those who, like the many "extremely useful" and "industrious" persons just noted, were an asset to their localities, and others who were the parasites of their neighborhoods. Individuals of the first class, Russell indicates, were known as "men of color"; those of the latter class were contemptuously called "free niggers." [40]

About 1850 the effort to save certain free Negroes shifted from the state legislature to the local units of government, especially the cities. In the meantime a new set of defenders began to answer the attacks on the free Negroes, especially in 1853 in connection with the legislative agitation to remove all free Negroes from the commonwealth. Foremost among the defenders were certain newspaper correspondents and newspaper editors.

Two correspondents of the Richmond *Enquirer* took the position that the expulsion bill of 1853 would have disastrous

[39] Petitions, Loudon, 1850. The free Negroes mentioned above by no means represent the entire number of those who petitioned the legislature for permission to remain in the state. There are in the archives of the Virginia State Library at least 150 petitions from the years 1830 to 1860 urging that certain free Negroes be allowed to remain in the commonwealth. Most of the petitions state openly that the labor of the person in question is their main interest; the others, although emphasizing some humanitarian question such as the separation of husband and wife, are also concerned with the value of the individual's past or present labor.

[40] John H. Russell, *Free Negro*, p. 159. Russell had the advantage of coming in contact with the original free Negroes, while the present writer has had to depend on interviews with the second and third generations.

consequences, since the free Negro in certain regions of Virginia was indispensable. "A Friend to Humanity" declared that the state was in great need of laborers. "Shall she," he asked, "at such a time suddenly expel from her borders fifty thousand of her laboring population and that too when the very demand for labor and increased wages are operating to improve the condition and character of those whom it is proposed to expel?" The people in the sections where the free Negro population was largest, he indicated, were not clamoring for the expulsion bill. Such people were the ones most willing to retain them. "One of the Constituency," the second *Enquirer* correspondent, took the position that even if the free Negroes were expelled, no white labor would come in, because of the presence of slave labor. "In lower Virginia," he continued, "there is not now, and never has been enough labor to clear, improve, and cultivate the finest strip of land—in the world." The free Negroes helped to overcome this shortage by performing "a great deal of labor for white people." Both of these writers denied that free Negroes were a danger and a menace to slave society. Although one of them admitted that some free Negroes were worthless and lazy, he asserted that one white man could do more injury to slaves than fifty free Negroes. Finally, he said that the freedmen deserved to stay because they had not been involved in the slave insurrection, and because they had fought in the Revolution "as long and as hard as white men." They had not been traitors.[41]

The editors of the Richmond *Times, Dispatch,* and *Whig* advanced similar arguments and made several other points. They voiced the opinion that a sudden removal of the free Negroes would ruin the planters in those sections where their number was greatest and where their labor was essential during harvest time and the season for gathering the tobacco crop. The editors felt that the free blacks were far more

[41] Richmond *Enquirer*, Feb. 17, 24, 1854; Richmond *Times*, Feb. 12, 1853; Richmond *Whig*, Jan. 25, 1853.

acceptable than the poor whites who would take their places and who would be the only substitutes, since no higher type of white men would work in competition with slaves. These writers felt it absurd to propose to remove a labor force as great as the entire labor force of Florida.[42]

In his opposition to the removal bill of 1853 and to Ex-Governor Smith, who had been an ardent advocate of such action, the editor of the *Whig* went so far as to say that many of the free Negroes "in all the relations of life," were "as respectful and good citizens as he the ex-governor . . . himself." [43] The general tone of these newspapers gives the impression that the free Negroes were not half so bad as the demagogues asserted, that they were perfectly harmless and were less to be feared than the slaves, who in several instances had instigated uprisings.

Some governors of Virginia also entered this controversy on the value of free Negro labor. Governor William Smith held that this class was worthless and should be expelled because of its competition with white men; Governor Giles, on the other hand, had previously declared that at least half of the free Negroes were valuable workers whose labor added to the wealth of the state. The contribution of this portion, he contended, would more than compensate for the evils of the dissolute among them.[44] A generation later Governor Wise asserted "that their labor is needed in many parts of the state where they are most numerous and that to get clear of them in any way is considerably to reduce *pro tanto* our population." [45] This governor thus took a position similar to that of many newspaper editors of the day.

Even the opponents and critics of free Negroes occasionally admitted that their labor was valuable. Rutherford of Goochland County, who strongly advocated their removal,

---

[42] Richmond *Times*, Jan. 17, Feb. 12, 1853; Richmond *Dispatch*, Feb. 15, 1853; Richmond *Whig*, Jan. 25, 1853.
[43] *Ibid.*, Jan. 25, Feb. 4, 1853.
[44] Giles, *Political Miscellanies; American Colonization Society*, p. 19.
[45] *Documents of the House of Delegates*, no. 1, 1857, p. 151.

acknowledged that in some counties in which they were numerous their labor was valuable to farmers at certain seasons of the year and that a sudden removal would be productive of great mischief. Fitzhugh, the well-known slavery protagonist, charged that the free Negroes were worthless but agreed that under the pressure of the laws against them they were much more careful than formerly. "Under the portentous signs of the time" they had intermarried with slaves, hired themselves to farmers, and attached themselves to white masters generally.[46]

In all this mass of testimony, the statement made by "A Friend to Humanity" is especially significant. His argument that the legislature of 1853 should not think of expelling the free Negroes at the very time "when the demand for labor and increased wages are operating to improve the condition and character of those whom it is proposed to expel," indicates the full force of the economic revival previously discussed. It was operating to make the free Negro more necessary than ever in the economy of Virginia.

Although free Negroes found employment in rural Virginia, opportunities for employment were not abundant for all of them. A study of occupational lists of the various counties indicates that at least 25 per cent had no particular occupation and probably remained idle much of the time. The free Negro group had its shiftless element; yet there is some truth in the observation of a contemporary traveler that the degradation of the free blacks was due not to themselves, but to the slavery of others: in other words, to the competition of slaves.[47] There is also some truth in the further contention of this observer that the freedom of all the slaves would have made the labor of all Negroes valuable.

In some instances the residence of free Negroes near a

---

[46] Rutherford, *Speech on Removal*, p. 8; Fitzhugh, *What Shall Be Done with Free Negroes*, p. 15.

[47] Ethan A. Andrews, *Slavery and the Domestic Slave-Trade in the United States*, p. 36.

plantation on which slaves were employed was thoroughly disliked by the owners of such property. The freedmen were compelled to meet the opposition not only of slave owners but also of slaves. At least one citizen of that day testified that slaves often objected to working beside free Negroes, since these received wages, and the slaves did not.[48]

In view of the fact, then, that free Negroes for one reason or another could not always obtain work in the country, they flocked to the towns. In some instances they went from a small town to a larger place like Richmond or Petersburg.[49] Free Negro mechanics in particular moved to the villages and towns where greater opportunity for their trades could be found.[50] The preference of free Negroes for residence in cities is shown by the fact that in 1860 there were at least 11,000 of them in cities of Virginia.

Among the several cities and towns of Virginia, Petersburg proved the most attractive to free Negroes. In 1790 there were 310 free Negroes in Petersburg; in 1810, 1,089. In 1830 the number was 2,032, a gain of nearly 100 per cent. Thirty years later, in 1860, the free Negro population reached the peak of 3,164, the highest among the cities of the State. The steady growth in the free Negro population of Petersburg did not fail to attract the attention of its of-

---

[48] *Ibid.*, p. 43; Russel, *Economic Aspects*, p. 134.
[49] Such was the case of Joseph Farrow, who left Charlottesville for Richmond, and later was the subject of the following letter of recommendation:

Charlottesville, Jan. 2, 1860

I take pleasure in recommending Joseph Farrow, a free mulatto & the bearer of this; whom I have known well, and whose deportment I have noted particularly for 12 or 14 years past. He was employed by my father in his carpenter shop, before he was grown, all the time under my direction & has since been in my employ until he left during last summer for Richmond; and I can conscienciously recommend him for his correct & honest deportment, and for his moral & industrious habits, ever since I have known him; as well as for his skill as a good workman.

G. W. Spooner.

A photostatic copy of this letter is in the possession of James Browning, Miner Teachers College, Washington, D. C.

[50] Pinchbeck, *Virginia Negro Artisan*, p. 66.

ficials; more than once they made efforts to limit the number of free Negroes, or to prevent them from coming in altogether. Richmond, facing the same problem, occasionally refused the applications of certain free Negroes to take up residence there.[51] Despite this opposition to a further increase in the free Negro population from the outside, this group, when once in the city, found opportunity for employment greater than in the country.

A significant fact in free Negro employment in cities was the preponderance of women. In the state at large in 1860 there were 27,721 males and 30,321 females, with an even greater disproportion of females in urban areas. In about one-third of the counties of rural Virginia, on the other hand, the males actually exceeded the females in number.[52] This disproportion in favor of females in cities had always been true. In Petersburg, for example, of 503 heads of families in 1830, 285 were women.[53] The approximate ranking of males and females in certain cities in 1860 may be shown as follows:

TABLE V

Percentage Distribution of Sexes in Certain Cities in 1860

City	Male	Female
Norfolk	35	65
Portsmouth	39	61
Winchester	41	59
Alexandria	41	59
Fredericksburg	42	58
Suffolk	42	58
Lynchburg	44	56
Petersburg	44	56
Richmond	44	56

[51] In 1848 the delegate from Petersburg to the legislature was instructed by the local court to procure the passage of an act giving this body power to refuse to register free Negroes. Minute Book, 1848–1851, p. 102. See also Minute Book, City Hall, Richmond, no. 19, pp. 45b, 134, 424.
[52] U. S. Census, Population, 1860.
[53] Woodson, *Free Negro Heads of Families*, pp. 169–171.

The preponderance of females as a whole meant a preponderance of women as heads of families and of the washerwoman as a bread winner. In Norfolk in 1860, of a group of 189 heads of families, men and women, eighty-four were washerwomen, about fifteen belonged to other women's occupations, and twenty-two persons were unclassified as to occupation. In all, over 100 of the 189 heads of families were women, with the occupation of washerwoman far in the lead. In Richmond, eight years earlier, of a total of 431 men and women "free colored housekeepers," 125 were washerwomen.[54] Petersburg presented a different picture in that about seventy women heads of families were tobacco stemmers, sixty-five were laborers, many others were unclassified, while only thirty-nine were washerwomen. As in the case of Richmond, women's occupations were equal to about half of all occupations.

Many free Negro women either lived with white men or supplemented their earnings by concubinage with them. Phillips rates the double activity of concubinage and the procuring of women by Negro men for the gratification of white men as one of the main vices of free Negroes. The white man could involve himself in this fashion with impunity since he, as the keeper of a Negro mistress, ordinarily lost no standing in society. The fact that census enumerators often assigned no definite occupation to many free Negro women, even when they owned considerable property, would lead one to assume the existence of such concubinage.[55]

With the exception of the legitimate occupations of washerwomen and factory hands which led all others, the ranking of occupations among free Negro women in cities ran about

[54] U. S. Census Bureau, *Free Inhabitants*, 1860; *Richmond City Directory*, 1852.
[55] Phillips, *Life and Labor in the Old South*, p. 172; Bassett, *Slavery in North Carolina*, p. 46. In one instance only has the writer found an open statement of sexual vice as a means of livelihood. Elizabeth Langley of Lynchburg is listed by the Federal census enumerator as "House of Ill Fame" (ms. census, 1860), and local tax assessors noted her as "Easy Virtue" (Personal Property, Lynchburg, 1851).

as follows: seamstress, miscellaneous domestic service, cook, and nurse. The number of seamstresses was surprisingly high. In Richmond, for example, they comprised about 12 per cent of all housekeepers who were reported with definite occupations.[56] Miscellaneous domestic service accounted for about 5 per cent of the free Negroes in cities. The occupation of cook in cities was apparently held largely by slaves rather than free women. In comparison with the washerwoman and seamstresses the number of cooks among the free Negroes was very small. Although nurses were not numerous, their services were highly valued by the community. In the opinion of a contemporary in a neighboring state, the free Negro women made better servants than slave women; consequently they enjoyed much employment.[57]

Regardless of sex, and regardless of residence in town or country, one line of employment excelled all others with reference to the number of free Negroes it attracted— namely, the tobacco industry. The history of the cultivation of tobacco in Virginia makes evident the very high place which Negro labor, slave and free, held in this industry. Contrary to his position in the cotton industry, in which he was confined largely to cultivation, the Negro was important in the manufacture, as well as in the cultivation, of tobacco. In its manufacture many women workers were engaged. In the factories of Petersburg, where the women were about half as numerous as men, they worked as stemmers, while the men worked as twisters.[58] According to the report on manufactures in Virginia of the 1860 census, there were at this time 261 tobacco establishments employing 11,382 workers at an annual cost of $2,123,732. At least 2,500 of

[56] *Richmond City Directory,* 1852.
[57] Rosser H. Taylor, *The Free Negro in North Carolina,* p. 25.
[58] Pinchbeck, *Virginia Negro Artisan,* p. 14. Negroes early held a prominent place in tobacco manufacturing. In 1820 a slave-hiring agent of Petersburg advertised: "I shall have a number of . . . Negroes for hire . . . among which are boys accustomed to the manufacturing of tobacco." Petersburg *Republican,* Dec. 19, 1820.

this number were free Negroes, who lived chiefly in Richmond, Petersburg, and Lynchburg, the leading centers of tobacco manufacture, and who worked side by side with slaves. In Lynchburg most of the free Negroes worked in the tobacco factories during the manufacturing season, "and then," said a public official of that town, "the males do whatever comes in their way the balance of the time." [59] In Farmville likewise the five tobacco establishments absorbed many more free Negroes than did any other line of employment. Richmond factories, for some reason, made so little use of women that during the fifties there were about 125 free Negro washerwomen in Richmond and only thirty-nine in Petersburg. The women of the latter place found their opportunity in tobacco factories rather than as washerwomen.

Most of the free Negroes in cities, like those in the country, were unskilled laborers. Those who were skilled, however, made an excellent record in their communities. Many of them, recent recruits from slavery, had already made reputations as skilled laborers and continued their steady habits as free men. In all such instances the white citizens of their communities objected to being without them.

Occupying a leading place in the group of skilled artisans in cities were the blacksmiths. Each of the larger cities contained from five to fifteen heads of families who were blacksmiths, but if all blacksmiths had been classified, this number would be doubled or trebled. The free Negro blacksmith in many instances was a man who had once been a slave but who later bought himself. He labored in a shop of his own, in the shop of another free Negro, or in the shop of a white blacksmith.

In some places the carpenters, exceeding the blacksmiths in numbers although not in income, became contractors and master workmen. Allied to these two trades were those of the cooper and the wheelwright. The cooper was most valuable to his own race and the larger white community he

[59] Personal Property, Lynchburg, 1851.

served.⁶⁰ Bricklayers were fewer in number than those in the other trades; some, as in Alexandria, where there were brickmaking establishments, worked as brickmakers and brickmoulders. Shoemakers ranked in number and importance with these other tradesmen. Richmond led all other cities in shoemaking, with twenty-three heads of families engaged in this trade. In many cases they were not simply cobblers but real shoemakers possessing a high degree of skill.⁶¹

A number of skilled mechanics of all kinds were located in Fredericksburg. Writing from this town in 1835, one observer remarked that the high degree of thrift and skill shown by these mechanics led some to the belief that they were more "moral and respectable" than many among the lowest classes of whites. He further stated that several of the master workmen among this group employed many persons of their own race. Fine traits of character and qualities of leadership in these artisans are shown by the fact that everywhere they held office in their churches and benevolent societies.⁶²

Ability in mechanical trades or useful services in other fields led some men to branch out into business. In this way Booker Jackson, a shoemaker of Farmville, went into the

⁶⁰ Deed books and will books frequently reveal the worth of the cooper to his community. The inventories of the estates of deceased free Negro coopers, found in the will books, tell the story of these artisans in considerable detail. See Clerk's Office, Orange County, Will Book 8, p. 58.

⁶¹ A well-known shoemaker in Petersburg was James Colson (1830–1892). In a later day he advertised his business thus: "James M. Colson, Manufacturer of Boots and Shoes, 17 Oak Street, Petersburg, Va. All work warranted to give perfect satisfaction. For a neat and good boot go to James M. Colson. Repairing done neatly and promptly." Petersburg *City Directory*, 1876–1877, p. 49.

⁶² Andrews, *Slavery and the Domestic Slave-Trade*, p. 162; Minute Books (mss.), Gillfield Baptist Church, Petersburg; First African Baptist Church, Richmond; First African Baptist Church, Lynchburg; Constitution of the Beneficial Society of Free Men of Color, Petersburg, 1852, in the possession of Mrs. Gertrude Jackson, Petersburg, Va. Such free Negroes as Jarratt, Elebeck, Page, Tayburn, Mathews, Stevens, Tinsley, Scott, and Garnes, deacons and trustees of the Gillfield Baptist Church in Petersburg, were also the leading contractors, bricklayers, shoemakers, painters, and boatmen of the town.

livery stable business; Edmund Kean, a skilled worker of Winchester did likewise.[63] Randle Evans of Winchester, who acquired a knowledge of hotel service while a slave, opened a very successful confectionery shop when he became a free man.[64] Jack McCrae of Petersburg, who first followed the trade of carpenter, later engaged in a similar business and prospered in it.

Free Negroes in cities operated various types of stores and markets. In Richmond, for example, they operated at one time seven grocery stores. Fruit vendors and saloon keepers were also found in cities, either in connection with restaurants or operating independently. From the large volume of fishing carried on by the boatmen of Petersburg on the Appomattox and James rivers, grew the business of operating fish markets in the city market house.

Many free Negroes flourished in their monopoly of driving cabs or drays. The draymen in the seaport of Norfolk numbered nine in 1860, and there were about five each in Richmond and Petersburg. Free Negro cab or hack drivers and those engaged in other lines of business advertised in newspapers as did the whites. One of these cabmen, Richard Kennard of Petersburg, advertised thus: [65]

Hacks for hire. If you want a very fine carriage, horse, and driver, send your orders to Richard Kennard, at Mr. Reuben Ragland's stable on Lombard St. Remember the name "Richard."

The occupations just named were important, but in none of them were more free Negroes employed than in the barber trade. One traveler of the day described this occupation as

[63] The same business attracted Robert Clark of Petersburg. He worked first at a hotel, saved enough money to buy his freedom, and afterwards opened a livery stable, which eventually became the best patronized in the town. Testimony of many white and Negro citizens of Petersburg still living. Clark died about 1875.

[64] Petition, Frederick, Jan., 1833.

[65] Petersburg *Daily Express*, Aug. 18, 1858. John K. Shore, a barber of Petersburg, advertised in this same paper. For an advertisement concerning the reopening of his shop he paid on May 18, 1857, $1. Colson Family Manuscripts, Petersburg.

"the birthright of the free Negro." His description of one shop in a hotel in Washington, D. C., is applicable to those in any town in Virginia. The establishment in Washington, he says, was operated by men of color, mostly mulattoes. They were "good looking, dressed in clean white jackets and aprons, smart, quick, and attentive." [66] With at least eighteen barbers, Richmond led all other places in this business during the decade of 1850. Because of their large patronage, the barbers constituted a free Negro aristocracy. Many of them could read and write, and a few even had a taste for general literature. Except in Norfolk, the white barber was almost unknown in the larger towns of the state, and the trade belonged almost exclusively to free Negroes.

How the urban free Negroes made a livelihood may be shown in tabular form by reference to one city, Petersburg, which had the largest free Negro population among the cities of Virginia. The occupations noted here may be regarded as typical except for the variations outlined in the preceding pages.[67]

TABLE VI

Occupations of Free Negro Heads of Families in Petersburg, 1860

Occupation	Number	Occupation	Number	Occupation	Number
Barbers	10	Fishmongers	4	Plasterers	3
Blacksmiths	12	Fruit sellers	2	Preachers	1
Boatmen	15	Firemen	5	Porters	1
Bricklayers	10	Finishers	1	Railroad hands	1
Brickmoulders	1	Fishermen	7	Stone masons	2
Butchers	2	Hackmen	3	Sailors	1
Cart men	3	Hotel waiters	2	Sawyers	3
Car hands	1	Hucksters	4	Seamstresses	10
Carpenters	21	Laborers	160	Tinners	1
Caulkers	1	Livery keepers	1	Train hands	1

[66] Sir William H. Russell, *My Diary, North and South*, 1:73-74.
[67] U. S. Census Bureau, Free Inhabitants, 1860. This table is approximate.

Occupation	Number	Occupation	Number	Occupation	Number
Cook shops	2	Midwives	2	Tobacco twisters	56
Coopers	8	Musicians	2	Tobacco stemmers	81
Ditchers	5	Machinists	1	Tobacco prizers	2
Draymen	5	Millers	3	Upholsterers	1
Engineers	1	Painters	1	Unclassified	105
Waiters	1	Wagoners	3	Whitewashers	1
Wheelwrights	1	Washerwomen	38	Well diggers	1

Free Negro labor was apparently considered valuable in urban areas. From Richmond, Petersburg, Lynchburg, Norfolk, Winchester, and other places a number of petitions were sent to the legislature on behalf of certain free Negroes and manumitted slaves. These appeals were especially numerous in the decade of 1830. Petitions had been coming in from the urban centers since about 1805, and the process was continued until about 1850, after which date, as has been noted, the courts were given power to decide such cases.[68] On p. 100 a table of the 1830 decade gives a summary of petitions to the legislature, on behalf of certain industrious free Negroes in urban communities.[69]

The arguments advanced by the citizens of these communities were so effective that in most cases the person concerned was allowed to stay in Virginia. But such was not the experience of Archibald Carey of Lynchburg, who was forced to move to North Carolina. The petition of 137 citizens in

---

[68] Among petitions from Petersburg, dated before 1830, were those on behalf of Major Elebeck, Uriah Tyner, James Butler, and John Brown. Both Elebeck and Tyner were mechanics. The latter was a blacksmith and an "extremely industrious man." The 115 signers of Tyner's petition maintained that his expulsion would be a loss to the town. Petition, Dinwiddie, Dec. 15, 1810. James Butler, a miller, had conducted himself with such "respect, honesty, and sobriety" that his white supporters felt that he should be emancipated without having to leave the state. John Brown should stay, his one petitioner felt, because he was a "long, tried, and faithful servant." *Ibid.*, Dinwiddie, Dec. 5, 1821. Intercessions were made, for similar reasons, for Benjamin Godwin of Portsmouth and Elvira Jones of Richmond.

[69] The petitions listed here are found in the Legislative Petitions (mss.), Virginia State Library.

TABLE VII
Petitions for Certain Industrious Free Negroes

Name	City	Occupation	Reasons for Petition	Remarks
Ned Keeling	Norfolk	Drayman	Supported mistress and her children for a while after master's death.	Bought himself.
Ackey White	Norfolk	Drayman	Indispensable—place can not be supplied by anyone else.	Emancipated 1824.
Rachel Collins	Norfolk	Cook-Washerwoman	Old age—worked faithfully in War of 1812.	Bought herself.
Ned Adams	Lynchburg	Cooper	"Very valuable to the community."	Emancipated by last will and testament.
Archibald Carey	Lynchburg	Hack driver	Owner of real estate; "respectable worthy man."	Sent out of the state.
John Elson	Richmond	?	Far advanced in life.	Bought wife and two children.
Robin Brown	Richmond	Blacksmith	"Very useful."	Emancipated by will of master.
Wilson Morris	Richmond	Cooper	"Useful person to the merchants and grocers of Richmond."	
Milly	Richmond	?	"Upright woman in every way."	Married to a slave in Richmond.
Baptist Saunders	Richmond	?	"Honest, sober and industrious man."	Married to a slave woman.
Jack Hopes	Richmond	Cooper	"Remarkable for fidelity and correctness of conduct."	Hired out when a slave.
Randle Evans	Winchester	Confectioner	Confectionery, "a source of great convenience and utility to our citizens."	Bought himself and buying members of his family.

Carey's behalf includes perhaps the most elaborate statements among all those made on behalf of free Negroes. Carey's petitioners spoke of him as follows: "There is not an honester or more upright man under the sun ... in leaving Lynchburg, Archy carries with him the good wishes of all who know him." Of his services as a hack driver in Lynchburg for the previous ten years they said: "In that capacity he stands higher than anyone else who has ever lived in this part of the world." The fight for Carey was also waged on the ground that "by honest toil" he had acquired a house and lot in Lynchburg and "a tract of land of considerable value in the county of Amherst." Carey in 1827 paid $700 for the Lynchburg property referred to by his petitioners, and sold it in 1840 through agents for $1,100. When Carey was compelled to leave Virginia, his white friends even wrote letters of recommendation for him. One letter read that he "is now in pursuit of a home," and expressed the wish that all good citizens would permit him to travel through the country and protect him as they would any other citizen. On the strength of these fine testimonials, officials in North Carolina agreed not to enforce the law against him.[70]

Such is the story of the free Negroes at work. Both as individuals and as a group they had made themselves indispensable in the economic life of Virginia. According to the federal census there were in the state in 1860, 236 barbers, 4,224 blacksmiths, 743 boatmen, 1,895 coopers, 1,567 factory hands, 30,518 farm laborers, 1,778 laundresses, 1,257 oysterers, 11,053 servants, and 3,728 shoemakers. Free Negroes were represented in high percentage in each of these occupations. They were a majority in number of barbers, boatmen, and laundresses, and they were a substantial fraction of the large group of factory hands, farm laborers, oysterers, servants, and shoemakers.

[70] Petitions, Amherst, Dec. 23, 1833; Clerk's Office, Lynchburg, Deed Book J, p. 97.

CHAPTER IV

THE FREE NEGRO FARMER AND PROPERTY OWNER

FREE Negroes enjoyed an income from the many occupations in which they were engaged, and some of them put their earnings to good account. They bought property, farm land, and town lots. The chief contribution of this group of people lay in the field of labor, but such activity promoted the by-product of property ownership. Virginia free Negroes in agriculture were divided into classes like the rest of the agricultural population in Europe or America. Most of them were farm laborers; some, more progressive, became tenants; and the most thrifty became farm owners. Free Negroes of each group maintained close contacts with neighboring farmers, cultivating some land for themselves and also working for their white neighbors when their help was needed.[1] Free Negroes thus fitted into each of the several areas of farm activity and moved from rung to rung of the farm ladder. The shifting position of members of this group is reflected in many of the state and county records and in the census returns.

The largest group in free Negro rural labor was the farm hands. Though free Negro mechanics or skilled artisans were to be found in practically every county, the laborers and farm hands always greatly outnumbered them. This preponderance may be shown by reference to some of the counties in which the free Negro population comprised 18 to 43 per cent of the entire Negro group. Of a group of 1,600 or more free Negroes above the age of twelve in Accomac in 1851, about 1,300 were farm hands. In this county especially there

---

[1] Ulrich B. Phillips, *American Negro Slavery*, p. 437.

were very few free Negro mechanics—apparently no carpenters and but two or three blacksmiths and shoemakers. There were, on the other hand, many white mechanics in Accomac. Prince William County presents a situation common in northern Virginia. In 1860, of the 100 or so free Negro heads of families living in this county, thirty-two, or about one-third, were definitely farm hands. Another large block, one-seventh of the total free Negro population, lived and worked as members of white families. Still others who were farm tenants labored regularly or casually for the whites. All told, well over half of the free Negroes of Prince William who were reported as having definite occupations, were farm laborers. Frederick County in this same region had free Negro blacksmiths, shoemakers, coopers, farmers, and at least one wagoner, but the large majority of these people were farm hands and were employed in many cases, as has been shown, with the slaves.[2]

The steady employment of free Negroes in farm labor raises the question of their wages. In some cases it is certain that the major consideration was not wages but maintenance, or food and clothes. In other cases all or part of the wages was paid in cash. Olmsted interviewed one farmer who used all free labor—Negro and white—and who, with only a few exceptions, paid his laborers at less than $100 a year. In this situation it may be surmised that the Negro division of his labor supply received not more than $40 annually. This farmer did say in reference to his Negro employees that two of them were worth $20 a year more than the others because they had been brought up in his family.[3]

[2] Personal Property, Accomac County, 1851; U. S. Census Bureau, Free Inhabitants (ms.), 1860; Personal Property, Frederick, 1851.
[3] Wright, *Free Negro,* p. 164; Olmsted, *Seaboard Slave States* (1863 ed.), pp. 99–100. The wages paid free Negro farm labor in Virginia in antebellum days seldom exceeded $40 a year, if they were comparable with the wages Negroes received in 1868 under Freedmen's Bureau contracts. In Henry County, under one of these contracts for 1868, Chaney Thomas and her children were to receive only $35 as a yearly wage. Freedmen's Bureau contract, manuscript in possession of the writer.

Either by means of money wages paid or as a substitute for wages, free Negroes came into possession of farm implements and work stock.[4] With this equipment some of them became farm tenants, cultivating twenty-five or more acres on their own account while still lending a helping hand to their white neighbors. The existence of tenantry among the free people of color is revealed by the records in deeds of trust, later called crop liens. The deed of trust involved a contract between three parties: the free Negro tenant, a trustee, and the merchant from whom the tenant had secured either cash or its equivalent in goods. For a tenant to offer his crops and chattel property to merchants in satisfaction of debts incurred was a common occurrence, especially in Westmoreland County. The families of Ashton, Rich, Tate, and others were frequently involved in this way. On one occasion Anderson Tate was in debt to Atwell and Hunt, merchants of Westmoreland. As security for his debt this tenant offered eleven hogs, two cows, one bay mare, one tumbler cart, his half of the undivided crop of wheat, and his growing crop of corn. About the same time Campbell Tate was in debt to his merchant to the extent of $61. He offered as security one yoke of oxen, other livestock, and his growing crop of wheat, corn, and fodder.[5]

In the adjoining county of King George, in the Northern Neck, similar contracts were made by tenant farmers. Each year between 1850 and 1854 William Shanklin found it necessary to alienate his personal property in order to satisfy certain claims against him. In one instance he pledged his en-

---

[4] The deed books do not give a systematic record of personal property transactions as they do of real estate. How and when a particular free Negro came into possession of such property cannot, therefore, be determined with accuracy.

[5] Clerk's Office, Westmoreland County, Deed Book 33, p. 19; 35, p. 180. Under similar circumstances Hopeful Tate offered the usual livestock and all his interest in the crop of corn growing on the land that he was then renting. For his debt of $44.69 to his merchant, P. C. Hungerford, John Tate offered one yoke of oxen, an ox cart, and his growing crop of wheat on the land of Hungerford during that year. *Ibid.*, 36, p. 1.

tire wheat crop; in another, his crop of corn and fodder "now standing in the field." At another time, when he owed $120, his security embraced not only his "present crop of corn" (100 barrels) and growing crop of wheat and rye, but also five head of horned cattle, two horses, five hogs, and various farming implements.[6] Farther south, in Elizabeth City County, Samuel Chisman, a tenant, made a contract offering for his indebtedness of $52.09 one horse, one horse cart, one cow, four hogs, and his crop of sweet potatoes and corn then growing on the land of one W. S. Smith.[7]

The transactions indicated here leave the impression that the system of tenantry among the poorer whites and free Negroes in Virginia was similar to that after the Civil War. Cash tenantry, rather than a system of share cropping, seems to have prevailed. The land itself was rented on a variety of terms. Sometimes the rental was merely nominal, like that of James Barber of York County, who in 1829 entered upon a life contract for twenty-five acres of land at the rate of $1 payable annually on the first of January.[8]

In almost every county in Virginia the farm population of free Negroes included all three types: the laborer, the tenant, and the owner. These types may be illustrated from a group of free Negroes in one section of Hanover County during the year 1830.[9]

Of these ten persons four were "at" and four were "on" someone's place; each of the remaining two was "on his own land." Thus four should be ranked as laborers, four as ten-

---

[6] Clerk's Office, King George County, Deed Book 17, p. 475; 18, pp. 54, 150, 188. On a larger scale still, John Lucas offered forty or more items of his personal property as security for a debt of $135. Among these items were two feather beds, three tables, eleven chairs, one bureau, one cupboard, one walnut case, two clocks, one looking glass, one saw, one plane and other carpenter's tools, three axes, two plows, one cultivator, four hoes, two wagons, two horses, one buggy and harness, three hogs, six hens, one spinning wheel, one corn sheller, one lot of shoemakers' tools, and one silver watch. *Ibid.*, 19, p. 228.

[7] Clerk's Office, Elizabeth City County, Deed Book M, p. 450.

[8] Clerk's Office, York County, Deed Book 11, p. 96.

[9] Personal Property, Hanover, 1830.

TABLE VIII
Types of the Farm Population

Cupit Austin	*at* Bowling Vaughan's
Daniel Cooper	*on* J. Hare's land
Ben Dickson	*at* Benjamin Vaughan's
Pleasant Freeman	*on* Thomas Haris' land
Ben Gilman	*on his own land*
Henry Goins	*on* E. B. Crenshaw's land
Stephen Genett	*at* William Lawrence's
Frank Harris	*at* Bowling Vaughan's
General Marshall	*on* Martin Strong's land
Thomas Smart	*on his own land*

ants, and two as farm owners. The one-fifth who were farm owners in this selected list from Hanover represented a frequent proportion of owners to laborers and tenants in many other counties.

Tenants, or those "on" the land of some one, often became the owners of that land or of other tracts. Examples of this change in position are legion among rural Virginia free Negroes. In Isle of Wight County Ben Bailey and Burwell Green owned one horse apiece, and no real estate, in 1830. In all probability at that time they were renters, or persons "on" the land of some owner. Twelve years later they had become the owners of fifty acre and sixty-three acre tracts respectively. In James City County there were six free Negroes each of whom in 1830 had little or no personal property but in 1845 owned tracts of land ranging from twenty-five to 100 acres. The adjoining county of New Kent recorded three free Negroes who had very little personal property in 1830, whereas by 1845 each held tracts from six and one-fourth to fifty acres.[10] About 1830 in Goochland County six other free Negroes owned such items as one horse, one yoke of oxen,

---

[10] Land, Personal Property, Isle of Wight, James City, New Kent, 1830–1845. The six free Negro landowners of James City mentioned above were Ashton, Carter, Davis, Dunston, Moore, and Wallis.

and other equipment; but ten and fifteen years later they owned tracts varying from nine and one-fourth to sixty-eight acres of land. Within twelve years (1830–1842) William Epps of Halifax County made the unusual advance from the ownership of one horse to the ownership of 595 acres of land and other equipment, purchased at the cost of $2,966.[11]

Of course, many free Negroes always remained tenants; and some of these acquired a reputation for thrift. One such man was Charles Cousins of Nottoway County, a farmer and shoemaker, who finally rose to the rank of manager of a plantation. While he was still a tenant his community styled him "a good tenant and faithful paymaster." [12] Other free Negro farm tenants in Virginia made great strides as owners of chattel property and as men of business acumen. Many of them were perhaps of more solid economic worth to their communities than farm owners, particularly than that large group of owners whose acreage was less than twenty-five; for the value of the tenant's livestock, implements, and household furniture in some cases exceeded the total value of the property of such small owners.

Facts about the chattel property owned and the crops raised in 1860 by some free Negro farm tenants may serve to indicate the economic position of the more advanced. Thomas Stewart of Brunswick County cultivated a farm of 250 acres and owned two horses, one mule, several head of cattle, and twelve hogs. His chief crops for 1860 were corn and 1,000 pounds of tobacco. The products of Theophilus Stewart of Dinwiddie County included oats, wheat, Irish potatoes, sweet potatoes, 250 bushels of corn, and 3,200 pounds of tobacco. His livestock included four horses, one cow, and six swine.

[11] *Ibid.*, Goochland; Clerk's Office, Halifax Deed Book 47, p. 315. Matthew Hill of this same county had no property of any kind in 1830, an accumulation of livestock and other equipment in the late thirties, and 110 acres of land in 1840. Land, Personal Property, Halifax, 1830–1845. John Epperson of Buckingham, a wheelwright, had one horse but no land in 1850; ten years later he owned 198 acres. Land, Personal Property, Buckingham, 1850–1860.

[12] Petition, Nottoway, Dec. 20, 1819.

John Chavous for a number of years operated a farm of 125 acres in Mecklenburg County. In 1860 he owned seven horses, three cows, three other cattle, and ten swine with a total value of $300. His chief crop in that year was tobacco. Colgate Whitehead of Southampton owned four horses, three cows, two oxen, three other cattle, and eighty swine worth $400. To feed these hogs he raised 750 bushels of corn. Aside from corn he raised ninety bushels of peas and beans, 100 bushels of sweet potatoes, and six bales of cotton. Farming on such a scale, Whitehead easily excelled many free Negro farm owners and indeed ranked in a class with many white farmers of Southampton.[13]

Naturally tenantry was most widespread in those counties where free Negro ownership was lowest—Westmoreland, King George, Accomac, and Caroline. There were never more than six Negro farm owners in Westmoreland during the entire period under review, but the number of tenant farmers ran as high as forty.[14] Though King George County had ten or more free Negro tenants in 1860, two or three of whom were prosperous, this county had only one free Negro owner at this time and, indeed, had no more than two at any time during the period from 1830 to 1860. The free Negro population of Accomac County, three times as great as in Westmoreland, comprised about twenty-five farm owners and forty or more tenants. In 1860 there were nine of these tenants on the 207 acre farm of one white man, each one having one or two horses or oxen, and small crops of corn and oats. Other Accomac farm tenants, however, were in better circumstances. Edward, George, and William Downing, for example, cultivated farms of 45 to 110 acres. Caroline

[13] U. S. Census Bureau, Agriculture (ms.), 1860, in the Virginia State Library. Generally speaking, these records do not label farm tenants as such nor do they indicate race. Information on race can be obtained, however, by checking these records with the personal property books of each county. The latter always indicate race and give much information on taxable personal property. Thus the property books serve as an excellent supplement to the census enumeration.

[14] Land, Personal Property, Westmoreland, 1830-1860.

County, with only seventeen free Negroes owning farms in 1860, had at least forty farm tenants, practically all of whom, however, owned fairly large numbers of cattle, hogs, and other livestock.[15] Some of the western counties of Virginia, with a very small free Negro population, had a few tenants but no owners whatever. Such were Bath, Botetourt, Roanoke, Shenandoah, Smyth, Tazewell, Warren, and Wythe, which had from one to six free Negro tenants apiece.

In the entire state the number of free Negro tenant farmers in 1860 may be computed, under one type of classification, at approximately 800; under another type of classification, however, there may have been as many as 1500.[16] The value of their personal property extended from a few dollars to $500 apiece. The usual amount was $50. Since many of these tenants occasionally worked for the neighboring white farmers for wages, they were of substantial value to their communities. Their value was further enhanced by the fact that in many cases they were tradesmen and cultivated small farms for their subsistence. An analysis of the farm owners in the 1860 group makes it clear that many of them had once been tenants.

An adequate discussion of free Negro farm owners in Virginia involves consideration of the amount and value of land in their possession in 1830 and in 1860; of the ways in which they obtained their land—whether by gift, inheritance, or purchase—and of their methods of farm operation.

In 1830 free Negroes in Virginia held 31,721 acres of land valued at $184,184; in 1860 they owned 60,045 acres

---

[15] U. S. Census, Agriculture (ms.), 1860; Land, Personal Property, Caroline, 1860.

[16] These figures are based on a compilation drawn from the ninety-seven land books, ninety-seven personal property books, and six or more volumes of the original U. S. Census agricultural enumeration. The number 800 is based on the state personal property records, which rated personal property only in terms of those items taxed by the state. Oxen, cows, swine, and farm implements did not usually come under their purview. Since a large number of families of that day, both Negro and white, owned oxen rather than horses, the number 1,500 is a fair approximation of the actual situation.

valued at $369,647. The acreage held by free Negroes in 1830 embraced 678 farms; thirty years later the total acreage comprised 1,202 farms. In the unincorporated towns and villages free Negroes owned thirty-seven lots in 1830, eighty-six in 1860. Thus it is evident that the property belonging to free Negro rural dwellers in 1860 had about doubled in value and quantity since 1830. This 100 per cent gain in property was accompanied by less than 20 per cent increase in number of rural free Negroes.

The largest farm owned by a free Negro in the state in 1860 was 1,100 acres; the largest owned by a free Negro during the entire period from 1830 to 1860 was 1,304 acres. In 1860 two free Negroes owned 600 acres or more; two owned 500; four, 400; eight, 300; and twenty-seven, 200 or more. Thirty-four such persons owned between 150 and 200 acres; ninety-five between 100 and 150 acres; eighty-eight between 75 and 100 acres; and 169 between 50 and 75 acres. Of the remaining 749 free Negro farm owners in the lower brackets, 230 owned from 25 to 50 acres, and 515—about 43 per cent of the total number of farm owners—had 25 acres or less.[17] With this large group in the lower levels it is obvious that the typical farm owned by a free Negro was not a commercial enterprise but a farm home.

Free Negroes in certain counties and sections of the state made rapid progress in farm ownership between 1830 and 1860, while elsewhere they remained at a standstill. Nansemond County, with its large free Negro population, made the most rapid increase. Acreage owned by Nansemond free Negroes, 475 acres in 1830 and 5,630 in 1860, increased ap-

---

[17] These data on farm ownership are derived from the study of the eighty-one land books for as many counties in 1830, and the ninety-seven land books for as many counties in 1860.

The present census definition of a farm is an area of land covering three or more acres. Under this classification the actual number of farms in 1860 was 1,132; since 67 (about 5.6 per cent of the 1,202) embraced tracts of less than three acres. In a few instances one person owned more than one tract of land. Under this classification the number of farms owned by free Negroes would extend to 1,300 or more.

proximately twelve times; in Amelia, six; in Amherst and James City, five; in Campbell, Cumberland, and Rockbridge, three; in Isle of Wight and Dinwiddie, two. The gain in land in all of these counties was accompanied by only a negligible increase in free Negro population; in four of them there was an actual decline. The free Negro landowners in Nansemond County advanced from eighteen in 1830 to thirty in 1835, forty-five in 1840, fifty-two in 1845, sixty-six in 1850, and ninety-two in 1855. For some reason the number in 1860 dropped to eighty-six.[18]

Although free Negroes gained in land ownership in certain counties, there were others, notably Accomac, Westmoreland, Northampton, King George, and Fauquier, where the rate of tenantry was high and where the ownership of land by Negroes was limited. Among the causes of this variation the principle of proportion of the free Negro population to the slave population seems to have had little bearing. In the two Eastern Shore counties of Northampton and Accomac, where the combined free Negro population was about one-third that of the slaves, the large population might seem to have worked against land ownership by free Negroes; on the other hand, in such counties as Nansemond, Surry, and Isle of Wight, where the proportion of free Negroes to slaves was about as great, a high rate of land ownership among free Negroes prevailed.

About two-thirds of the counties showed gains in Negro ownership of land from 1830 to 1860; one-third showed decline or no change. This latter condition may be explained on the ground that ten or more of these counties, located in the west and southwest, always had a very sparse Negro population, although in a few of these counties showing loss in farm land the loss was offset by the appearance of free Negro ownership in town lots.

The attitude of the whites toward land ownership among free Negroes was more decisive than the ratio of the free

[18] Land, Nansemond, 1830–1860.

Negro population to the slave population, and indeed this attitude affected land ownership among Negroes in the period after 1865 as well as before the Civil War. In all probability the whites in certain sections encouraged such activity, while in others they condemned it.[19] Documentary evidence tends to show that for a time the whites of the Eastern Shore of Virginia, with its large free black population, were opposed to Negro land ownership.

The practice of not allowing free Negroes to hold land is linked with the larger subject of physical violence toward the group and of attempts at expulsion. As a result of the Nat Turner insurrection and other factors a considerable migration of free Negroes took place from various points in Virginia, especially in the years from 1830 to 1835, with a more even migration throughout the rest of the period under review. A previous chapter has shown that large numbers of Virginia free Negroes migrated to Ohio because of persecution in their native State or for other reasons. This fact may have had some bearing on Negro land ownership in Virginia, in cases where the migrants secured property in their new homes. In other words, if these migrants had remained undisturbed in Virginia, or if conditions had been as favorable to property ownership in Virginia as in their new homes, these persons might have owned property in their native state.

It is interesting, therefore, to see how much property Virginia-born free Negroes acquired in certain parts of Ohio, the state to which they went perhaps in largest numbers. A number of Virginia Negroes, many of whom were progressive, migrated to Jackson, Ross, Greene, Franklin, and Brown counties in Ohio. First-hand information concerning them is found in the original United States census enumera-

[19] W. E. MacClenny of Suffolk in Nansemond County reported to the writer that in his boyhood days Elijah Hare, a white man of this county, was known as the "free Negro's God." This epithet was given to Hare because he always defended free Negroes and attempted to promote their progress.

tion for the year 1860. At this time Jackson County had forty Virginia-born free Negro heads of families, who held property ranging in value from $300 to $6,000. All but four of these persons were farmers. Half of them held property valued at $1,000 or more. Ross County, Ohio, had thirty Virginia-born free Negro heads of families with property ranging in value from $500 upwards. Greene and Franklin counties, with a smaller number of Virginia free Negroes, maintained an even higher record in property holding.[20]

Allowing for the common practice of over-valuation by census enumerators, one is impressed with the successful showing made by these Virginia migrants. In many cases all or some of the children of these heads of families had been born in Virginia. In the particular counties named, the majority of the free Negroes were property holders. Within this particular limited area of Ohio, the Virginia-born free Negroes made greater advancement than did their people back in Virginia. They forged ahead as useful citizens despite the fact that although the laws against them were not quite so severe as Virginia's, public sentiment was perhaps even more hostile. The characterization of free Negroes as

[20] Noah B. Nooks led the roll of free Negro heads of families in Jackson County, with real estate valued at $6,000 and personal property at $800. This man and his Virginia-born wife went to Ohio sometime in the late thirties. In Ross County, William Cunningham, a farmer who went to Ohio about 1830, accumulated an estate valued at the unusual sum of $12,000 and personal property valued at $1,500. Robert Jackson and Richard Johnson, farmers, held property valued at $3,000 and $1,800 respectively. In one of the towns in this county lived Tucker Isaacs, a painter from Charlottesville, Virginia, whose real estate amounted to $4,000; and William Langston, a carpenter, with property valued at $3,000. Samuel Brown and Peter B. Bolling of Greene County were six-thousand-dollar farmers, while Laura Anna Smith held an estate valued at $26,000. In Franklin County lived James A. L. Clarke, a farmer with a property of $17,000, who had come to Ohio in the forties with his Virginia-born wife. Pleasant Literford, a Virginia-born farmer of the same county, held property valued at about half as much as Clarke's. In Brown County lived James Ellis, with farm property valued at $4,000. U. S. Census Bureau, Free Inhabitants, Ohio, 1860. For progressive Negro farmers in Northern states, regardless of their place of birth, see Martin R. Delaney, *The Condition, Elevation, Emigration and Destiny of the Colored People of the United States*, ch. 15.

the drones and pests of society was quite as frequent in Ohio as in Virginia.[21]

Still another reason for the low rate of landowning by free Negroes in certain counties in Virginia was the usual shiftless element and the presence of large groups of families who apparently lacked any desire to advance. Much of the free Negro population of Richmond County, one of the low-ranking counties, centered in three families: Venie, Thompson, and Rich. There were twenty-four families of Venies in 1860, but only two or three of them ever owned land. With two landowners and several flourishing tenants, the Thompsons were slightly better off. In the neighboring county of Essex the general average was lowered by the Bundy families, among twenty or more of whom between 1830 and 1860 only two ever became landowners. Only one of these families possessed real estate in 1860, and that amounted to only one and one-fourth acres in the hands of Baldwin Bundy. In the light of this condition there is perhaps truth in the derogatory statement made by a group of Essex petitioners concerning the free Negroes: "There are from 400 to 500 free Negroes here of the most indolent habits and degraded character which tend to swell greatly the poor rates of the county." [22]

[21] For hardships of Negroes in Northern states, see Carter G. Woodson, *A Century of Negro Migration*, ch. 3, and for their success despite handicaps see *ibid.*, ch. 5. It is difficult to determine whether the prosperous free Negroes indicated here were born free or whether they went to Ohio as recently emancipated slaves. In the case of slaves money was frequently given them by the former white owner. Occasionally aid was also extended to Negroes born free in Virginia. It is possible, therefore, that in some of the cases cited the start in life was based on this past relationship.

One instance of a Virginia-born free Negro in Ohio receiving financial assistance from a Virginia white father is that of John M. Langston. By a will made in Louisa County, 1833, Ralph Quarles, the white father, gave him and his brothers a plantation with all its equipment. The income from the sale of this land was presumably to be used to support Langston during his schooling in Ohio. Clerk's Office, Louisa County, Will Book 9, p. 110. For other examples of Virginia Negroes who received land or money in Ohio, see Beverly B. Munford, *Virginia's Attitude toward Slavery and Secession*, pp. 66–68.

[22] U. S. Census Bureau, Free Inhabitants, 1860; Land, Richmond, 1860; Clerk's Office, Essex County, Deed Books 42–51; Petition, Essex, Jan. 3, 1846.

THE FARMER AND PROPERTY OWNER 115

In considering free Negro landowners, the question of color—that is, of the proportion of white blood among them—arises. The United States census classified these persons under two heads: black and mulatto. In the entire state the mulattoes in 1860 numbered 23,485; the blacks, 34,557. In the cities the proportion in favor of the blacks was two and three to one. As this discussion will later show more fully, the general opinion in American society has been that all advance made by Negroes during the slavery period rested with the mulatto element, both slave and free. It has been generally assumed that the bulk of land owned by free Negroes was in the possession of the mulatto element and had come to them through their white kindred. For Virginia with its 58,000 free Negroes this assumption is highly incorrect.

According to the United States census, among the ninety-seven counties of Virginia the mulattoes outnumbered the blacks in forty-nine counties, one county was exactly half and half, and in forty-seven the blacks outnumbered the mulattoes.[23] These same counties may be examined with respect to landownership by blacks and mulattoes. Certain counties in southeastern Virginia—Dinwiddie, Isle of Wight, Nansemond, Norfolk, Prince George, Southampton, Surry, and Sussex—contained 10,375 free Negroes, or about 21 per cent of the rural free Negroes of the state. This region also contained 385 free Negro landowners, about 33 per cent of the total for the state, with an acreage of 19,359 constituting 32 per cent of the acreage held by Negroes within the state. The blacks among the free Negroes in this section outnumbered the mulattoes more than three to one. In so far as the records indicate, the majority of the Negro landowners in each of these counties was black. In Isle of Wight, where the records are most complete, 80 per cent of the landowners were black rather than mulatto. Such extensive land-holding families as Bailey, Butler, Holloway, Judkins, Pretlow,

[23] U. S. Census, *Negro Population*, 1860.

Ricks, and Tynes were all people of dark complexion.[24] A similar situation existed in Sussex County.

In other sections of the state with an appreciable free Negro population similar conditions prevailed. Goochland, James City, King and Queen, New Kent, and Powhatan were all counties in which the blacks outnumbered the mulattoes and in which the number of black landowners exceeded that of mulatto landowners. Ransom Harris of King and Queen, with his 475 acres, and Arthur Lee of Alleghany, with his 413 acres, were dark men. In contrast to these counties with a heavy landownership by blacks there was King George County, with a free Negro population, all mulatto, with only one Negro land holder, while Essex and Fauquier with their preponderant mulatto population contained a few only. The reverse of the shield, however, shows Amelia and Amherst, mulatto counties, with a high rating in Negro landownership, while Accomac, with a large black population, ranked the lowest in the state in its proportion of Negro landholders. If the preponderant black ownership of property in the cities of Virginia is added to that in the country, the total result runs strongly in favor of the black element rather than the mulatto as owners of property.[25]

[24] Some proof of this statement may be found in the complexion of the descendants of many of these families today. The preponderance of the black element in these counties may have its origin in the great number of manumissions executed in this region during the revolutionary period by Quakers and Methodists. Cf. Wesley M. Gewehr, *The Great Awakening in Virginia, 1740-1790,* chs. 6, 10. Presumably the Negro race as a whole was darker in the revolutionary period than at the present time. Therefore, since fewer mulattoes were manumitted in the early period than persons of darker hue, this latter element would still be predominant in the period from 1830 to 1860. One striking example of a wholesale manumission of "non-mulatto" slaves was that made by Timothy Tynes of Isle of Wight. In 1802 his will gave freedom to eighty or more slaves who, judging by the classification given them in all the records (U. S. Census, deed books, marriage record books), were persons of dark complexion. There are many Negro Tynes families in Virginia and elsewhere today. The Tynes family also acquired land by this will in 1802 and have remained landowners in Isle of Wight until the present day. The Tynes will is found in Clerk's Office, Isle of Wight County, Will Book 11 (1794-1802), pp. 587-588.

[25] The prominence given by historians to the mulatto element and its achievements perhaps grows out of the high ranking of this group in Louisiana and in Charleston, S. C.

THE FARMER AND PROPERTY OWNER

The great majority of the free Negroes obtained their land by purchase rather than by inheritance or gift. A tabulation of the method by which the landholders of 1860 in one county obtained their property is sufficient to illustrate the general tendency. In the following table, for Sussex County, the grantee is the free Negro purchaser, the grantor is the seller.

TABLE IX
Acquisition of Property, Sussex County

Grantee	Grantor	No. of Acres	Price	Date	Reference Deed Book	Page
Polly Andrews	J. Nicholson	65	Hire of son for 8 years	1852	V	178
Absalom Baird	Peter Thomas	95	$106.88	1825	O	308
Henry Bowling	E. S. Davis	23	70.00	1829	P	401
Sally Brown	Harris & Faison	10	100.00	1857	V	594
Dudley Graves	Charles Hill	123	1.00	1842	T	105
Lucy Graves	Fred Hill	7½	14.00	1839	S	249
Ben Hamlin	B. W. Johnson	45	45.00	1851	U	632
Milly Hamlin	T. L. Johnson	75	60.00	1853	V	183
Chesman Hargrave	S. Marable	114½	100.00	1856	V	434
Johnson Hargrave	E. Nicholson	20	18.50	1851	V	191
Ned Hargrave	John White	34	137.60	1825	O	408
Penine Hargrave	John Ellis	8	8.00	1845	T	474
Abraham Hill	Miles Horn	76	219.00	1851	V	67
Charles Hill	Anthony Parham	320	800.00	1841	T	25
Fred Hill	Henry Evans	12	30.00	1834	B	43
————	H. W. Eppes	99	84.90	1835	R	278
Mary Hill	D. J. Mayes	30	225.00	1857	V	585
Moses Hill	T. L. Johnson	85	400.00	1839	S	496
Edmund Judkins	John Owens	21	39.98	1851	V	326
————	Amy Ellis	13	12.00	1839	U	3
Jordan Judkins	Wm. Harrison	20	24.00	1850	R	548
Sancho Moore	J. M. Presson	40	25.60	1835	L	221
Tom Moore (estate)	B. Moore	45	£56	1807	U	442
Arthur Myrick	William Milby	18	36.00	1847	V	174
Mary Nicholson	John Nicholson	50	200.00	1858	V	647
Melinda Nicholson	Martha Hart	34	24.50	1851	V	30
John Owen	Charles Hill	14	31.50	1855	V	363
Anthony Parham	Fred Hill	8	24.00	1851	V	73
Jesse Parham	Elizabeth Wynne	46	200.00	1858	V	676
George Roberts	William Pegram	25	37.50	1851	V	55
Edwin Sampson	————	100	Acquired by will from B. Sampson			
John Sampson	————	175	Acquired by will from B. Sampson			
Wiley Turner	Wright Turner	30	16.08	1848		
Madison Welborne	John Pitts	95	360.00	1858		664

The free Negro purchased his land under a variety of contracts, usually by a full payment but sometimes by time payments. Several examples of the latter may be cited. In 1848 Charles Rich of Westmoreland paid $150 for sixty-seven acres of land by means of a deed of trust for three payments of $50 each. Eight years later, after having met all three of these payments, he was granted a deed of release. In 1851 George Roberts of Sussex paid $37.50 for twenty-five acres—one-half down, the rest in notes. Still later Fleet McCoy of Lancaster paid $425 for twenty-three acres—$100 in cash and the rest in installments. In 1859 Peter Jenkins of Cumberland paid the handsome sum of $1,000 for ninety-two and one-quarter acres by one down payment and two installments, and the next year Thomas Arrington of Madison paid $900 for seventy-nine acres, $500 in cash and eight annual payments.[26]

Usually the terms of the deeds of sale followed customary provisions, but occasionally some of the terms restricted the use that the free Negro purchaser might make of his land. An example of extreme restriction is the terms imposed in a certain fifty-dollar purchase of one acre of land at the Goochland County court house. Benjamin Anderson, the white grantor of the property, sold it to John Pierce, the free Negro grantee, on condition that none but members of Pierce's family were to live on this ground without Anderson's consent; no house of entertainment might be erected on it; no spiritous liquors might be sold; the house on the land was to be kept free from visits of disorderly persons; and the land was to be kept well enclosed so as to keep out fowls. Finally, if Pierce himself became disorderly, Anderson might repossess the property.[27]

Free Negro owners of property disposed of it as white persons did, frequently by making wills. Thus, in a county or

[26] Clerk's Office, Westmoreland County, Deed Book 32, p. 213; Sussex, R. p. 55; Lancaster, 42, p. 18; Cumberland, 28, p. 636; Madison, 23, p. 289.
[27] Clerk's Office, Goochland, Deed Book 24, p. 355.

city list of property holders for a given year, one or more owners can usually be found who came into possession of their property by bequest from a free Negro parent, grandparent, or other relative. Both in the 1830 and in the 1860 state lists there are a number of free Negroes whose ownership of property extends back more than one generation.[28]

The Jarvis family of York County is a case in point. William Jarvis, one of the wealthiest free Negroes in Virginia, died in 1825, leaving to members of his family an estate valued at $6,656. His wife received by bequest $500, and his sons Thomas and John inherited the bulk of his landed estate with its appurtenances. This land embraced two tracts, one of 135 acres and the other of 300 acres, which Jarvis, like most free Negro property owners, had himself purchased. Sixteen years later, one of his heirs passed on to others the property he had received from his father.[29] The Owen property of fifty acres found in the 1830 Brunswick County list had come to the family by inheritance. In 1817 Robert Owen had provided that his "beloved wife," Polly, should have all of his stock of every description, plantation implements, the tract of land whereon he then lived, and the mill belonging to the same.[30] Owen, like Jarvis, had come into possession of this property by purchase.

In Sussex County a free Negro, Lewis Turner, in the early years likewise accumulated a competence sufficiently large to keep it in possession of his descendants until 1860 and later.

---

[28] There are at least seventy-five Negro families in Virginia today whose ownership of farm land began with their free Negro ancestors in the slavery period. In the case of the Brown family of Charles City County this continuous ownership extends back to 1769 or even earlier. The Watts family of Norfolk County likewise owned land very early. Among these seventy-five families today seven live in Charles City County, three in Cumberland, four or more in Gloucester, three or more in Isle of Wight, six or more in Nansemond, four in Northumberland, four in Middlesex, and five in Surry.

[29] Clerk's Office, York County, Will Book 11, pp. 44-48; 10, p. 503; 12, p. 427; 7, p. 492; 9, p. 133.

[30] Clerk's Office, Brunswick County, Will Book 10, p. 284. John Stewart of Brunswick in 1860 owned 421 acres, at least part of which he had received by the will of Dempsey Stewart, made in 1848. *Ibid.*, 15, p. 231.

Between 1800 and 1814 this man bought three tracts of land in Sussex ranging in size from twenty-eight to ninety acres. He later made other purchases and left a personal estate valued at $505. Turner provided in his will (1818) that his wife should receive the greater part of his estate, that one plantation was to go to his brother after his wife's death, and that his children should be given money from the sale of a part of his land. The 1830 Sussex County list of property holders shows that his wife, Aggy Turner, was in possession of three tracts of land willed to her while his brother was in possession of the other.[31]

In Surry County, adjoining Sussex, there were a number of cases in which free Negro parents made provision for their children and relatives through their wills. The 1860 list of property holders for this county accordingly shows an unusually large number of owners who had inherited their possessions. For example, the Debrix property of 130 acres in 1860 had come to the three holders through two generations. In 1829 John Debrix had bequeathed fifty acres of his estate to his son, Major; eight years later this same son bequeathed his plantation to his wife, Polly, and directed that after her death it was to be conveyed to his son, Thomas, one of the 1860 property holders.[32]

Scattered cases of inheritance of land by free Negroes in other counties may be noted. John Kelley of Lunenburg re-

---

[31] Clerk's office, Sussex County, Deed Book I, p. 436; J. p. 386; L, p. 401; H, pp. 534–537. Edwin and John Sampson of Sussex also acquired land by the will of their free Negro father, Ben Sampson.

[32] Clerk's Office, Surry County, Will Book 8, p. 384; 7, p. 410. Similar cases are those of the Pretlow, Brown, and Charity families. Henry Pretlow's fifty-three acres and Lysander Pretlow's seventy-eight acres, listed for 1860, were inherited from their mother, who had in turn inherited the land from the father, William Pretlow. *Ibid.*, 8, p. 241. The Brown property of 1860, in the hands of two of the family, consisted of 170 acres that in 1850 had been bequeathed by Benjamin Brown, who had given to his "beloved wife, Susan Brown, the land and plantation . . . and also all . . . other estate, both chattel and personal." *Ibid.*, 9, p. 515. In 1860 three members of the Charity family owned land that in 1828 had been bequeathed by Squire Charity, a shoemaker, who in addition had provided that the sum of $50 be paid to each of his three sons at the age of twenty-one. *Ibid.*, 6.

ceived his eighty acres from his mother by her will in 1855; the three Pierce heirs of Goochland inherited their ninety acres from their mother, Mildred Pierce, who made her will in 1850. Charles Wilson of Campbell County received 200 acres through the 1852 will of his father, James Wilson; and the fifteen or more Brown families of Charles City inherited all or part of their small tracts by the wills of Isaac, Peter, and Abraham Brown, made during the thirty years before 1860.[33]

Although William Daniel of Louisa County did not own real estate in 1860, his inheritance is none the less interesting. His wife, Lucinda Daniel, in 1847 made a will in which her chief bequest to him was the following: "I manumit and set free my husband William Daniel, who was sold, and the title to him transferred to me by Peter M. Daniel." She also left him all of her estate of every kind and description. Among the items of personal property in the estate were a bay mare, a cow and calf, a bed and furniture, a writing desk, a spinning wheel, a loom, a carryall, and shoemaker's tools. The last item was no doubt especially valuable in that William Daniel earned his living at shoemaking.[34]

A discussion of the source from which the free Negroes of the years 1830 and 1860 obtained their property leads to a consideration of the part which white men played in furthering such ownership. As has been noted earlier, the major portion of the free Negroes' possessions came through purchase by themselves. Possession by inheritance from free Negro relatives was limited; that which came by gift or bequest from the whites was perhaps still more limited. The channels through which white people bestowed land on free Negroes were two in number: first, by gift at the time of the

[33] Clerk's Office, Lunenburg County, Will Book 14, p. 56; Goochland, Deed Book 36, p. 222; Campbell, Will Book 11, p. 183; Charles City, Will Book 3, p. 407; 4, pp. 375, 447.
[34] Clerk's Office, Louisa County, Will Book 12, pp. 160, 270. William Daniel's son, Charles J. Daniel, became the secretary of the Virginia Normal and Collegiate Institute at Petersburg. His grandchildren today hold important positions in the field of education.

manumission of slaves, and second, by bequest to persons who had long been free. This second occasion was frequently the result of concubinage.

One convenient method for discovering land given by white persons to free colored persons is the size of the estate. Free Negroes in Virginia rarely obtained land in excess of 500 acres by their own efforts. The existence of such holdings in most cases therefore would indicate that the land in question came into the hands of the Negro owner from white sources. When the investigator finds a Priscilla Ivey with 1,304 acres of land, an Alfred Anderson with 670 acres, and a Frankey Miles with 1,100 acres, he may well infer that such holdings are of white origin, and in these cases further investigation proves his inference correct. All told, however, not more than forty families in Virginia throughout the history of free Negro land ownership in the thirty years prior to 1860 received their lands from white persons. A careful examination of the entire list of free Negro property holders in all the counties and cities of the state for 1830 indicates that ownership based on white origin is limited to that number.[35] The number for 1860 is less than that for 1830.

Acts of manumission were common in Virginia and were occasionally accompanied by provision for the material welfare of the persons manumitted. One strong deterrent, however, to the granting of property to manumitted slaves was the uncertainty, after 1806, that they would be allowed to remain in the state beyond the legal twelve months' period.

[35] This statement is based on a complete study of all property ownership in five or more counties not only for the years 1830 and 1860 but for intervening years as well. Besides studying farm property ownership, the writer has examined the origins of practically all ownership by free Negroes, more than 500 cases, in the cities of Richmond, Petersburg, and Fredericksburg. The securing of land by purchase rather than by bequest is even more pronounced in cities than in the counties. Aside from making this complete study in certain counties and cities, the writer has examined the subject of property origins to some extent in each of the forty-five county and city clerks' offices consulted for this treatise. The result is the same in all cases. The manuscript deed books and will books in these local archives therefore give the complete story.

Thus it happens that among these free Negroes of the 1830-1860 period whose land was willed to them by white persons the bequests were made prior to 1806. Liberal-minded slaveholders frequently provided by will that their executors should purchase for the manumitted slaves land outside the state, or that they should apply the proceeds from the sale of land to the transportation and establishment in Liberia of manumitted slaves. So celebrated are some of these provisions that there is a general impression that these liberal allowances extended throughout the period of slavery and that manumitted Negroes as legal residents of Virginia were allowed to hold such property during this whole span of time.

Several cases, however, give a different impression. In 1819 Samuel Gist of Richmond manumitted 113 slaves in Hanover County, and 150 in Goochland and Amherst counties. He left these people two tracts of land, not in Virginia but in Brown County, Ohio, bought for $4,000. This same year Edward Coles of Albemarle freed a large number of slaves and provided them with land in Illinois, 160 acres for each head of a family. John Ward of Pittsylvania manumitted seventy slaves, provided them with money, and settled them in Lawrence County, Ohio. In this instance, however, the testator desired that with the court's permission two of his most faithful slaves should remain in Virginia and enjoy the 300 acres of land and $150 with which he provided each. Although James Bray of Chesterfield County willed his twenty-five slaves several tracts of land and a mill in the county, the legislature by an act of 1830 directed Bray's executor to sell this property and invest the money in land outside of Virginia wherever the emancipated slaves should remove. Similarly, the commonwealth intervened in the case of Abraham Depp of Powhatan, a blacksmith, who inherited valuable property from his master. In 1832 the legislature allowed him a period of only two years to continue residence in Virginia so that he might have time to dispose of the property "devised him by his late master." The case of John

Randolph of Roanoke has received considerable attention from historians. At his death this statesman freed all his slaves, about 385, and settled them on land in Ohio, at a cost of $13,000.[36]

In contrast to the masters just mentioned a certain group of slave owners freed their slaves without reference to residence and property outside the state. They presumably did so in the expectation that the manumitted slaves would enjoy their freedom and property in Virginia. But in many instances, such freedmen were compelled to lay themselves at the mercy of the local courts or the state legislature for permission to remain in Virginia and enjoy the property given to them.

Other slaveholders, mindful of the law, frankly left property to manumitted Negroes on condition that the freedmen secure the permission of the courts to remain. In this general category fell the slaveholders Emanuel Fentress of Princess Anne, James Ross of Middlesex, and Richard Sandridge of Louisa, who, in 1829, requested that the legislature allow his emancipated slaves to remain but provided that if it did not, certain property of his should be sold, and from the proceeds, lands outside the state should be bought for them.[37] Some ten years later similar efforts were made by Thomas Purdie of Isle of Wight and Sarah Jenkins of Elizabeth City. In the latter instance the testatrix gave her house and lot to

---

[36] Munford, *Virginia's Attitude toward Slavery*, pp. 66, 68; Petition, Pittsylvania, 1827; *Acts of Assembly*, 1830, ch. 129; 1832, ch. 248. Similarly John Warwick of Amherst, Travers and Thaddeus Herndon of Fauquier, and Theodore Gregg of Dinwiddie sent their many slaves to Ohio, Michigan, or Liberia. Munford, *Virginia's Attitude toward Slavery*, p. 70; Woodson, *Century of Negro Migration*, p. 27. Other masters who freed their slaves did not assign definite destinations for them, but like John Rawles of Nansemond County indicated that the money and property left to them should be used for establishing them "where they may enjoy the blessings of liberty unmolested." Clerk's Office, Nansemond, Deed Book 1, p. 145.

[37] Clerk's Office, Princess Anne, 1814; Middlesex, 1826; Louisa, 1829. Edmund Littlepage of King William, Jane Barr and James Bishop of Prince George, and Robert L. Bailey of Surry, contemporaries of Sandridge, made the same provisions. Clerk's Office, King William, 1825; Prince George, 1827, 1830; Surry, 1829.

her four slaves with the "hope," she said, "that the county court will let them remain." [38]

The holding of land by manumitted Negroes through bequests from white persons was thus, after 1806, feasible beyond the borders of the state but uncertain within the state. The manumissions and bequests made prior to the law of 1806 lay on safer ground, and these earlier bequests had the greater bearing on the property holding lists of 1830 and 1860; those coming after 1806 had practically none.

As might be expected, some manumitted Negroes who received gifts or bequests of land from white persons gradually lost or dissipated their holdings; others kept their land through several generations. In 1799 the will of Thomas Haynes of Bedford County freed seventeen or more slaves and gave each of them land, the whole of his estate, in this county. In 1830 twelve Haynes families held this land, averaging approximately forty-five acres each. By 1860, however, only three of these families still owned their property.[39] In 1800 William Jones of Henrico liberated thirty-one slaves and settled them on land that received the name of Jonestown. In 1810 the holdings of the Jones Negroes amounted to twenty-six small tracts averaging twelve acres; in 1850 only three tracts remained in the Jones family; by 1860 all of the tracts had been alienated.[40] In 1797 the will of Richard Randolph of Cumberland and Prince Edward, "to make retribution . . . to an unfortunate race of bond men," liberated all his slaves, about seventy-five, and gave them collectively 400 acres of land near Farmville in Prince Edward County. This land was surveyed and divided among heads of families,

---

[38] Clerk's Office, Isle of Wight, 1839; Elizabeth City, 1842.

[39] Land, Bedford County, 1830–1860. A copy of the will of Thomas Haynes is in the possession of Mrs. Ariel Haynes Eberhardt, of Institute, West Virginia. The late Charles D. Haynes, a descendant of the group freed by Thomas Haynes, once stated to the writer that the dwindling of this property was due to the chicanery of certain white persons. This informant was born about 1860.

[40] Clerk's Office, Henrico County, Deed Book 6, p. 440; Land, Henrico, 1850–1860.

who, with their descendants, kept it until 1860 and later.[41] Another wholesale manumission in which the freedmen involved kept their land was that resulting from the will of Timothy Tynes of Isle of Wight, in 1802, liberating eighty or more slaves and providing each with land.[42] In 1805 the combined Tynes estate amounted to eighteen tracts with an average of about forty-five acres to each family. Three of the Tynes slaves, however, received 100 acres each; one received 199 acres; another received 800 acres, or a whole plantation. Some of these beneficiaries disposed of their holdings at once, yet in 1860 there were twelve families of Tynes who still held land embracing nineteen tracts in Isle of Wight County. The largest of these owners' tracts were 161 acres valued at $1,610, owned by John Tynes, and 150 acres valued at $1,100, owned by Cyrus Tynes.

This review of the extent to which free Negroes acquired land through manumission would be incomplete without consideration of the second way in which Negroes acquired land through white sources, namely, the miscegenation of whites and free Negroes. Though property was not often transferred in these cases, a few free Negro landowners were affected. The Lipscombs of Powhatan and Cumberland, prominent property holders of 1830 and 1860, came into possession of property originally through the will of Henry Lipscomb of Cumberland, made in 1825. In this instance eleven persons were well provided for, with "Nancy, a free woman

---

[41] Clerk's Office, Prince Edward County, District Court Will Books I & II, p. 4. This particular allotment of land to manumitted slaves has received unfavorable comment both from contemporaries and from historians. Cf. Phillips, *American Negro Slavery*, 436. The recipients of this property are said to have entered upon a long career of moral and physical degeneracy and to have become known as the worthless "Israel Hill" Negroes of Farmville. The better element of Negroes in Farmville today substantiate this statement, but emphasis on this one case and a few others scattered throughout the South obscures the fact that many other families who came into possession of land in this manner did not degenerate. On the contrary, they multiplied in number, held to their land, and made progress. Such is the case of the Lemons of Gloucester, the Tyneses of Isle of Wight, the Andersons of King William, and many others previously cited in this chapter.

[42] Clerk's Office, Isle of Wight, Will Book 11, pp. 587-588.

THE FARMER AND PROPERTY OWNER 127

of color, called Nancy Lipscomb" heading the list with fifty acres and other valuable personal property. All of the "plantation tools, household and kitchen furniture" of Henry Lipscomb, the white testator, went to another of these eleven, namely, Billy, "called Billy Lipscomb." [43] In 1821 Priscilla Ivey of Mecklenburg came into possession of 1,304 acres of land and valuable personal property, the entire estate devised by Frederick Ivey. She and her children kept the property as a life estate until her death in 1856.[44] Frankey Miles of Amelia County in a similar manner received from Nathaniel Harrison a plantation of 1,100 acres with all its equipment. She had once been his slave. He also made provision for certain of her married children.[45]

Once free Negroes had obtained their land, by whatever method, they entered into farming operations. Some engaged in commercial and some in subsistence farming; they raised various types of crops and made varying amounts of progress between 1830 and 1860.

[43] Clerk's Office, Cumberland, Will Book 8, pp. 121, 365.

[44] *Ibid.*, Mecklenburg, Will Book 9, p. 189; 19, pp. 16, 38. Priscilla Ivey's case is a puzzle to the investigator. In 1795 she was lawfully (or unlawfully) married to Frederick Ivey, and he spoke of her as "my wife," and of the children by her as "my children." This woman, who lived to be about seventy-five years old, has descendants in Mecklenburg and elsewhere today.

[45] Original will, in possession of Marguerite Anderson Richardson of Amelia, great-granddaughter of Frankey Miles, who now lives on a part of Frankey Miles's land. Judging from the testimony of the older white and Negro citizens of Amelia the relation of Harrison and Frankey Miles was a striking case of concubinage.

Other free Negroes who received property from whites were Francis and Alfred Anderson, who came into possession of land and other property at different times through the wills of the white Andersons, one of them Henry Anderson, who made his will in 1848.

By deed of gift made in 1850 James Jackson, a white man, conferred upon Patty Jackson and her children Peter and Arena lands amounting to 950 acres; Patty had been manumitted many years before by James Jackson. The gifts, said Jackson, were motivated by "the love and affection . . . I bear to my old Negro woman, Patty." Clerk's Office, Southampton, Deed Book 28, p. 24. In 1819 Patty Jackson had to face the question of getting permission to remain in Virginia after her manumission by James Jackson. Because of her "extraordinary merit" she and her seven children were granted such permission the following year by the local court, with James Jackson giving bond that she would not become a charge on the public. Minute Book, 1819, p. 47.

Commercial farming developed several specialities: tobacco-raising, hog and corn raising, and truck-gardening. Most commercial farmers concentrated on the raising of one crop, but a few engaged in diversified farming. The type of farming adopted by different free Negroes was of course determined in any given area by the system prevailing among all the farmers of that area.

Tobacco was raised most extensively by free Negroes in Amelia County. Here the Andersons and some of the persons connected with the Frankey Miles estate raised crops comparable to those of the average white farmer. In 1860 Alfred Anderson produced 12,000 pounds of tobacco, 200 bushels of wheat, 650 bushels of corn, 480 bushels of oats, and 40 hogs on his farm of 700 acres, a little less than half of which was under cultivation. At the same time John Pleasants of this county produced 6,000 pounds of tobacco; Edwin Harrison 2,600 pounds; and Francis Anderson, brother to Alfred, 7,000 pounds. Each of these men raised a substantial amount of wheat, corn, and oats; each owned five to ten horses, six or seven cows, two or more oxen, and about thirty sheep.[46] Seven of the eighteen free Negro farm owners in this county, including Frankey Miles with her 1,100 acre plantation, thus easily ranked as commercial farmers. Not more than two, among eleven, had so ranked in 1830.

The twenty-two or more Negro farm owners and tenants of Amherst County also grew tobacco extensively. Fully half of the seventeen owners of this County in 1860 cultivated farms commercially, as contrasted with only four such owners in 1830. But with the exception of Tarleton Johns these men had an individual yield of only about half that of the tobacco farmers of Amelia. Some of this deficiency was counter balanced by the raising of hogs, of which Peter Curry raised twenty and Fred Beverly twenty-five. Each of these Amelia County farmers owned live-stock ranging in value from $50

[46] U. S. Census, Agriculture (ms.), Amelia, 1860.

to $460. Foremost in this group were Fred and Sam Beverly with a number of horses, cows, and other cattle.[47]

Other counties in which free Negroes were engaged in tobacco cultivation were Bedford, Caroline, Cumberland, Dinwiddie, Halifax, and Louisa. Nine such farmers in these counties operated establishments ranging from 75 acres to 575 acres.[48] One of them, William Epps of Halifax, aside from raising tobacco on a large scale, made other successful ventures. His livestock, including fifty hogs, was valued at $650. Other crops and yields of this man included 120 bushels of wheat, 525 bushels of corn, 280 bushels of oats, 20 bushels of Irish potatoes, 300 of sweet potatoes, 400 pounds of butter, and 100 pounds of honey.[49] Cultivating about as much acreage as Epps, the two Wilkerson brothers of Louisa raised less produce. In all of these counties from one-sixth to one-third of the farm owners may be classified as commercial farmers. In almost all of them the number of free Negro farm owners and commercial farmers more than doubled in the thirty-year period under review.

In the southeastern part of the state, where by reason of population the greatest amount of farming among free Negroes was undertaken, the cash product was hogs and corn. In 1830 this region—embracing the counties of Prince George, Dinwiddie, Sussex, Surry, Nansemond, Southampton, Isle of Wight, Norfolk, and Princess Anne—had 246 free Negro farm owners; in 1860 the number was 376. Excepting Prince George, all of these counties in 1860 had a greater number of large scale farmers than in 1830. The increase was especially marked in Nansemond County. About half of the seventy-five farmers in Nansemond and Isle of

---

[47] *Ibid.*, Amherst; Personal Property, Amherst, 1860.

[48] These farmers were R. Haines of Bedford, Susan Grimes and Washington Jeter of Caroline, Peter Jenkins and Frank Lipscomb of Cumberland, Becky Ampey of Dinwiddie, William Epps of Halifax, and two brothers, Cyrus and Ned Wilkerson, of Louisa.

[49] U. S. Census, Agriculture (ms.), Halifax County, 1860. In this year Epps had $500 in cash also. Personal Property, Halifax, 1860.

Wight counties in 1860, raised hogs in excess of ten, and slightly over half produced 200 or more bushels of corn. Colegate Whitehead of Southampton, the tenant noted above, grew 750 bushels of corn and raised sixty hogs in 1860. Second to Whitehead in this region was Dempsey Hare of Nansemond, who raised thirty-one hogs and 400 bushels of corn.[50]

North of the James River in the counties of Henrico, King and Queen, and Warwick there were three prominent corn and hog farmers: William C. Scott, Ransome Harris, and Thomas Wright. Scott of Henrico perhaps held the record for the state in corn production among free Negroes, 1,000 bushels in 1860. He also raised 450 bushels of wheat, 100 bushels of oats, and thirty-five hogs. This farmer lived only about a mile from Richmond so that in all probability he sold his grain and hogs there. In 1860 Scott's farm of seventy-five acres was worth the unusual sum of $15 an acre or a total of $1,115. Ransome Harris of King and Queen had a $2,243 farm of 475 acres with 150 acres under cultivation. In 1860 he raised 625 bushels of corn and seventeen hogs. He also had nine cattle and three sheep.[51]

A smaller number of free Negro farmers engaged in truck farming, with potatoes and other vegetables as the cash crops. These farmers lived in the same section as the corn and hog farmers, with a certain number also on the Eastern Shore. In 1860 Dempsey Hare of Nansemond led the sweet potato growers with 300 bushels; Samuel Tucker of Norfolk ranked second with a smaller amount. Nevertheless, Tucker raised 300 bushels of Irish potatoes and orchard products valued at $100, while the total value of the products of his market garden for this year amounted to $400.[52]

Certain other free Negroes of Virginia engaged in large-scale general farming. Jacob Sampson of Goochland County

---

[50] Personal Property, 1860, Nansemond, Isle of Wight, Southampton.
[51] Land, Personal Property, Henrico, 1860; King and Queen, 1860.
[52] *Ibid.*, Norfolk. The brothers Joseph and John Tynes of Isle of Wight were farmers of this same type, though on a smaller scale.

and John T. Collins of Northampton were outstanding in this respect. On his 535 acre farm Sampson raised in 1860, 400 bushels of wheat, 1,500 bushels of corn, 1,000 bushels of oats, 2,000 pounds of tobacco, eighty pounds of wool, fifteen bushels of buckwheat, 200 pounds of butter, five tons of hay, two pounds of beeswax, and sixteen pounds of honey. His stock consisted of eleven horses, three mules, four cows, two oxen, four other small cattle, forty sheep, and fifty hogs. The cash value of Sampson's farm was $4,000; the value of his livestock was $960; the value of his animals slaughtered was $220. Over a period of thirty years Sampson bought his estate piece by piece.[53] In diversified farming, this man perhaps stood first among the free Negroes of Virginia. Aside from his farming outfit, in 1860 Sampson had $1,000 in cash, for which he was duly taxed. In the same year John T. Collins had a farm of 330 acres with the unusually high cash value of $8,000. His horses, mules, cows and oxen numbered from one to five each, while he had also nine sheep and twenty hogs. At this time he raised 1,500 bushels of corn and the same amount of oats.[54]

On his farm of 115 acres Madison Welborne of Sussex County engaged in a variety of undertakings. He owned eight head of cattle from which he produced 300 pounds of butter. His diversified crops included corn, oats, and hay with a small amount of molasses, flax, flax seed, and clover seed. The value of his animals slaughtered and home manufactures in general ranked above the average of the farmers of his county.[55]

[53] Land, Personal Property, Goochland; Clerk's Office, Goochland, Deed Book 30, p. 512; 32, pp. 294, 295; 33, pp. 193, 194; 34, p. 364; 37, p. 734. By his will made in 1854 Sampson conveyed half his estate to his three daughters; his seven sons received the other half. In addition his son Moses received $500. Deed Book 41, p. 566.

[54] U. S. Census, Agriculture (ms.), Northampton, 1860.

[55] U. S. Census, Agriculture (ms.), Sussex, 1861. Welborne was only thirty-four years old in 1860. He lived in the Reconstruction period following the war and became a leader in the party politics of that day.

The farming operations of Lot Langston of Nansemond and Lorenzo Robinson of King and Queen were similar to Welborne's. Robinson raised sheep

Richard Parsons of Campbell County rivaled Jacob Sampson of Goochland in the variety and quantity of his produce. His smaller farm of 175 acres was valued at $3,500; his livestock of horses, mules, cows, and oxen was valued at $600. Parsons produced in 1860, 300 bushels of wheat, 250 bushels of corn, 200 bushels of oats, and fifty tons of hay. Parsons, like Sampson, and the great majority of the farmers mentioned here, had bought his land. In 1845 he paid for his farm the handsome sum of $3,000.[56]

One or two unusual types of farming among the free Negroes may be mentioned. Sally Scott of Isle of Wight, the owner of an orchard, in 1860 produced 130 gallons of wine; Fred Beverly of Amherst, like some other general farmers, produced twenty pounds of beeswax and 400 pounds of honey; Samuel Thompson of Loudon County produced about the same amount of honey and large quantities of butter as well.

Some of these persons were versatile not only with respect to their farm operations but also with respect to occupation. Madison Welborne was a carpenter; Jacob Sampson, as has been shown, operated a well-patronized tavern at the Goochland County court house; Richard Parsons operated a line of boats on the James River; and there were many other large scale farmers with other occupations.[57]

Successful landowning and farming, as has been noted, increased as the year 1860 approached, yet a certain degree of

---

and produced a small amount of wool. Peter Curry and Henry Peters of Amherst County raised sheep and produced wool along with small crops of wheat, rye, oats, and a quantity of butter beyond the family needs. Samuel Hampton of Charles City, with a 350-acre farm, owned many kinds of livestock, including two mules.

[56] Clerk's Office, Campbell County, Deed Book 6, p. 212.

[57] Such were Jesse Booker of Pittsylvania, operator of a tannery, with 185 acres; William Hayes of Mecklenburg, a wagoner, with 106 acres; John Epperson of Buckingham, a wheelwright, with 198 acres; Richard Hill of Dinwiddie, a carpenter, with 137 acres; William Leftwich of Bedford, a blacksmith, with 80 acres; Phillip Cousins of Goochland, a boatman, with 90 acres; Anderson Stewart of Lunenburg, a wagoner, at one time with 429 acres; and Arthur Lee of Alleghany, a blacksmith with 413 acres.

this existed in 1830 and the years preceding. Some families, such as the Stewarts of Brunswick County, engaged in high-grade farming through several generations; and by a process of inheritance or by thrift, increased the quantity of land in the family. In 1806 William Stewart, for example, bought a small tract of land; by 1830 he owned 315 acres. John Stewart, building on a legacy from Dempsey Stewart, who owned 144 acres in 1830, later became the owner of several farms amounting in all to 421 acres. At his death, about 1860, he left, besides his landed property, a big variety of personal property valued at $744.[58]

The farm operations discussed above were those of the prosperous men only, who engaged in farming as a business or whose possessions placed them in the class of commercial farmers. Most such men owned farms of 150 acres or more. An attempt to compare the numbers of commercial farmers and subsistence farmers presents some difficulties. One standard of measurement is acreage. Of the grand total of 1,202 free Negro farm owners in Virginia in 1860, 428, or about 36 per cent, owned farms of from fifty to seventy-four acres.

---

[58] Clerk's Office, Brunswick County, Will Book 18, pp. 96–97. Among the items of personal property in the inventory of John Stewart's estate are the following:

Article	Value	Article	Value
2 axes	$ 2.00	parcel old ploughs	$ 1.50
cart and wheels	5.00	contents of smoke house	2.00
horse cart and wheels	5.00	9 hogs	36.00
parcel wheat	60.00	parcel wheat straw	1.00
parcel seed cotton	25.00	mule	100.00
parcel salt and sack	1.00	sow and 6 pigs	5.00
cross cut saw	1.00	parcel unstripped tobacco	45.00
saddle and bridle	1.50	fan mill	3.00
5 meal bags	1.00	parcel old tobacco	7.50
pair traces	.75	tobacco hogshead	1.50
large chain	.50	lot baskets and barrels	.50
parcel short corn	10.50	lot weeding hoes	.50
parcel corn (65 bbls.)	227.50	2 grub hoes	.50
horse	20.00	parcel peas	.25
3 cows, 1 calf and yearling	35.00	7 shoats	10.00
7 geese	2.00	3 sows	10.00
5,000 bundles fodder	37.50	8 chickens	1.50

Two hundred sixty, or about 22 per cent owned tracts seventy-five acres or more. On this basis it is reasonable to say that 25 per cent, or one-fourth of the free Negro farm owners in Virginia, maintained a commercial type of agriculture.

The fact that one-fourth of the owners had commercial farms does not indicate that all of them were independent. The vast majority of the Negro farm owners as well as the tenants cultivated land on their own account and at the same time worked as hired laborers for the many white farmers. Commercial farmers, furthermore, did not necessarily have the highest incomes in the group of Negro farmers. Ranking with them or even above them were the many free Negro farm owners with less than fifty acres who enjoyed a cash income from other sources. Such men were Thomas Trent of Buckingham, William Wheely of King William, and Beverly Combs of Fluvanna, shoemakers, with ten, fifteen, and twenty acres respectively; William Jimmerson, Samuel Driver, Braxton Drummond, and James Morris of Gloucester, oysterers, with fifteen, twenty, thirty-eight, and fifty acres respectively; Schuyler Staunton of Buckingham, boatman, with thirty-seven and three-fourths acres; Carrington Tyler of Goochland, ditcher, with nineteen acres; James A. Martin of King and Queen, bricklayer, with twenty acres; Solomon and Robert Greenhow of James City, bricklayers, with twenty-seven and fifty acres respectively; and John Ashlock of James City, teamster, with thirty-three acres. In a few cases farm owners were even day laborers by occupation. In this class was George Lee of Frederick County with seventeen acres and Samuel Stone of Hanover with fourteen and one-fourth acres.

Rural free Negro blacksmiths who, like Arthur Lee, incidentally owned farms were frequently very successful. Samuel Charity of Charles City, another blacksmith, with fifty acres was a prosperous man, and George McCowen of Fluvanna with his twenty-eight and a half acres was the most prosperous of all the free Negroes of this county. Among his possessions in 1860 were four horses and carriages, which made him the talk of his community.[59] In like manner several millers with small farm holdings, such as Holland Wood of Lancaster, owning thirty-eight acres, were well-to-do.[60]

The progress made by some farm owners and farm tenants, though commendable, is significant only when seen in relation to the progress or lack of advancement in the whole free Negro group. Approximately 35 per cent of the total number of free Negro heads of families either owned or rented land; 65 per cent were mere laborers, without any claim to the soil whatever. This 65 per cent is the class which so deeply impressed the many unfriendly contemporary critics of this group.

Failure to own land, of course, was not confined to the free people of color. White heads of families, engaged in agricultural pursuits as laborers or tenants, frequently owned no property. In Isle of Wight County in 1860, for instance, seventy-seven white farmers who were heads of families owned no real estate whatever; as many more held property with a value of less than five hundred dollars.[61] In Sussex County about a hundred white heads of families were in a similar plight. As the reports of the overseers of the poor reveal, the free Negro held no monopoly on poverty. In Lancaster County during the decade of 1850 nearly all the persons on poor relief were whites. Indigent whites outnumbered indigent free Negroes ten to one.[62] Though many rural free Negroes were propertyless, a large number of them lived in a state comparable to that of many whites.

From an economic point of view, the year 1860 found free

[59] Interview with S. C. Abrams, grandson of a prominent Fluvanna free Negro. It is to be noted in this connection that draught horses were relatively rare at that time. The ox was the usual beast of burden among the poorer classes. There were many white families of average means without horses.
[60] Clerk's Office, Lancaster, Will Book 30, p. 40.
[61] U. S. Census Bureau, Free Inhabitants (ms.), 1860.
[62] Clerk's Office, Lancaster County, Annual Report of the Overseers of the Poor (ms.).

Negroes further advanced than in any period in the previous history of the group. They were twice as well off as in 1830, and perhaps three times as prosperous as in 1800 or 1810. It has been thought that Negroes have made progress in property ownership only since the emancipation of the entire race in 1865. In proportion to its numbers, however, the Virginia free Negro group of 1860 held as much land as the entire race held in this state in 1891. The small free Negro element of 1860 owned 60,045 acres, while the whole race in 1891 owned only 698,074 acres.[63] This elevenfold increase in land owned, however, was accompanied by an elevenfold increase in free Negro rural population. Some counties in the state, including Amelia, Goochland, King and Queen, New Kent, Powhatan, Prince George, Rockbridge, and Sussex, contained proportionately even more free Negro land in the earlier period than in the later. The position attained by free Negroes in these counties and others in 1860 was comparable to the position attained by all Virginia Negroes in these counties in 1900. The free group of 1860 was even better off than the larger group of 1891 in reference to land value, for land was worth on the average $6 an acre in 1860, whereas thirty-one years later the average value was only $4.

In the light of these facts students of history must revise their thinking on the economic status of the rural free Negro, particularly with respect to the thirty years preceding the Civil War. Though the laws enacted seemed to spell the doom of this group, the prevailing economic conditions nullified the severity of the laws. The free Negro farmer and property owner is a reality in Virginia history, and very probably, in other states of the South.

[63] *Report of Virginia State Auditor,* 1891, Table 30.

CHAPTER V

THE CITY PROPERTY OWNER

IN cities and towns, between 1830 and 1860, free Negroes made distinct progress in property ownership, even greater than the advance made in owning farm land or rural property. In 1830, 157 free Negroes owned town lots; thirty years later the number of such owners was 693.[1]

City property—described in the records as town lots— was found in most of the counties as well as in the cities proper. Free Negroes owned such lots in about half of the counties and in all of the cities. About nine-tenths of this ownership was concentrated in Richmond, Petersburg, Norfolk, Portsmouth, Alexandria, Winchester, Lynchburg, Fredericksburg, Farmville, and Suffolk. These larger centers are therefore especially important for this study.[2] The actual accomplishments of free Negroes in city property ownership are summarized in the table on p. 138.

This table demonstrates the great gain made during the period from 1830 to 1860, a gain of more than 400 per cent in the number of owners, and of more than 600 per cent in the value of property owned. Such progress was made de-

---

[1] This statement is based on a study of the land books of all the counties and cities of Virginia for the two periods under consideration. These manuscript records are found in the archives division of the state library.

[2] The term "Richmond" in this study embraces all the territory within the present limits of the city of Richmond. It includes Manchester, the district now known as South Richmond, and a strip of territory in Henrico County east of the city of that day but now within the city limits. Alexandria in 1830 was a part of the District of Columbia. On the basis of population each of these ten cities except Farmville and Suffolk would meet the present census classification of urban areas: incorporation and a minimum population of 2,500. Farmville and Suffolk were incorporated under state laws, but each had fewer than 2,500 inhabitants. These two places are included in the treatment here because they had a relatively large number of free Negroes.

TABLE X

Free Negro Ownership of Town Lots

	1830		1860	
	Number of Owners	Value	Number of Owners	Value
Richmond	50	$18,435	211	$184,971
Petersburg	25	16,035	246	142,030
Norfolk	10	12,450	13	10,250
Portsmouth	5	2,100	5	3,500
Alexandria	—	—	41	27,950
Winchester	5	3,625	40	29,975
Lynchburg	2	3,000	18	12,552
Fredericksburg	21	7,500	15	5,850
Farmville	1	415	7	2,400
Suffolk	1	300	11	5,408
(All others)	37	10,683	86	38,078
	157	$74,543	693	$463,016

spite the fact that the free Negro city population increased only 50 per cent between 1830 and 1860. On the whole, the number of owners in most cities was equal to the number of lots owned; although, in Richmond, especially, it was not uncommon for one individual to own several houses and lots.

It is noteworthy that practically all of the property listed above came into the hands of the owners by purchase. Possession of city property through gift from white persons was well-nigh unknown, though occasionally an owner came into possession of houses and lots by inheritance from a free Negro relative or friend. Free Negroes frequently bought property from one another. The following table, comprising twenty-three of the twenty-five owners in Petersburg in 1830, illustrates how property was obtained by purchase rather than in other ways. The "grantee" is the free Negro purchaser.[8]

[8] The references made in this table are to the deed books in the clerk's office, Petersburg.

TABLE XI
Property Owners, Petersburg, 1830

Grantor	Grantee	Date	Price Paid	Deed Book	Page
William Wilkinson	Jane Allen	1817	$350	5	214
Peter Fagan	June Bailey	1824	300	7	246
Joseph Cooper	John Booker	1815	600	6	317
Isaac Scott	Shadrack Brander	1817	250	5	144
Richard Jarratt	Rebecca Brown	1829	150	8	231
Edward Stabler	Plato Cook	1794	75 pounds	2	385
John Wilder	William Curl	1814	150	4	277
Cook & Randall	Susan Curl	1822	350	7	80
William Corling	Thomas Elliott	1826	450	8	31
James Eppes	William Eppes	1824	80	7	252
Henry Markes	Mary Eppes	1819	900	6	40
Peter Fagan	Martha Hall	1809	50 pounds	3	446
Edward Lee	Cyrus Hill	1820	50	6	233
William Moore	Sylvia Jeffers	1821	435	6	317
David Cary	Richard Jarratt	1828	300	8	165
Luke Tayburn	Daniel Jackson	1823	360	7	216
Joshua Poythress	Robin Jackson	1820	500	6	242
Peter Fagan	Elizabeth Joiner	1826	160	7	322
Robert Bolling	Eliza Kennon	1818	500	5	292
M. B. Pillsborough	Polly Lee	1817	600	5	198
Ransdell & Cook	Charles Lewis	1821	100	7	9
Joseph Shepherd	Elizabeth Matthews	1820	325	7	188
Robert Crook	Kitty Smith	1826	60	8	3

As in the case of farm property, free Negroes began to acquire city property at an early date. The buying of houses and lots extended over a period of eighty years—from about 1785 to 1865. Some of the gains made before 1830 are important inasmuch as the free Negroes of two cities—Fredericksburg and Norfolk—owned more property in the thirty years before 1830 than in the thirty years afterwards. The records of Richmond, Lynchburg, and Petersburg before 1830 should also be considered as a background for the advance made in these cities in the later thirty year period.

Beginning with four free Negro owners of property in 1809, Margaret Evans, James Ferguson, John Minor, and Thomas Carey, Fredericksburg advanced to twenty-one owners in 1830. In 1809 both Margaret Evans and James Ferguson owned property with a yearly rental value of $20; John Minor's property had a rental value of $50. Thomas Carey, a blacksmith, had two houses with a rental value of $250; he bought two other houses and lots for 200 pounds and 250 pounds in 1813; he leased property in 1819; in the following year he bought one more piece, for which he paid $397.50. Altogether, by 1824 this thrifty blacksmith owned nine pieces of property.[4] Carey's houses and lots were rented out to others. In 1816 the total rental value of his real estate amounted to $767.33; his real estate tax was $23.02. Two years later the rental value of his property had increased to $1,050.66, and his tax to $52.53. In a will made in 1824 Carey bequeathed to his wife, Sarah, all his holdings, which upon her death should go to their children and one other relative in equal proportions.[5]

In Fredericksburg four other free Negroes, William Jones, Fred Dawson, William Brown, and John Lewis, were property owners, three of them with property valued at $400, and the fourth with property valued at $500. Aside from owning his home, late in life William Jones was granted an annual pension of $60 from the state for his services as a soldier in the American Revolution. Another group of thrifty free Negroes was the DeBaptist family consisting of Benjamin, the father, and his three sons. This family, owning a number of horses and carriages as well as real estate, accumulated their wealth by serving the town as contractors.[6]

In 1830 two men, James West and James Wilkins, were outstanding among all the free Negro property owners in Fredericksburg, each of them holding property valued at more than $1,000. West, a blacksmith, owned a two-story brick dwelling house on Princess Anne Street, which he gave to his wife and sons at the time of his death. During a fifteen

---

[4] Clerk's Office, Fredericksburg, Land Book, 1809; Deed Book D, p. 166; E, pp. 26, 86; G, p. 34.

[5] Clerk's Office, Fredericksburg, Will Book B, p. 180.

[6] Guild, *Black Laws of Virginia*, 193; Land, Spotsylvania County, 1815–1830.

year period, Wilkins bought property eight times and sold property four times. On different occasions, when in need of funds, he granted several deeds of trust upon his holdings.[7] With this constant growth in the number of free Negro property holders, one family out of three held property in the town of Fredericksburg in 1830.

In Falmouth, a town adjoining Fredericksburg, free Negroes also accumulated property. Only a few such persons lived in the town, yet by 1830 ten of them had become owners of property. Abram Howard and Daniel Lewis headed the list with property valued at $750.[8]

Before 1830 property ownership among the free Negroes in Norfolk was not so general as in Fredericksburg, yet certain owners in this town displayed the business acumen common to most of the early free Negro property holders in cities. Representative of these were Francis Drake, Samuel Bailey, and Thomas Knight, barbers; and Henry Jackson, pilot.[9] Some of these men first secured property during the 1790 decade; by 1810 they had become well known. Three years after his manumission in 1792, Francis Drake bought a house and lot for fifty pounds; in 1803 he owned four houses and lots and paid $22 in taxes, more than did any other Negro in Norfolk. When he died in 1812, his personal property included one buffet with a "parcel of china and glassware," two dining tables and a tea table, looking glasses, mantelpiece ornaments, Windsor chairs, and many other articles.[10] Samuel Bailey, a business associate of Drake's, bought property in 1802 from Levi Johnson for ninety-four pounds and ten shillings; when Bailey's wife inherited this

---

[7] Clerk's Office, Fredericksburg, Will Book D, p. 268; Deed Books, I, J, K, L.

[8] Land, Stafford County, 1830.

[9] Other free Negro property owners in Norfolk were George Johnson, John Wiles, and Aaron Rogers, shoemakers; George Scott, house carpenter; Levi Johnson, shopkeeper; and Lewis Armistead, livery stable operator. Ned Keeling, a drayman, held property valued at $1,000 in 1830; and John Blye (or Bligh) held property valued at $2,000.

[10] Clerk's Office, Norfolk, Deed Book 3, p. 189; Will Book 3, p. 65.

property, she immediately sold it to Joseph Bartlett. All the parties to these several transactions were Negroes. Thomas Knight amassed more real estate than any other person of his race in Norfolk during the entire period of slavery. In 1820 he paid $960 for the lease of his barber shop on Commerce Street; five years later he paid $2,845 for his residence on Main Street. He bought one of his houses from Henry Jackson, the free Negro pilot. In 1830, eight years before his death, Knight held six pieces of property.[11] Henry Jackson began his career as property holder in the 1790 decade. He lived in one of his two houses and rented the other. His son Henry also owned property, which in 1830 was valued at $950. Despite the success of individual Norfolk free Negroes, the total number of property owners during any of these early years was not more than ten; though in the smaller town of Fredericksburg the number was twenty-one.

Among the leading free Negro property holders of Richmond in the early years were William Cocke, Joseph Dailey, Peter Hawkins, and Nathaniel Anderson. These individuals and several others owned real estate during the 1790 decade. In 1786 Cocke purchased a half-acre lot for ten pounds from the trustee of William Byrd's estate. Joseph Dailey, a fisherman, owned land "on the Main street leading from the river up to the capitol" and conveyed this lot by will to his daughter. At the same time he directed that his fishery of five acres should be sold and the proceeds divided equally between his children.[12] Peter Hawkins was a dentist or "tooth drawer," who went about the streets of Richmond pulling teeth. His trade necessitated the use of a vehicle, and horses and carriages formed a part of his personal estate. He acquired several houses and lots, the rental of which advanced between 1796 and 1803 from twelve to forty pounds. In 1814 the total value of his property was $3,500.[13] Nathaniel

---

[11] Clerk's Office, Deed Book 17, p. 480; 18, pp. 98, 487; 20, p. 202.
[12] City Hall, Richmond, Deed Book 3, p. 415.
[13] Land, Richmond, 1796-1814; Mordecai, *Richmond,* p. 205.

Anderson, who operated a livery stable and owned five horses and two carriages, made his first purchase of real estate in 1797 and a second ten years later.[14]

During the period from 1800 to 1820 other free Negro property owners, such as Humbro Gallego, Lewis Armistead, Lott Carey, and John Elson, began to appear in the Richmond records. Gallego, who had been the slave of Joseph Gallego the flour miller, owned a home on Broad Street and other valuable properties, some of which he sold in 1810 for $1,940.[15] Lewis Armistead came from Norfolk about 1815, set himself up in the livery business, and six years later bought a lot on Carey Street for the sum of $1,450, on which he operated his livery stable.[16] In connection with this business he owned, of course, horses and carriages. Lott Carey was known during his day primarily as a preacher and missionary to Liberia in the first years of that republic. But in worldly affairs he had much the same activities and experiences as other successful free Negroes. By his work as foreman in a tobacco factory he was able to buy first his own freedom and later that of the members of his family. During this process he also bought a small farm on the outskirts of Richmond for $693.[17] John Elson was one of Richmond's first Negro grocerymen. With the earnings from his business he accumulated a small amount of property, which he willed to his daughter and his granddaughter.

The free Negroes of Lynchburg, fewer in number than those of the other cities, made less headway in the early years. Archer Carey, hackman, and Claiborne Gladman, barber, were the only two who became property owners. As a result of his unusual industry Carey was able to buy real estate in 1827 at the price of $700. Eight years earlier, Glad-

---

[14] City Hall, Richmond, Deed Book 4, p. 562. William Brown compared favorably with Anderson in that in 1803 the yearly rental value of his real estate amounted to thirty pounds.

[15] *Ibid.*, 6, p. 513.

[16] *Ibid.*, 18, p. 511.

[17] Clerk's Office, Henrico County, Deed Book 15, p. 501; 17, p. 605.

man had begun the property holding that has extended through his direct or collateral descendants continuously to the present. He made his initial purchase for $1,312 and another in 1824 for $500.[18]

Before 1830 in Petersburg, as in most of the cities, the ratio of free Negro property owners to the total numbers was small; some of the men and women of this place, however, acquired property at an early date.[19] One of the first Negroes in Petersburg to acquire property, Richmond Graves, bought real estate in 1797 and again in 1799, each time for the sum of 150 pounds; and later he transferred it to his daughters.[20] Richard Jarratt also bought houses and lots and laid the foundation for real estate ownership that has come down to the present. Daniel Jackson paid $600 for a house in 1817 and lived in it until after 1865, paying taxes in Petersburg for nearly fifty years. Uriah Tyner, another progressive free Negro, acquired ownership of a residence valued at $1,000. "By honest industry" Jack Booker acquired an "equitable right to property of considerable value in Petersburg." Upon his death in 1831 his personal estate included such items as four blacksmith bellows, three sledge hammers, three anvils, one cow and calf, and one secretary and bookcase valued at $20.[21] His widow owned a sloop, the *Margaret,* a house and lot, and considerable household furniture. Shadrack Brander owned property in excess of $1,000 and left a personal estate valued at $533. Among the items of his estate were 1,300 barrel staves, one lot of cooper's tools, one sideboard, one writing desk, one wagon

---

[18] Clerk's Office, Lynchburg, Deed Book E, p. 342; G, p. 494.
[19] A list of the leading free Negro property owners of Petersburg, with their occupations, includes: Graham Bell, shoemaker; Richmond Graves, livery stable operator; Jack Booker, blacksmith; Shadrack Brander, cooper; James and William Colson, barbers; Major Elebeck, mechanic and business man; Betsy Allergue, storekeeper; Richard Jarratt, boatman; Daniel Jackson, preacher; Joseph Shepherd, school teacher; Uriah Tyner, blacksmith; and Colson Waring, preacher and missionary.
[20] Clerk's Office, Petersburg, Deed Book 3, pp. 555, 633.
[21] Clerk's Office, Petersburg, Will Book 3, p. 48.

and gear, two plows, two cows, one gray horse, one sorrel horse, and one roan horse.²²

As the table of ownership of town lots indicates, Richmond in 1830 had fifty free Negro owners; Petersburg, twenty-five; and Norfolk, ten. But the number of owners of property in a given locality has significance only when considered in relation to the number of those without property. From this point of view the proportion of free Negro property owners in 1830 in nearly all of the cities was very low. Petersburg, for example, had a population of 2,032 free Negroes divided among 503 families, but only 25 families or about 1 in 20, held property. Richmond had a proportion of about one in fifteen. All told in 1830, with the exception of Fredericksburg, the success of the few rather than the success of the many was the chief characteristic of property holding among city free Negroes.

The main explanation for this condition lay in the fact that the 1830 generation of free Negroes had not been free long enough to establish themselves as property owners. Just as the 1890 generation of Virginia Negroes failed to reach the stage of material progress attained by the generation of 1920, so did the 1830 group fail to reach the mark attained by the 1860 group. Then again, a large part of the 1830 population was made up of men who had only recently been drawn to the cities from the surrounding counties. With them the buying of property would naturally come later.²³

Another deterrent to property ownership in these cities

---

²² *Ibid.*, p. 82. James Colson bought property in 1804 and began the process whereby real estate remained in possession of his descendants through most of the slavery period and on to the present. Major Elebeck bought property early and in like manner left his descendants in comfortable circumstances for several generations. His son operated a barber shop in partnership with William Colson.

²³ The percentage of increase in the population of all the cities from 1820 to 1830 was greater than that in any other decade. Richmond is typical. Whereas from 1810 to 1820 the free Negro population of this city grew from 1,189 to 1,235 only, from 1820 to 1830 the increase was from 1,235 to 1,956. The increase in this single decade was slightly greater than that of the three decades from 1830 to 1860.

was the relative lack of employment. The year 1830 was not only too soon for this group to get a foothold, but in addition, in one town at least, the 1820 decade was one of business stagnation. According to a Petersburg newspaper, long lines of storehouses were closed and "for rent" signs could be seen all over this town. Many dwelling-houses were then dead property to their owners.[24]

Still another deterrent to property ownership in 1830 was the colonization movement to Liberia. Though in later years the vast majority opposed the plan bitterly, the scheme appealed to a fairly large number of free Negroes in Richmond, Petersburg, and Norfolk during the 1820 decade. The largest number of emigrants to leave Richmond and Petersburg set sail in 1824 and 1829, the first group in the ship *Cyrus* and the second in the *Harriot*. Most of the 103 persons who went out in the *Cyrus* were from Petersburg. One writer said: "The accession of this company was hailed by all as a joyful event . . . especially as it comprised an unusual amount of intelligence, industry and morality." The *Harriot* sailed with 155 passengers, about forty of whom had been slaves. The other passengers had long been free and had acquired considerable property.[25]

Among the persons going to Liberia from Petersburg with "considerable property" were Amelia Roberts and Joseph J. Roberts (mother and son), Joseph Shepperd, and Colson Waring; among those from Richmond were Lott Carey and Colin Teague. Colson Waring's property in Petersburg was valued at $1,037.50; Joseph Shepperd's and Amelia Roberts' property had about the same value. These individuals sold their houses and lots shortly before emigrating to Liberia.[26] These emigrants were teachers, preachers, and mis-

[24] *The American Constellation* (Petersburg), Nov. 24, 1834.
[25] Library of Congress, American Colonization Society Manuscripts, Board of Managers, 2:13.
[26] Clerk's Office, Petersburg, Deed Book 5, p. 237; 7, pp. 188, 309; 8, pp. 164, 179.

sionaries, but they were not unmindful of the commercial opportunities which the new land presented.

Some free Negroes sold their property in Virginia simply because they were leaving the state; others sold because they desired to invest their money in productive enterprises in Liberia. Some of them, having succeeded in business in America, made plans for further operations in the new country. Conscious of the fact that colonies in the early stages of economic development offer unusual opportunities in the field of trade and commerce rather than in agriculture, certain Virginia Negroes invested their savings in ships and merchandise in the United States preparatory to trading between Liberia and this country. Thus there arose in Liberia a group of Negro merchant traders.

One of these concerns was Roberts, Colson, and Company. This enterprise consisted of Joseph Jenkins Roberts, boatman, whose parents had accumulated a little wealth in Petersburg as owners and operators of boats on the James and Appomattox rivers; and William Nelson Colson, barber, whose father had been an owner of property and a successful barber also. With this substantial background, and with the profits from William Colson's well-patronized barber shop in Petersburg, these young men were in a position to take advantage of the opportunities offered in Liberia.[27] The articles of agreement leading to the organization of Roberts, Colson, and Company were drawn up in Petersburg before Roberts left the country permanently in 1829. He thereupon became the resident member of the company in Liberia, while Colson, still in Petersburg, financed the venture further and bought merchandise from Petersburg, Philadelphia, and New York merchants to ship to the house in Liberia.[28] In turn, Roberts and other members of the company at Monrovia ex-

---

[27] Clerk's Office, Petersburg, Accounts Current (ms.) 2, p. 70; 3, pp. 24, 28.
[28] See account of the transactions of Colson with various merchants in *Journal of Negro History*, 12: 373–375 (1927).

ported certain raw products from Liberia to New York and Philadelphia merchants. In order to conduct this import and export business these Petersburg Negroes bought a ship, the schooner *Caroline*. On one occasion they made a shipment of cainwood, palm oil, and ivories to Grant and Stone of Philadelphia, which was worth $3,389.80. In the fall of 1835 Colson made his first visit to Africa, where he died only two months after arriving. This man's death resulted in a series of negotiations between Colson's widow in Petersburg and Roberts regarding her share and future status in the partnership of Roberts, Colson, and Company. At the same time the Petersburg hustings court appointed the widow the administrator of her deceased husband's personal estate in Petersburg. This task involved the appraisal and sale of toilet articles and equipment in a well-stocked barber shop, and personal property in a well-furnished five-room house.[29]

Another firm of Negro merchants traders in Liberia, apparently operating on a wider scale, consisted of Colson Waring and F. Taylor. Whereas Roberts, Colson, and Company were dealers in articles of clothing and fancy goods, and shipped to the United States the native products named above, Colson Waring and his partner offered for sale such commodities as firearms, ale, and rum imported from Liverpool. In the year 1830 alone, Waring is reported to have sold goods to the amount of $70,000.[30] Waring's progress in Liberia was founded on his advancement in Virginia. He married into the well-to-do Graves family and shared in the ownership of one of their valuable residences on Market Street in Petersburg. Waring died in Liberia about the same time as William N. Colson; Roberts, however, throve in this climate and became the first president of the republic of Liberia in 1847. The coming of Joseph J. Roberts, Colson

---

[29] Clerk's Office, Petersburg, Accounts Current 3, pp. 187–189; Colson Family Papers, in possession of different members of this family.

[30] American Colonization Society, *Fifteenth Annual Report*, p. 43 (1832); Eugene P. Southall, "Arthur Tappan and the Anti-Slavery Movement," in *Journal of Negro History*, 15:166 (April, 1930).

Waring, William N. Colson, Lott Carey, and others to Liberia was a boon to that infant colony, but their going from Virginia meant a loss of the money and talent which these men might have used in the future development of the Negro in their native state.

Though property standing was low among the free Negroes in 1830, and opportunities for employment were not abundant, better days lay ahead. Whereas the year 1830 was characterized by the success of the few rather than the success of the many, as time passed there came a change toward the well-being of all. In the different cities of Virginia under discussion, twofold, fourfold, eightfold, and tenfold gains were made in free Negro property holding by 1860. And the free Negroes made these gains despite all the hostility of their unfriendly critics.

In Petersburg the first decade of the thirty years under review brought little additional property to the free Negroes, but the second showed improvement. In the third, the decade of the fifties, there was a great increase in free Negro buyers. In 1840, the first year of improvement, five purchases of property, all on the same street, were made by free Negroes of this town. A few years afterwards such persons as Eliza Gallee, Catherine Cook, and William Walker entered the ranks of property owners. Eliza Gallee became the owner of two houses and lots valued at $750 and $1,500; Catherine Cook acquired valuable property worth $1,200; William Walker, a shoemaker, acquired three separate pieces, the most costly of which was valued at $1,000.[31] Walker's trade is made evident by the inventory of his estate, which contained one lot of boots and shoes, one lot of leather, and last blocks. Shortly after this shoemaker's death his former residence was sold at auction for $2,450.[32] During the whole of the 1840 decade thirty-five or more free Negroes emerged

---

[31] Clerk's Office, Petersburg, Deed Book 11, pp. 36, 37, 355; 14, p. 497; Land Books, 1841-1845.
[32] Petersburg *Daily Express,* June 27, 1859.

as additional owners of property, half of them in the space of two years only.

The landslide of the 1850 decade increased the number of owners in Petersburg from fifty-six to 246, an addition of 190 persons. Beginning in 1853 and continuing to 1860, the rate at which the free Negroes of this town acquired property amounted to twenty-three a year. The value of some of this real estate exceeded $1,000, but most of the individual properties were valued at less than $500. To be exact, 129 of the 190 purchases made in the period fell within this lower group. Thus the "masses"—washerwomen and tobacco factory workers—were acquiring homes as well as the relatively well-to-do. In many instances the purchase price was less than $100. All told, Petersburg free Negroes by 1860 had advanced far beyond their low standing of 1830; therefore, any effort to appraise the property standing of free Negroes in Petersburg and in the state must take into account the difference in status of this group in the two periods under consideration.[33]

Richmond, like Petersburg, had relatively few free Negro owners of property in 1830. On the outskirts of the Richmond of the early day, however, there was always a fairly large body of owners; ranging in number from about thirty to eighty. Situated in Henrico County, originally as slaves, it is likely that they were swept along to freedom by the very strong antislavery sentiment among the Quakers of this county. Samuel Pleasants and John Pleasants, members of the sect, were strong antislavery leaders. Freedom came to these Negroes from the Quakers as a voluntary gift in the

---

[33] These facts are drawn from the land books and deed books of the period from 1830 to 1860, in the clerk's office, Petersburg. The land books in this office, unlike many others, are complete from 1820 to the present. For the land books as a source of study for this entire work, the author has depended mainly on the complete collection in the state archives. Though duplicate copies of these books are sometimes found in the county clerks' offices, they are usually scattered.

See the table in the appendix for the names of the 246 free Negroes who owned property in Petersburg in 1860.

belief that freedom is the natural right of all men, but in the matter of the ownership and possession of homes the freed people provided for themselves.[34]

The increase among free Negroes owning real estate in Richmond closely paralleled the growth in Petersburg. The number of Richmond owners increased as the years passed, as did the value and size of their homes. By 1860 seventy-one free Negroes in Richmond held property of a minimum value of $1,000. Forty-one of this number owned property valued between $1,000 and $2,000; the remaining thirty exceeded the two-thousand-dollar mark. Fifteen of these, by frequent purchases of real estate, accumulated property worth $4,000 or $5,000.[35] The most prosperous individual was Reuben West, a barber, whose real estate holdings amounted to $7,000.[36] Some of these persons frequently did their buying and selling of property among the members of their own race. Some of them disposed of property by will to heirs and relatives; others died intestate, leaving their heirs to inherit through the regular laws of succession.

The rapid growth of Negro land ownership in Richmond and Petersburg is significant, because the combined free Negro population of these cities represented about 12 per cent of the entire free Negro population of the state and about half the total urban free Negro population. Expressed in terms of families rather than individuals, in Petersburg

[34] The records for the accumulation of property by free Negroes on the outskirts of Richmond are found at the Henrico County Clerk's office on Main Street in Richmond. The deeds recording transfers of property from 1830 to 1860 are found in Deed Books 32–72.

[35] Over a period of fifteen years Fields Cook bought property on three different occasions. City Hall, Richmond, Deed Books 63, p. 32; 70B, p. 728. William B. Lyons did likewise. *Ibid.*, 72A, p. 223; 74A, pp. 186, 550. Virginia Cunningham and George W. Ruffin purchased property four times each; Thomas Hall and George Gray, five times; Lomax Smith and Benjamin Judah, six times; Reuben West, seven; and John Ferguson, eight. John Adams led all others with thirteen purchases of houses and lots before 1860 and eight from 1860 to 1871. City Hall, Richmond, Deed Books 46, p. 57; 47, p. 126; 63, pp. 415, 416; 65, p. 124; 70A, pp. 736, 737; 70B, p. 690; 73A, pp. 213, 558; 75A, p. 179; 76A, p. 83; 78B, p. 182.

[36] City Hall, Richmond, Deed Books 43, 46, 49, 52, 56, 64.

property ownership increased so that about one-third of the 811 free Negro families became property-owning families; in Richmond the proportion increased to about one-fourth. There were still other signs of growth. With the appearance of the large number of new property holders, certain street blocks in Petersburg and Richmond became "colored" blocks.[37]

In the towns of Winchester and Suffolk, also, real estate buying among free Negroes increased. The number of such owners in Winchester grew from five in 1830 to forty in 1860, representing at least a fourth of the free Negro families. Five among the forty Winchester owners had property worth $1,000 or more. The most widely known of these Winchester owners, and indeed one of the best known in the state, was Edmund Kean, operator of a livery stable, who will be discussed later. The town of Suffolk probably drew some of its eleven property holders from Nansemond County, in which it is located. As has been shown, free Negroes accumulated more farm land in this county than in any other in the state. Some of this same thrift was exhibited in Suffolk, where free Negro owners increased from one in 1830 to eleven in 1860. Jack Douglas, the foremost, owned not only a farm of 268 acres in the county, but also two houses and town lots valued at $1,458.

A remarkable record in property holding was made by free Negroes in the small town of Hampton. Although one or more free Negroes of this town held property as early as the decade of 1790, no individual of this group held property there in 1830.[38] The Hampton free Negroes resumed

[37] One of these blocks in Petersburg was located on Perry Street. Here a few Negroes began to buy as early as 1815; in 1860 there were fifteen or more owners on this street. Included in this free Negro property was a very important church, the Gillfield Baptist, the membership of which embraced many free Negroes. This short block in Petersburg today is largely owned by colored people.

[38] One free Negro woman of Hampton, however, Nancy Tarrant, daughter of Cæsar Tarrant, owned 2,666 acres of bounty land in Ohio through a grant from the state for her father's distinguished services as a pilot in the Virginia

the buying of property about 1845. The number of owners increased from one in that year to eight in 1860, with a total property valuation of $5,600. These eight owners were useful in this town of 1,848 inhabitants as carpenters, blacksmiths, teamsters, oystermen, and storekeepers. James Bailey, one of the number, owned one lot in 1852 and four lots in 1860. His personal estate included two horses, two carriages, and $200 in cash. This man, like Douglas in Suffolk, owned a farm in the country also.

Williamsburg, a still smaller place than Hampton, had in its population in 1860 four free Negroes with property valued at $4,600, about half of which was owned by Alexander Dunlop, a blacksmith.[39]

Though free Negroes made rapid gains in property ownership in most of the urban communities, there were three in which only a little advance or even a small decline occurred between 1830 and 1860. These cities were Norfolk, Portsmouth, and Fredericksburg. One other, Alexandria, showed advancement for the period as a whole but none at all during the last ten years, when the larger centers were progressing so rapidly. There were probably two reasons for the lack of progress in these places: lack of industrial opportunity, and migration.

If Negro property ownership in Norfolk had developed after 1830 as fast as it did in Richmond and Petersburg, on the basis of the 1860 population there should have been in Norfolk about seventy-five owners instead of thirteen. In all probability Negroes failed to advance in Norfolk because of the competition of the white mechanics. As previously noted, with perhaps one or two exceptions all the blacksmiths

---

navy during the American Revolution. Land Office, Richmond, Military Certificates (ms.), 3, 1811–1876, p. 242.

[39] After the war Alexander Dunlop was summoned to Washington to give testimony to the Joint Committee on Reconstruction regarding Southern conditions. His statement to this powerful body was that during the war he had all of his "belongings" taken from him, and that since that event hostile persons were determined to "get" him. Report of Joint Committee on Reconstruction, *House Reports*, 39 Cong., 1 Sess, No. 30, Pt. 2, p. 58.

and bricklayers of Norfolk were white. In 1860 there were only three free Negro carpenters. Even in the barber trade, which Negroes virtually monopolized in other places, Norfolk white barbers outnumbered the free Negro barbers. It is significant that in the one field in which the free Negroes of this city faced no white competition, that of draying, several property holders appeared, notably Ackey White, Edward White, and Ned Keeling. In 1860 only one Negro barber in Norfolk held property, in contrast to the many in Richmond and Petersburg. White supremacy in the trades was only another indication of the ever-increasing white population in this city. The Negro population, slave and free, was relatively declining.

Norfolk's situation may also be explained in terms of the predominance of women as heads of families. The 189 heads of families in this town included over 100 washerwomen, whose earnings were too meager to lead to property ownership.[40] Furthermore, it must be remembered that Norfolk never became a manufacturing center comparable to Richmond and Petersburg. A railroad connection with the interior of Virginia was not opened until 1850.

Fredericksburg exceeded all other cities in 1830 in free Negro property owners but afterwards declined. The town itself deteriorated prior to 1850, but the strongest deterrent to the continued progress of free Negroes in this place was the migration of its leading Negro property-holding families to Detroit, Michigan, and to other centers. Among the migrants from this place were the DeBaptist family, Louisa Moore, and Maria Richards. Just before leaving, Maria Richards sold for $1,050 the house and lot on Sophia Street for which she had paid $120 about twelve years earlier.[41]

---

[40] In 1860 women constituted 65 per cent of Norfolk's free Negro heads of families. Women were in the majority everywhere as family heads, but their majority in Norfolk was greater than in any other city. The preponderance of women as heads of families throughout the state suggests the possibility that the husbands of most of these women were slaves.

[41] Clerk's Office, Fredericksburg, Deed Book Q, p. 172. The migration of

Other property holders and prospective migrants also sold their real estate. The most prosperous free Negroes of Fredericksburg left the town, apparently because their petition for a continuation of formal school instruction in 1838 was denied by the state legislature.

Alexandria free Negroes found the laws and government of the District of Columbia more satisfactory than those of Virginia. Having lived a long period of time in Alexandria as a part of the District, they disliked the retrocession of this town to Virginia in 1847. Because the laws of Virginia were too "obnoctious," many of the property-holding and taxpaying free Negroes left the town for Washington, D. C. Of a group of forty-six property holders in Alexandria in 1850 only sixteen held property at this place ten years later. Not all of the thirty who were missing had died; many had migrated to the capital of the nation. But for this, the number of free Negro property holders in Alexandria would have been larger. However, even after the migration, of a group of some 283 families in this town in 1860, forty-one were owners of real estate.[42]

Further insight into the securing of property by free Negroes in cities may be gained by showing the relation of property holding to certain occupations. Such an approach gives a general view of the state rather than the record of any particular city, and is more significant for the later years of the period under discussion, especially the year 1860.

By far the greatest property-producing occupation among free Negroes in cities was the livery stable business. There were about six operators of livery stables in the state who were men of fairly large means. Edmund Kean of Winchester, the most prosperous of these, owned four pieces of prop-

---

the Fredericksburg free Negroes is told by W. B. Hartgrove in *Journal of Negro History*, vol. 1 (Jan., 1916).

[42] In a few instances the ante-bellum property of certain free Negroes of Alexandria is still owned by Negroes either as direct descendants or as purchasers. Among these are the families of Birkley, Hamilton, Lyles, and Pritchett.

erty valued at $7,300. One of these properties alone, perhaps his residence, was valued at $4,500. This man's taxable personal estate at one time included fifteen horses, six hogs, seven carriages, and $400 in cash. All told, Kean's real and personal estate amounted to at least $10,000. Robert Clark of Petersburg, Booker Jackson of Farmville, and William Peters of Harrisonburg were also prosperous. Each of these men owned property, real and personal, to the extent of $3,000, and each of them used employees in their business enterprises.

Just as every livery stable operator owned real estate, so did most of the small shopkeepers, such as grocerymen, confectioners, barkeepers, and restaurant proprietors. In this general field, Isaac Gray of Winchester led all others with town real estate valued at $2,500 and a farm of sixty-nine acres in the country. Randle Evans of Winchester operated a confectionery shop and owned property valued at $1,000. Mary Savoy of Alexandria and Russell Thomas of Lynchburg, keepers of grocery stores, were almost as successful as Evans. As a business man, Thomas frequently found occasion to borrow money through deeds of trust on his property.[43] William Gray of Alexandria operated a butcher shop and owned real estate. Jack McRae of Petersburg, the operator of a flourishing restaurant, owned two houses and lots valued at $1,550, and fixtures and equipment valued at $2,287.36 in the inflated currency of the Civil War period.[44]

The barber trade also was important in leading to property ownership. There were about fifty Negro barber shops in the cities of Virginia, and most of the proprietors owned considerable property. Reuben West of Richmond and Robert Campbell of Staunton, each with six or more pieces of real estate valued at $7,000, owned more property than any other barbers in the state. Aside from real estate, Reuben West at one time possessed $7,000 in cash or its equivalent

---

[43] Clerk's Office, Lynchburg, Deed Book W, p. 84.
[44] Clerk's Office, Petersburg, Will Book 5, pp. 220–221.

in bonds.⁴⁵ Nearly all of the barbers in Richmond owned real estate, ranging from one to eight pieces. In Petersburg, Henry Elebeck owned several houses and lots; John Berry, James Auter, John K. Shore, and James Ford owned one house and lot each. Elebeck's three-thousand-dollar residence was located on one of the principal streets. Armistead and William Pride of Lynchburg accumulated property and were well-to-do for more than a generation.

The occupations of drayman, teamster, and hack driver produced almost as many property holders. Caleb Pitts and Edward White of Norfolk owned less than $1,000 worth of real estate; Dawson Gardner and James Robinson of Richmond and Phil Sewell of Petersburg owned more. Thirty years earlier Ackey White and Ned Keeling of Norfolk had likewise become men of substance. These draymen and hack drivers perhaps owned as much personal property as real estate; each owned several horses, carriages, and wagons, for which he was duly taxed.

Blacksmiths in cities became property owners too, although not so generally as men in the foregoing occupations. Gilbert Hunt, Robert Hill, and Abraham Brown of Richmond owned property worth $1,000 or more, as did Berry Bonner and Armistead Wilson of Petersburg. Fully one-third of the shoemakers secured real estate. Benjamin W. Judah of Richmond came into possesison of more real estate than any other man of this trade in the state. His six or more houses and lots had a valuation of $4,300.⁴⁶

A few free Negroes became successful contractors. Outstanding among them was George Seaton of Alexandria, whose combined holdings amounted to more than $4,000. Thomas Scott of Petersburg, and the DeBaptists of Fredericksburg, a generation earlier, had ranked equally high. So successful was John Adams of Richmond, a plasterer and contractor, that he became the owner of thirteen houses and lots, the largest number of separate pieces of property held

---

⁴⁵ Personal Property, Richmond, 1856.   ⁴⁶ *Ibid.*, 1860.

by a free Negro in the entire state. The total valuation of his property, however, amounted to less than that of a few other well-to-do free Negroes in the state. Because of the good wages paid, most of the bricklayers in cities became property owners.[47]

Among women the seamstress ranked high as an owner of property. Certain Richmond women successfully practiced this skilled occupation.[48] Nurses, like seamstresses, frequently did well, but the numerous washerwomen held very little property until about 1860.

Of the hundreds of free Negroes employed in the tobacco factories, a few emerged as property holders. In Petersburg, nine tobacco twisters bought property; three women, tobacco stemmers, did likewise.[49] In almost every instance, these tobacco workers of Petersburg and a similar group in Richmond came into possession of property during the fifties. Patsey Brooks of Richmond even reached the one thousand dollar class.

The fact that greater numbers of free Negroes began to own urban property in the fifties and that the thirty years as a whole showed an upward trend may be explained by the general prosperity of the period. The economic revival in Virginia, previously discussed, stimulated free Negro prosperity. At this time land values were appreciating, wage levels were rising, banking capital was growing, old factories were operating constantly, and new ones were being established. The value of slaves and slave hire moved up corre-

---

[47] Such at least was the status of Thomas Garnes, John Warren, and Coy Quivas of Petersburg. Nelson Vandervall of Richmond was a plasterer, and he too became a property holder.

[48] Virginia Cunningham held property valued at $3,452; Elizabeth Beatty, $2,315; Ann Wallace, $1,950; Mary J. Sullivan, $1,644; Mary Hope, $1,630; and Rhoda King, $1,255. Personal Property, 1860, City Hall, Richmond, Office of the Commissioner of Revenue.

[49] The nine men were Thomas Berry, Collin Bland, Ambrose Bonner, Phillip Evans, William Finney, Joseph Jenkins, Israel Jones, Robert Penn, and Robert Smith. The women purchasers were Martha McKenna, Mary Scott, and Susan Valentine.

spondingly. In short, the opportunities for work, especially in Richmond and Petersburg, had never been greater.

Travelers and correspondents commented on these points. One correspondent reported in 1859 that he visited a tobacco factory in Petersburg which employed 230 hands, all of whom were Negroes. They worked at this factory not more than seven or eight hours a day as regular time and frequently had overtime employment. On this visit he was shown hands who earned $10 every week for overtime work alone.[50] Olmsted reported similar conditions. On one occasion he was told that slaves in the factories earned from $5 to $20 a month extra for themselves and that free Negroes did equally well. On another occasion in Virginia, during the prosperous fifties, he met a free Negro whose wages during one year alone amounted to $900. This traveler believed that because of the high wages, any free colored man in Virginia could accumulate property faster than any Northern wage-earner.[51] With due allowance for exaggerated statements by casual observers, it is certain that the trend of wages during the fifties was upward, that employment was steady, and that some Negroes put their earnings to good use by investing in property. This boom would have led to still greater investment in real estate but for the shiftless element, especially among the tobacco factory hands.

Prosperous conditions among free Negroes and hired slaves was reflected in the purchase of church property as well as individual residences. Free Negroes and slaves might unite their small earnings for the purchase of church property, but the legal title to it might be held by free Negroes only.

Negroes owned churches in the period before 1830. In 1818, for example, the members of the Gillfield Baptist Church of Petersburg secured title to the land costing $550,

---

[50] Petersburg *Daily Express,* Sept. 29, 1859.
[51] Olmsted, *Seaboard Slave States,* pp. 141, 142.

upon which their new church was later built.[52] In the same year, the congregation of the Elam Baptist Church at Charles City received title to their church property, not by purchase but by gift from Abram Brown and his wife, Susannah, free Negroes of this place.[53] In Norfolk in 1830 the ten free Negro trustees of the First Baptist Church bought their present ground for the sum of $250.[54] In addition to the Gillfield Baptist there was organized in Petersburg the African Baptist Church, which made efforts at property ownership later.

In the thirty years from 1830 to 1860, additional Negro Baptist churches were established in the cities of Virginia, and in most cases the members of these bodies became the owners of their church edifices with the land attached. At the same time the earlier churches made additional purchases or improvements in their old property. All told, the Negroes of Virginia advanced in church ownership, just as they did in individual ownership, in this period of prosperity.

Three of the older churches, the First Baptist or Bute Street Church of Norfolk, and the Gillfield Baptist and the African Baptist churches of Petersburg, undertook campaigns for new structures and general improvements. The building campaign in the Norfolk church, begun in 1850, extended over a period of nine years, during which time several thousand dollars was raised, deposits were made in the bank, and fire insurance was secured for the newly erected building. The new brick edifice was opened and dedicated in 1859.[55] In Petersburg the Gillfield congregation completed in the same year a seven-thousand-dollar brick structure, for which one of its members, C. B. Stevens, served as con-

---

[52] Clerk's Office, Petersburg, Deed Book 5, p. 261.
[53] Clerk's Office, Charles City, Deed Book 6, p. 214. Abram Brown, the grantor of this church lot, became a landowner in 1769 with the purchase of 150 acres. Charles City County, Records, 1766–1774, p. 155. This record book is in the State Library.
[54] Clerk's Office, Norfolk County, Deed Book 19, pp. 270–271.
[55] First Baptist Church, Norfolk, Record Book (ms.), Feb. 10, April 21, 1850; Oct. 9, 1853; Feb. 6, 1859, in possession of the Reverend Richard Bowling of Norfolk, pastor of this church.

THE CITY PROPERTY OWNER

tractor. One unusual aspect of this enterprise was that before erection of the building was begun, the members had on hand about half the cost, and at the time of the dedication the entire cost had been paid. The money raised in this campaign came from a tax of $5 per member on 500 members, and from the proceeds of fairs and concerts staged among the white people. Finally the women members were instructed "to go forward in any honest way not to bring reproach upon the church to get up money for the purpose of building the new church." The African Baptist Church of Petersburg bought a lot for $1,440 in 1860 and completed a church edifice on it several years later at a reported cost of $11,000.[56]

The Negro Baptist churches instituted after 1830 were the First African, the Second African, and the Ebenezer churches in Richmond; one African church each in Alexandria, Lynchburg, and Fredericksburg, and the Bank Street Church in Norfolk. The members of the First African Church of Richmond paid to their white former members $5,902.08 for the property once used by the two races jointly.[57] The Second African Church was organized in 1847 as an overflow from the First African. In this instance a group of thirty or more free Negro trustees became the owners of the church property.[58] Another overflow from the mother church, the First African, produced the Ebenezer Church in 1856. In this year the distinguished white pastor of the First African Church, the Reverend Robert Ryland, bought the church property for the new congregation in his own name. Six years later, with John Adams, the well-to-do

---

[56] Gillfield Baptist Church, Petersburg, Record Book (ms.), Aug. 1, 1858, in possession of Lewis Wells of Petersburg, deacon of this church; Petersburg *Daily Express,* April 3, Aug., 1859; Clerk's Office, Petersburg, Deed Book 26, p. 756.

[57] First African Baptist Church, Richmond, Record Book (ms.), May 4, June 21, 1846. In this instance $2,752 of the purchase price was donated by white citizens of Richmond. In this particular purchase the free Negro members were not allowed to act as trustees of the church in a legal capacity. The attorney general of Virginia advised the pastor that such action would be inexpedient. *Ibid.,* Feb. 4, 1849, p. 142.

[58] City Hall, Richmond, Deed Book 52, p. 555.

plasterer, and Richard C. Hobson, the barber, serving as trustees, the Negroes paid back to Ryland $8,100 and became owners apparently in their own right.[59]

These solvent, well-established church organizations of Richmond and Petersburg frequently made contributions toward church property in the smaller cities of Virginia. In this way the First African Church of Richmond, beginning about 1850, contributed toward the ground or the meeting house of Negro communicants in Staunton, Lynchburg, Petersburg, Fredericksburg, and Williamsburg. For example, on Sunday, May 21, 1854, a collection of $11.30 was raised toward the erection of a church "for the colored people" of Fredericksburg. With such assistance these colored people of Fredericksburg in 1857 acquired legal title to church property once used jointly by both races.[60]

The free Negroes and slaves of Alexandria and Norfolk bought churches apparently without contributions from other cities. In Alexandria, after only eighteen months' separation from the white Baptist church, the Negroes erected a new house of worship and finished paying for it within a year.[61] In Norfolk during this same period the Bank Street Church, after its secession from the Bute Street Church, paid $2,700 to the white Presbyterians of that city for their old edifice.[62]

Small efforts at group property ownership are illustrated also by the free Negro benevolent societies in the cities of Virginia. Typical of these was the Petersburg "Beneficial Society of Free Men of Color" which was in existence from about 1815 until the Civil War. In 1818 this organization through its trustees bought a lot for a burying ground at the price of $100.[63] In 1840, under a different set of trustees,

[59] *Ibid.*, 78B, p. 250.
[60] Clerk's Office, Fredericksburg, Deed Book S, p. 257.
[61] Potomac Association Minutes, 1857, p. 31, in the Virginia Baptist Historical Society Library, University of Richmond, Richmond, Va.
[62] First Baptist Church, Norfolk, Record Book. Unlike the Negro Baptists, the congregations of the African Methodist denomination received their church buildings as a gift from the supervising white Methodist church.
[63] Clerk's Office, Petersburg, Deed Book 5, p. 306. The trustees were Uriah

this society bought additional property of the same type for $200.⁶⁴ Such efforts as these were in accord with the purposes of the members to support each other in sickness and death and to provide for each member a square in the cemetery wherein he might bury his free parents.⁶⁵

Although this study is concerned primarily with property owned by free Negroes as individuals, it is worth noting that the free Negroes of Virginia cities held legal title to about $60,000 worth of church property, to which the slaves also contributed something, and about $1,000 worth of property for burial purposes. These churches were actually Negro churches, which means that they possessed a considerable degree of independence. The Negroes managed all the finances of the church; in Petersburg and Norfolk they kept the records; they paid the white pastor out of their own resources; they chose him in some instances; they sponsored the various auxiliaries of the church; they disciplined their own members; in short, they did everything except the preaching which the law forbade.⁶⁶ The very men cited as the leading mechanics and property holders in these cities were also the leaders in the churches and the fraternal societies.

It is significant, too, that this forward movement in free Negro church life and ownership took place in the period from 1830 to 1860, when the reactionary state legislation of 1831–1832 is generally thought to have left the free Negro group prostrate. Some valuable privileges were curtailed at this time, but this action did not weaken the economic position

---

Tyner, Major Elebeck, James Colson, John T. Raymond, and John Stewart, all individual property holders.

⁶⁴ *Ibid.*, 11, p. 321.

⁶⁵ Constitution of the "Beneficial Society of Free Men of Color," in possession of Mrs. Gertrude Colson Jackson of Petersburg. This constitution provided that on the death of a member his family should have $15 from the funds of the society. The wife of such a member was entitled to $1 a month so long as she remained a "prudent widow."

⁶⁶ These statements are based on a study of the original minutes of several of these churches.

of the free Negro in the life of the state nor did it destroy some important phases of leadership in church life. Indeed, the period under review was the heyday of economic prosperity for the free Negro in Virginia.[67]

Free Negro ownership of property involved a variety of interests and motives. The effort to obtain property sprang from desire for personal advancement, concern about the welfare of others, and the wish to realize certain ideals. One of the strongest of these interests was the maintenance and perpetuation of the family. The ownership of property welded the family together and enabled the holder to share his possessions with his family circle. Evidence of concern for the family relationship is revealed in the legal instruments of property conveyance: the last will and testament, and the deed.

Several free Negroes of Petersburg evinced in their wills the desire to provide for their families. Loudon Cary, a boatman and owner of property, left to his "loving wife" Judith Cary all his real estate; after her death his lots and appurtenances with all the "rents, issues, and profits thereof" were to be equally divided among his six daughters. Cary also provided that his wife "keep and run my water craft called the *Shark* as long as this vessel is capable of running to enable her the more easily to raise and educate our children." Jane Cook, likewise an operator of boats, made provision by will for her husband, Peter Mathews, who was a slave. Her two lighters, the *Democrat* and the *Experiment,* were made over to him, since in operating them she had merely served as agent for her slave husband; and another free Negro, Charles Lewis, was appointed as agent. Lewis also had the

[67] The economic progress made by free Negroes, especially in property holding, has been overlooked by many writers, who have stressed rather the free Negroes' lack of achievement. See for example Phillips, *American Negro Slavery*, pp. 436-437; Ballagh, *Slavery in Virginia*, p. 147; Whitfield, *Slavery Agitation*, p. 7. Whitfield even says that the free Negro "scarcely owned the dust on the clothes he wore." Phillips conceded progress to certain mulattoes and quadroons here and there in the country, but he sees no economic advancement made by the entire group of free Negroes.

responsibility of acting as guardian for Jane Cook's daughter and of providing the child with an education. Susannah Graves, widow of the very prosperous free Negro Richmond Graves, expressed her concern for the welfare of her children in her will: "[I] recommend that [my] executor rent out the home in which I now live annually for the benefit of [my] children and that [they] may be kept together in the other house which is now occupied by Mr. Claiborne." Education of their children was a subject frequently mentioned by these city property holders.[68]

Outstanding among those persons in Richmond who were concerned about their homes and the proper rearing of their children were Peter Hawkins, the "tooth drawer," a Negro, and Christopher McPherson, a mulatto. Hawkins, owner of several desirable pieces of property, directed his executor to "make an inventory of my estate and rent out all my houses except the dwelling house wherein my wife resides out of which to have my children schooled and supported and if any surplus money [is left] for it to be put out at interest for their benefit." Christopher McPherson, a highly skilled clerk and bookkeeper employed by leading merchants and lawyers, owned real estate "in and about the city of Richmond." His will directed that three of his children should receive $200 each. As for his two other children, who were slaves, McPherson provided that they should be purchased and freed and that his close friend Thomas Griffin should take them under his paternal charge "and bring them up in

[68] Clerk's Office, Petersburg, Will Book II, pp. 149, 193, 30. In this group in Petersburg was Moses Cook Brander, who besides leaving his son Arthur two lots, also provided for Arthur's education. *Ibid.*, p. 153. The will of Henry Boyd, free Negro doctor of the same city, made in 1829, appointed David May as executor and continued: "as I am indebted to Elizabeth Graves daughter of Richmond Graves and wish to show her my gratitude [I] do leave [to her] the home I now reside in with my household and kitchen furniture during her life and at her death the same to be divided between my nieces Charlotte Warren [and] Cora Seaman of New York. . . . I wish the balance of my property real and personal to be sold the personal estate at 1, 2, and 3 years credit and the proceeds after paying my just debts to be equally divided between my son Dick (a slave of James Dunlop) and my nieces Charlotte Warren and Cora Seaman." *Ibid.*, III.

the path of duty they owe to their maker and themselves." [69]

Edward Jackson of Fredericksburg made some unique provisions concerning his property, because a part of his family were slaves. He directed that his house and lot should go first to his mother for her lifetime and then to his wife. After the death of his wife the proceeds from the sale of the property were to be given to his four sisters, not directly, because they were slaves, but to their owners.[70]

Aside from willing property to their relatives, free Negroes made bequests to organizations to which they belonged. Jones Mitchell of Petersburg willed that his property should be sold at public auction, his just debts and funeral expenses should be paid, his sisters Nancy and Suckey should receive $50 apiece, and the Gillfield Baptist Church of Petersburg should receive $100. The will then provided that "the balance" should go "to my wife Molly to her and her heirs forever." Hannah Brown of Richmond left all her real estate to the Baptist Relief Society of the First Baptist Church and appointed certain Negro members of this church as her executors.[71]

---

[69] City Hall, Richmond, Hustings Court, Will Book II, p. 199; III, p. 131. Richard Traylor of this same city bequeathed to his wife Virginia, in recognition of his "sincere regard for her" all of his estate, real and personal, with "entire confidence that she will do justice to my dear children." John Ferguson, owner of more than eight pieces of property in Richmond and in the country willed one or more pieces to each of his eight children, and bequeathed $450 in cash to one child. City Hall, Richmond, Circuit Court, Will Book 3, p. 253.

[70] Other Fredericksburg free Negroes who willed property to their families were Thomas Carey, who left his property to his wife Sarah with the proviso that if she remarried she was to have merely the use of his furniture, and John Minor, who bequeathed to his wife Betsy two houses and a lot, which upon her death were to pass to his children. Clerk's Office, Fredericksburg, Will Book D, p. 232. Anthony White of Farmville appointed his Negro friends Booker and John Jackson as trustees to administer his estate on behalf of his wife Milly during her life and to settle the estate and divide the proceeds among his children at her death. Clerk's Office, Prince Edward County, Will Book IX, p. 374. Edward Miller, a caulker of Norfolk, willed his whole estate to his wife Sarah and provided that at her death it should pass to his children and grandchildren.

[71] Clerk's Office, Petersburg, Will Book IV, p. 191; Clerk's Office, Henrico County, Will Book 10, p. 127.

Concern about the material welfare of husband, wife, and children was expressed by free Negroes during life as well as at death. Thus they conveyed property to one another both by deed and by will. Of particular importance in this class in early Petersburg was the family of James Roberts. As has been noted, Roberts accumulated property as a boatman, and he owned several vessels including a schooner. In 1817 he gave one of his lots to his wife for the consideration of mere "love and affection." [72]

Family solidarity was a constant trait of the Jarratts of Petersburg. Industry and thrift in the operation of boats and other water occupations on the Appomattox and James rivers made this family property owners and taxpayers for about 125 years. Beginning with the marriage of Richard Jarratt to Betsy Rollins in 1803 and his first purchase of property in 1815, this family, as previously noted, has owned property in Petersburg to the present day. As early as 1815 Richard Jarratt was paying $5.50 in taxes to the city government alone. Like the other persons named here, members of this family frequently gave away personal property to one another. Family interest among the Jarratts is further illustrated in the following letter which Alexander Jarratt, son of Richard, wrote to his wife in 1838.[73] He was then in Norfolk while his wife, Nancy, was visiting in New York. The message of this mariner is as follows:

My Dear Wife

I have now sit down with but a short time before me to address you with a few lines to enform you of my health which is very good

---

[72] By a deed of gift Joseph Shepard of Petersburg gave his daughter Caroline "all his goods, chattels, and personal estate, all whatsoever in whose hands ... they may be or in whose custody and possession ... they may be found." Uriah Tyner "for natural love and affection" granted his son not only items of personal property but his twelve-hundred-dollar house and lot as well. The personal property consisted of such articles as chests of drawers, a sideboard, a dining table, a tea table, and a card table, all of mahogany, and a dozen Windsor chairs. Clerk's Office, Petersburg, Deed Book VI, p. 175.

[73] Jarratt Family Papers.

at present and i am en hopes when they comes to hand they may find you and Lucinda enjoying the same Blessing of Health Your mother father sisters and brothers [in Norfolk] are well Sister Becky say that she is very much pleased with her basket and thanks you ontel you are better paid She expects to leave when her month is up to assist your mother in market Mother was much pleased with your presant and says that you are very nice they wants to see you very much indeed and says they shall expect you on my return trip . . . give my love to Lucinda sister Aby and except the greater part yourself i could say a great deal more but time will not admit therefore i must conclude with remaining your sincere and loving husband ontel Death us do part.

Occasional reference has been made to items of personal property owned by city free Negroes. Personal property sometimes passed from deceased persons to members of their families and the general public by the action of administrators in the settlement of estates. Administrators' sales, and the accounts rendered to the court by such functionaries in the settlement of the estates of deceased persons, furnish information on this point. Several cases from Petersburg may be cited to illustrate a condition common to the whole state.

Among the many items left in the home of Richmond Graves, the livery stable operator, were the following: a cherry desk, a book case, pictures of Washington and Jefferson, a dozen Windsor chairs, a mahogany dining table, a sideboard, three decanters, three brass candlesticks, china bowls, a large glass tumbler, china cups and saucers, silver tea spoons and table spoons, a wire safe, a copper kettle, and other kitchen utensils. Aside from household articles Graves left six horses, harness, saddles, and bridles. The sale of this property brought the sum of $654.53, which with certain debts due the Graves estate brought the total to $960.78. Although there were debts against this estate, there was a favorable balance of $329.51. The purchasers of the Graves personal property included his free Negro friends as well as his relatives. Thus James Colson, the barber, bought a half dozen of the Windsor chairs, and a horse and bridle; Graves' own daughters bought the dining tables, the book case, a looking glass, the pictures of Washington and Jefferson, and other articles.[74]

Graham Bell, the shoemaker, left items of personal property including a dining table, a tea table, a sideboard, a chest of drawers, and also horses, cattle, and a carriage.[75] Betsy Allergue's effects included a mahogany sideboard, a silver ladle, one dozen table spoons, tea spoons, other silver ware, and also scales and weights, sugar boxes, show glasses, jugs, and demijohns, which had been used in her store. As in the case of Graves, purchases of these and other articles were made at the administrators' sales by members of the respective families.

William N. Colson, of similar personal estate and business ability, was exceedingly intelligent and well read. He offered his family unusual advantages during his life; his real and personal property left them in good circumstances at his death. Among the opportunities Colson gave his family were education and travel: on one occasion he paid out $191 to cover a half year's instruction of his daughter and his wife's traveling expenses. Colson's furniture consisted of a mahogany sideboard, dining table, breakfast table, and sofa; also silver-plated candle sticks, venetian blinds, bureau and book case, wine glasses, glass tumblers, dinner and breakfast plates, and silver spoons. Reflecting his cultural interests, his library contained such volumes as the revised code of Virginia, volumes on the life of Washington and the History of Virginia, Goldsmith's Rome, a history of Greece, a history of

---

[74] Clerk's Office, Petersburg, Accounts Current I, p. 30–31.
[75] *Ibid.*, p. 88. Bell's funeral expenses, which formed one item in the settlement of his estate, were $78—$50 for a coffin, $8 for the grave and hearse, $5 for the services of a minister, and $15 for miscellaneous items.

Ireland, biographies of Jonathan Edwards and Whitfield, and a testament.[76]

The experiences of the many free Negroes discussed in this chapter leave the impression that this class of people fared well in the period from 1830 to 1860. But they were not alone. The economic revival in Virginia produced a condition in the urban industrial areas whereby a fairly large number of slaves could also become free men and own property.

[76] Clerk's Office, Petersburg, Will Book III, pp. 107–113; Accounts Current III, pp. 187–189; Colson Family Papers.

CHAPTER VI

FROM SLAVERY TO FREEDOM IN URBAN VIRGINIA

DURING most of the period before 1860, slavery remained slavery in the agricultural South, but the institution experienced considerable modification in the manufacturing and urban areas.[1] Hundreds of slaves became free persons in the cities of Virginia, and the thousands who did not become free found themselves living and working under a system different from that of the plantation belt. Because of the existence of a favorable labor market, slaves became freedmen, and freedmen became property owners. This was a continuing process; of the property mentioned previously, not all was obtained by the 1830 generation of free colored persons; some was acquired by the manumitted Negroes of the new day.

The transition from slavery to freedom is a story that reveals human nature at its very best. It shows the slave striving to rise to a higher level and to advance his relatives and friends correspondingly; it shows the slave often unwilling to seek and maintain freedom if freedom meant separation from members of his family. In the bondmen's seeking of individual advancement, in his building of home ties, some of the finer relations between masters and slaves were stimulated. Although the slave owner's public attitude toward slavery in the abstract was damaging to the slave, this same owner stood ready to extend favors to his individual slave and even, under some circumstances, to liberate him.

Acts of manumission had multiplied in the period of the

[1] Phillips, *American Negro Slavery*, p. 405; Wesley, *Negro Labor*, pp. 13, 21 ff.

American Revolution. Between 1782 and 1810, according to one estimate, the number of free Negroes in Virginia increased from about 3,000 to 30,000.[2] This striking growth was common to the urban centers as well as to the state as a whole. Influenced by the theories of natural rights and of freedom as the birthright of all men, many slaveholders in cities liberated their bondmen. During the twenty-four year period from 1782 to 1806, owners of slaves in Petersburg executed eighty-six acts of manumission, freeing about 100 slaves; owners in Richmond during this same period executed 108 manumissions, freeing still more.[3]

The motive and general character of manumissions in this early period is illustrated by certain cases. In one instance, in 1785, "being fully persuaded that freedom is the natural right of all men agreeable to the Declaration of the Bill of Rights," Gresset Davis of Petersburg emancipated his slave Ishmael. Similarly, Joseph Harding, a merchant of this town, believing like Davis "that God created all men equally free," provided in 1788 for the emancipation of Susannah and her five children. Stith Parham, another slaveholder of Petersburg, "being deeply conscious of the impropriety of slavery," set free at once his slave Gilly, and later four others.[4] In like manner Charles Copeland of Richmond in 1790 liberated three slaves, "being fully conscious from natural reason, that God created all men free; and that all laws made to subjugate one part of the human race to the absolute dominance of another are totally repugnant to the clearest dictates of natural justice." Copeland spoke the language of most of the hundred or more slaveholders of his community.[5]

---

[2] John H. Russell, *Free Negro*, p. 61.
[3] Clerk's Office, Petersburg, Hustings Court, Deed Books 1-6; City Hall, Richmond, Deed Books 1-4.
[4] Clerk's Office, Petersburg, Deed Book 1, pp. 22, 433; 2, p. 508.
[5] *Ibid.*, Richmond, 1, p. 456. After 1806 and continuing until about 1830, the number of acts of manumission in most of the cities and counties declined considerably. Norfolk was one exception.

For the whole period from the Revolution to the Civil War, manumission in Virginia had a checkered career: at one time the lawmakers sanctioned it; at another time they banned it. The manumission of slaves, therefore, was frequent at one period; rare at another.

Divergent views on the frequency of manumissions in different periods of Virginia history have been expressed by Beverly Munford and by John H. Russell. Munford takes the position that manumission was as widely operative in the period from 1830 to 1860 as in the liberal days of the Revolution. Russell on the other hand indicates that manumission definitely declined in the years from 1830 to 1860. He divides manumission activity into three periods, of which he says that preceding 1800 a slave in Virginia had about ten chances in 100 of manumission; from 1800 to 1832, about four in 100; and after 1832, about two in 100.[6]

Other writers, referring to the South at large, speak of a reaction against manumission after 1830 because of the abolition movement. Lewis C. Gray indicates that late in the decade of the fifties the sharpening controversy led to almost complete halting of manumission.[7] In like manner Ulrich B. Phillips holds that there was a slackening after 1830, although occasionally the liberation of a large number at one time took place.

There is an element of truth in the assertions of all these writers; yet each is apparently unconscious of the lively manumission movement that operated in Virginia's urban localities from 1830 to 1860, regardless of the abolition attack on the one hand and the high price of slaves on the other. Russell is perhaps correct in his statements concerning Virginia as a whole; Munford, though thinking in terms of the state as a whole, is correct concerning only one limited area of the state, namely, the urban communities. In urban Virginia

---

[6] Munford, *Virginia's Attitude toward Slavery*, p. 109; John H. Russell, *Free Negro*, 82.
[7] Gray, *Agriculture in the Southern United States*, 1: 526.

manumission did go forward in the later period on at least as large a scale as in any preceding period.

Three cities of Virginia—Richmond, Petersburg, and Fredericksburg—may be taken as representative of the urban trend. Their record of manumissions is approximately as follows:[8]

TABLE XII
Manumission in Cities

City	Number of acts of manumission			Number Slaves manumitted
	1782–1806	1807–1830	1831–1860	1831–1860
Richmond 90		12	225	352
Petersburg 86		37	161	270
Fredericksburg 28		25	67	86

These figures show that each of these cities yielded more acts of manumission during the last thirty years before the Civil War than during the previous forty-eight years combined. Over 600 slaves received their freedom in Richmond and Petersburg alone during the later period, and considerably more than a thousand were liberated in urban Virginia as a whole.

The frequency of manumission in the cities of Virginia during the thirty years before the Civil War assumes still

---

[8] These data on manumission in urban Virginia are based on the following sources:

Richmond, City Hall, Deed Books, 78 vols., 1783–1860; Minute Books, 1830–1860.

Petersburg, Clerk's Office, Deed Books, 25 vols., 1783–1860.

Fredericksburg, Clerk's Office, Deed Books, 19 vols. (A–S), 1783–1860.

Norfolk, Clerk's Office, Deed Books, 10 vols. (31–40), 1850–1860.

The two parties in a deed of manumission were the grantor and the grantee: the slaveholder and the slave to be manumitted. Such deeds were filed in the city which was the residence, temporary or permanent, of the slave. An act of manumission appearing in city records might involve a slaveholder who lived in one of the counties of Virginia or outside of the state altogether. For example, Lucy T. Bowles of Hanover County in 1856, John T. Foster of Amelia County in the same year, and Robert M. Briggs of Ohio in 1859, liberated respectively Jordan Morris, Sterling Harris, and James Actor of Richmond; and all of these manumissions are recorded in Richmond. City Hall, Richmond, Deed Books 70A, pp. 27, 286; 74A, p. 325.

greater significance when contrasted with the rarity in the counties at this same time. Acts of manumission were numerous in the counties during the Revolutionary period, but rare from 1830 to 1860. In Sussex County, for instance, during the decades of 1780 and 1790, slaveholders executed sixty acts of manumission, thereby freeing 240 slaves; but during the decades of 1830, 1840, and 1850 such acts were fewer than five. In Powhatan County thirty or more acts were executed in the long period between the Revolution and 1830, but only eight after this time. Richmond County, like the others, had many manumissions in the early period but scarcely more than one after 1830. Dinwiddie County in the early years rivaled Sussex in the number of manumissions, but after 1830 had not more than three.[9]

Manumissions in the early period were prompted by ideal motives. For example, Howell Chappell of Sussex County, "after full and deliberate consideration . . . and fully persuaded that freedom is the natural right of all mankind," liberated eleven slaves at one time. Manumissions after 1830 in the counties, as in the cities, lost this high character. Many of them were negotiated on a money basis like those executed in Orange County by Robert Dunaway in 1839 and Robert Wilson in 1840, who liberated one slave each for $300 and $400 respectively.[10]

[9] Clerk's Office, Sussex, Deed Books F, G, H, I, J; Clerk's Office, Petersburg, Register of Free Negroes and Mulattoes (ms.), 1794-1831. This valuable record of Petersburg free Negroes shows many instances of slaves manumitted in Dinwiddie County and elsewhere who afterwards came to Petersburg to live.

[10] Clerk's Office, Orange County, Deed Book 37, pp. 249, 380. The channel for the study of manumission in Virginia court records is either the index volume of each set of deed books, or the index in the separate volumes. In the column for deeds of all kinds, including deeds of bargain and sale, gift, trust, release, etc., these records show also "deeds of emancipation." An invaluable aid in the further pursuit of this subject is the Minute Books of the courts. The Minute Books frequently reveal what became of the slave after he was manumitted. In particular they show whether he was permitted to remain in Virginia or whether he made application for such permission. The discussion of the drive for "permission to remain," as given later in this chapter, is made possible largely by the existence of the manuscript Minute Books and

The fact that after 1830 manumission in Virginia was confined largely to the cities, is accounted for by certain forces operating in these restricted areas. These were: the prevalence of slave hiring on a wide scale in cities, the freedom of movement of hired slaves and other slaves in cities, and the concentration of free Negroes in these same areas. In short, the city was a magnet for both free Negroes and slaves. So many slaves worked in cities as persons hired to individuals and business concerns that their number may have exceeded the number who worked for their own masters. The exact ratio between the two cannot be determined, for federal census enumerators and state officials disregarded mere hirers of slaves and classified all persons having slaves as owners. Despite this difficulty it can safely be said that a large proportion of the slaves working in cities were really owned by masters living in the country, who sent their slaves to Richmond, Petersburg, Lynchburg, and other cities for employment, because their services were not needed on plantations. Thus around New Year's Day the streets of Richmond and other cities were filled with thousands of Negroes brought in from the country for hire.[11]

Slaves filtered into the cities particularly from northern Virginia. Frederic Bancroft estimates that from 10 to 12 per cent of the slaves in Fauquier County and fully 25 per cent of those in Fairfax were annually hired out. Slaves from these and other counties were hired in largest numbers in Richmond—fully 5,000 annually for work in or near this city. With eighteen hiring agents located there in 1860, Richmond ranked as a great market for the hiring as well as for the selling of slaves.[12]

The extent of slave hiring in cities may be examined fur-

Order Books. Some counties and cities use the term "Minute Book"; others use "Order Book."

[11] Richmond *Daily Dispatch*, Jan. 3, 1853; Richmond *Enquirer*, Dec. 28, 1854; Bancroft, *Slave Trading*, p. 404; Olmsted, *Cotton Kingdom*, 1: 50.

[12] Bancroft, *Slave Trading*, pp. 150-151, 404. It is significant that, according to Bancroft's estimate, the larger part of the slave hiring in the South was done in the state of Virginia.

ther by reference to the census enumeration of the urban slave population. In 1860 Petersburg had 5,680 slaves and Richmond 11,699. Petersburg's number embraced about 3,157 taxable slaves, those beyond the age of twelve.[13] Of this number of taxable slaves, 737, or nearly one-fourth, were employed by tobacco factories, railroads, and other enterprises. Three hundred and forty-five slaves were held by two railroads alone, probably not owned by the railroads, but hired from the surplus number owned by farmers in the country. Besides the slaves hired by factories, there were many rural slaves hired for work in private homes, and another large group of slaves hired as mechanics. Hiring in all of its phases furnished a favorable opportunity for the bondman to pass from slavery to freedom.

The hiring out of slaves in towns by rural owners is illustrated in the papers of particular individuals. Dr. B. H. Walker of King and Queen County furnishes one example. For several years around 1860 at Christmas time this man attended the annual slave hiring and selling at Stevensville in King and Queen County. On these occasions he hired out some of his slaves to persons in the country, and also one by the name of Edmund to agents in Richmond. His record of Edmund is: "I've sent him as usual to Richmond." Walker's agent reported to him on one occasion that one William Jenkins in Richmond hired Edmund for $140 a year, payable quarterly. Ben, another slave of Dr. Walker's, was sent to Petersburg under the care of an agent there.[14]

Elijah Craghall of Goochland County hired out a slave by the name of Beverly to Robert Francis in Richmond. That Francis found Beverly useful is indicated in a passage from a letter he wrote to Craghall:

Sir: You will let me know how long I can keep him Beverly— he is a good boy & I would like to keep him for five years & I will

---

[13] Personal Property, Petersburg, 1860.
[14] Virginia State Library, Diary of Dr. B. H. Walker (ms.), King and Queen County, Jan. 1, 1859; Jan. 1, 1861.

learn him to read and write & all the barber trade & I will make him a good man—if you ever call down to Richmond come to see me.¹⁵

Among the many other persons who hired out their slaves in one of the Virginia cities were Edmund Allen and John B. Ailsworth of Accomac County. In 1860 these partners in business hired out twenty or more of their bondmen in Richmond to thirteen different persons.¹⁶

One of the main employers of hired slaves in Richmond was the Tredegar Iron Works. In 1846 this establishment under the management of Joseph R. Anderson held forty taxable slaves, most of whom were hired. This iron master always followed the practice of hiring more slaves than he purchased. Because of good treatment the slaves were eager to work at the Tredegar mills. They came to Anderson in Richmond from various points in the state.¹⁷

The employment of slaves by persons other than their owners was complemented by the practice of slaves employing themselves, or self-hire. Phillips explains that the system of self-hire arose because some kinds of work, such as operating a blacksmith or cobbler shop, did not lend themselves to supervision, while there were certain other tasks involving limited, temporary employment which necessitated a modification in the slave system. Unless the slave system was altered to absorb such opportunities, free Negroes and whites would monopolize these tasks. As time passed, the practice of hir-

---

[15] Photostat copy in the possession of James Browning, Miner Teachers College, Washington, D. C. The original is in the possession of Mrs. Mamie Allen of Cardwell, Va. It is significant that despite the law to the contrary this hirer of Beverly speaks of teaching him to read and write.

[16] City Hall, Richmond, Deed Book 75A, p. 185.

[17] Personal Property, Richmond, 1846; Bruce, *Virginia Iron Manufacture*, pp. 242–245. Slave hiring assumed such proportions in Virginia that the system required the services of brokers. The practice is revealed by numerous advertisements in the newspapers of the day. One of these dealers, for example, announced to the public: "I have for hire the ensuing year, many slaves of both sexes, among them two good blacksmiths, two good cooks, house servants, field and factory hands." Petersburg *Daily Express*, Jan. 8, 1856.

ing slave carpenters, blacksmiths, barbers, and draymen to themselves grew in Virginia and in the South, despite the fact that all the states had laws against such liberal treatment of slaves. The significance of such a system, from the point of view of this study, is that self-hire was primarily an urban practice which frequently led to self-purchase and which encouraged some slaves to work with zest and save as much as possible in order to buy their freedom. In the larger sense this practice was made possible because town industry led to a modification of slavery.[18]

Both forms of slave hiring produced a situation which gave such slaves all the appearance of free men. Under self-hire the slave often operated a shop, made his own bargains, and received wages.[19] In like manner the slave hired to someone else frequently enjoyed privileges unknown in a system of bondage under his own master. In the factories of Richmond and Petersburg, for example, hired slaves worked under a task system whereby they were paid wages for all work done beyond the task assigned. In the towns they frequently found their own places of board and lodging, worked at odd jobs at night, gave suppers, and looked out for themselves in other ways.[20] Such was the condition of thousands of slaves in Virginia.

The wages earned by hired slaves had, of course, an important bearing on their ultimate attainment of freedom. Wages were relatively high in the fifties, higher even, in some cases, than the amounts paid Negroes immediately after the entire race had been freed. For example, a large group of

[18] Phillips, *American Negro Slavery*, pp. 339, 411, 413, 414; Bancroft *Slave Trading*, pp. 162, 163; Guild, *Black Laws of Virginia*, p. 70; R. Q. Mallard, *Plantation Life before Emancipation*, p. 48; *Atlantic Monthly*, 57:27 (Jan., 1886).

[19] One of the finest examples of a slave under self-hire managing his own affairs is that of Albert Brooks, the keeper of a livery stable in Richmond. Brooks was first hired by his master to a Presbyterian minister; later he persuaded his master to allow him to hire himself. Self-hire in the livery business enabled Brooks to accumulate a sum sufficient to purchase his wife and three young children. City Hall, Richmond, Deed Book 78A.

[20] *Southern Planter*, 12:377 (1852).

Richmond and Manchester tobacco factory hands petitioned their employers for higher wages in September, 1865, and showed that although as free men they then earned less than $5 a week, they had earned much more money in 1858 and 1859 as slaves, under a liberal task system.[21] According to one observer the amount paid to slaves for extra work in these years was greater than that paid as hire to their owners.[22]

These favorable conditions sometimes led to insubordination among the slaves. There are instances of slaves refusing to be hired to persons they did not like, or putting certain restrictions on their prospective employers independent of those made between the owner and the hirer. The following interview related by an observer illustrates the tendency of the times. One Judge Scott of Richmond inquired of a slave, "Are you for hire?" "I am, sir; what is your name?" asked the slave. "John Scott," said the Judge. "Very well," rejoined the black, "I'll enquire into your character, and if I like it, I'll come and live with you." It is evident that the excessive demand for slaves in the fifties enabled the prospective hired workers to exercise a voice in the terms of their hire.[23]

The tobacco factory slaves especially had considerable freedom of movement, a freedom that gave much concern to some observers, at what appeared to be a weakening of the slave system. An editorial in a Petersburg newspaper protesting the new condition is typical of many others. The editor asserted that slaves in Petersburg were losing their sense of deference and that the cause of this was the supine indifference of owners of slave property. According to this complainant, the code of Virginia on slaves, free Negroes, and mulattoes had broken down. This editor charged that,

[21] Trowbridge, *The South*, p. 230.
[22] Robert Ryland, in *The First Century of the First Baptist Church in Richmond*, p. 271. This writer, a white man, could speak with authority since he had been the successful pastor of a Negro Baptist church in Richmond with a membership in 1860 of 3,260 slaves and free Negroes.
[23] Robert Russell, *North America, its Agriculture and Climate*, 151; *Southern Planter*, 12:377 (1852); 13:23 (1853).

in defiance of this code, numerous slaves hired their own time, set up business on their own account, received the profits of their own labor, and, in short, did everything that white men could do. He said that some slaves even owned real estate with the legal title resting in some white person and furthermore that such property had been bought with money raised by the slave. The writer deplored this situation and warned that if the South intended to retain its peculiar institution, "all such approaches by the blacks to the condition of the whites must be abolished." [24]

Slave hiring and the freedom of movement which grew out of it thus stimulated the manumission of slaves in cities. An increasing ability to earn made it possible for an increasing number to secure their freedom. The place for this activity was the industrial city, the kind of city Virginia was developing in the generation preceding the Civil War. Manumission took place because, as one student of this subject notes, slavery and industrialism have always been incompatible.[25]

If the forces discussed were not sufficient in themselves to promote manumission, the presence of many free Negroes in cities aided their action. They too flocked to the cities and they too were employed. There was every opportunity, then, for one class to help the other. Free Negroes could be of great assistance in the promotion of the freedom of their slave kindred. The two classes intermingled and intermarried on such a scale that the union of a free Negro woman with a slave husband, or a slave woman with a free husband, was a common occurrence.[26] Such a union frequently led to freedom for the slave partner.

The subject of manumission always provokes a number of

[24] Petersburg *Daily Express*, May 13, 1852.
[25] Wesley, *Negro Labor*, pp. 21-22.
[26] The wide gulf that separated free Negroes and slaves in Charleston, S. C. appears not to have existed in urban Virginia. Because of the separation of these two classes during slavery, Charleston for many years after emancipation had a triangular race problem. Social distinction between free Negroes and slaves was even less in the cities of Virginia than in the rural areas.

questions. One vital question is whether the slave or the owner took the initiative in promoting the act. As has been noted, during the liberal period of the American Revolution the penitent owner, proclaiming that slavery was "contrary to God," "contrary to reason," or "contrary to the rights of man," took the initiative; the slave was merely a passive recipient of the freedom granted him.[27] Fifty years after the Revolution, however, in urban Virginia, the process seems to have been reversed. Whereas the manumissions of the early period were frequently based on moral or philosophical grounds, those of the later period often were made "in consideration of five hundred dollars," or some other money payment. It is clear that in this latter type of manumission the Negro sought his own freedom.

There are several indications that Negroes promoted their own freedom during the period from 1830 to 1860.[28] One of these is the rise in the price of slaves. This presumably made it unlikely that a slaveholder, except in the case of blood ties, would free his slaves as a gift. But if an industrious slave could pay the high price, the slaveholder would free him willingly. Because of less favorable circumstances, rural slaves might not be able to purchase their own freedom, but city slaves, under the favorable conditions previously described, could do so. Some of them found no great difficulties in meeting the price set on them; some, like Burwell Mann of Richmond, struggled for years and obtained their freedom only after a series of bitter disappointments; still others never received their freedom.[29]

[27] Cf. Clerk's Office, Sussex County, Deed Book F, pp. 148, 152, 172, 341.

[28] One exception is to be found in the manumission of mulatto slaves by their white parents or relatives. Among the 225 acts of manumission in Richmond, thirty-eight were possibly influenced by kinship. The thirty-eight slaves involved are described as "very light," "bright mulatto," or "bright mulatto with straight black hair." The deeds in the court records rarely indicate openly a blood relationship with the white race, but in view of the miscegenation that took place during the slavery period, the investigator is led to believe that many of these manumissions were motivated by blood ties.

[29] Burwell Mann was a mechanic and factory hand who sought to go to Liberia as a missionary. His chief difficulties were that his owner demanded

Another indication which points to manumission by some kind of purchase is the infrequent occurrence, in cities, of manumission by last will and testament. Throughout the history of slaveholding in the United States there were always some masters who felt that slavery was wrong. Such persons often soothed their consciences by providing by will for the freedom of their slaves. Russell asserts that for the state at large, manumission by will was more common than manumission by deed. In the cities of Virginia, however, manumission by will was rare. Among the 225 acts of manumission executed in Richmond from 1830 to 1860, only nineteen were by this method. In Petersburg a still smaller proportion, only about five among the 161 manumissions during this same period, were by last will and testament. Freedom by will was a pure gift; freedom by deed frequently involved a commercial transaction.[30]

Slaves undertook to free themselves through one of three methods: by direct bargaining with their individual owners, by bargaining with owners through the agency of a free Negro relative or friend, and by bargaining with owners through the agency of a white person. The second and third methods were frequently accomplished by the agent's acquiring temporary ownership of the slave through the money which the slave in question furnished him. But in many cases where the temporary owner was a free Negro relative, this person, rather than the slave, appears to have advanced the money.

The way in which slaves obtained their freedom by direct bargaining with their individual owners is well illustrated in

---

a very high price for his freedom and that several white Methodist ministers and church bodies who promised him financial aid failed to carry out their promises. Through his own savings and the assistance of white Baptists he finally accumulated the sum demanded by his owner. Carter G. Woodson, ed., *The Mind of the Negro as Reflected in Letters Written during the Crisis, 1800–1860*, pp. 15–47.

[30] John H. Russell, *Free Negro*, p. 84; Clerk's Office, Petersburg, Deed Book 13, p. 198; 14, p. 459; 15, p. 289; 18, p. 145.

the case of Hubbard Winn of Petersburg. G. G. Johnson, the owner of this slave, said of him:

> In consideration of the good conduct, industry, and fidelity of my man slave called Hubbard Winn, and in consideration of the fact that by industry and economy he hath paid me out of his extra earnings the full amount of the purchase money which I paid for him [I manumit] and forever set free . . . my said slave Hubbard Winn.[31]

The following table gives a partial list of slaves in Richmond, Petersburg, and Fredericksburg who, during the period under discussion, purchased themselves through direct bargaining with their individual owners.

TABLE XIII

Slaves Who Purchased Themselves

RICHMOND

Slave or Slaves	Master or Mistress	Purchase Price	Year	Reference Deed Book	Page
Richard Binns	Edward Marshall	$300	1833	32	401
John Buckner	Lewis Whiting	100	1835	34	40
Catherine	William Allen	300	1836	43	250
Sally Smith	Joseph Adkins	150	1837	38	56
Armistead Hamilton	Benjamin Belt	600	1840	41	229
Richard C. Hobson	Nicholas Mills	100	1841	43	158
Edloe Baker and wife and child	Curtis Carter	371	1845	49	318
Henry Walker	Cornelius Crews	700	1847	51	513
Collier Harris	Nicholas Mills	600	1848	53	412
David Robinson and wife Sarah	William Allison	700	1849	56	480
Robert Gordon	Alexander Duval	450	1848	54	20
Daniel Wight	Thomas Sampson	500	1848	55	146
Archie Burrel	William B. Standard	100	1850	59	97
Burwell Mann	John Cosby	500	1850	57	243
Jacob Smith	Joshua Fry	500	1850	57	146
Cornelius Turner	Sarah Munford	750	1851	59	573
Jefferson Rogers	Robert Edmund	630	1851	60	260
Thomas Sidney	R. C. Gawthney	300	1851	60	195
Frances Quivers & five children	John F. Tanner	750	1852	63	126
Mortimer Robinson	Archer Cheatham	800	1853	64	85
Walker Lewis	Jane Nicholas	510	1854	67A	319

[31] Clerk's Office, Petersburg, Deed Book 18, p. 481 (1851).

ACQUIRING FREEDOM IN THE CITY

RICHMOND (continued)

Slave or Slaves	Master or Mistress	Purchase Price	Year	Reference Deed Book	Page
Charlotte and two children	Benjamin Totty	850	1855	70B	566
William Dandridge and wife	Joseph Courtney	837	1857	71A	491
Franky and two children	Jane McKenzie	300	1857	71B	551
William Brown and wife	John B. Crenshaw	900	1858	73B	436
Jefferson Page	Charles Thompson	370	1858	73B	246
Lizzie	Louis Finney	250	1861	78B	360
Richard Thompson	Winston Jones	850	1861	76B	316
Lucy Brooks and 3 children, Robert, Alberta and Lucy	Daniel Vongroning	800	1862	78A	394

PETERSBURG

Slave or Slaves	Master or Mistress	Purchase Price	Year	Reference Deed Book	Page
James Bolling	John E. Mead	750	1838	10	
Coy Quivers	Abby Nelson	560	1848	16	688
Hubbard Wynn	G. G. Johnson	?	1851	18	481
Eliza Thornton & her 3 children	John Donnan	700	1852	19	409
Armistead Wilson	John F. May	800	1856	22	656
Doctor Walker	Ann Gill	500	1857	23	590
George Parker	Parmelia K. Briton	800	1858	25	251
Vine Robertson	James McD. Anderson	150	1860	26	29

FREDERICKSBURG

Slave or Slaves	Master or Mistress	Purchase Price	Year	Reference Deed Book	Page
Patsy Garnett	Edward C. McGuire	200	1831	J	12
Levi Barnes	Richard I. Walker	500	1833	J	356
Arthur Jackson	Alexander Phillips	700	1842	M	307
Henry Hunter	Eliza French	600		S	440

More slaves gained their freedom by bargaining through agents, who acquired temporary ownership of them, than by the direct method just indicated. Thus it appears that though many original owners of slaves might refuse to free them directly, they apparently had no objection to having freedom conferred upon their slaves by another individual.[32]

[32] It is significant that frequently the same individuals acquired temporary ownership of slaves to be emancipated. Members of the May family, a white family in Petersburg, often served as temporary owners. Thus they assisted fifteen or twenty slaves on their journey to freedom. Clerk's Office, Petersburg, Deed Book 10, p. 540; 11, p. 130; 13, p. 346; 16, p. 637; 18, p. 15; 19, p. 502; 22, p. 107; 24, p. 499.

Some of the deeds of manumission openly state that the way to freedom was cleared by a temporary owner; others imply this method. An open statement is made in the deed of emancipation of Jones Mitchell, a slave in Petersburg:

> Whereas I, Armistead Harwell [free Negro] of the county of Prince George did in the year 1843 purchase from William W. Wynn, a Negro man named Jones Mitchell, with money furnished for that purpose by the said Jones, and upon agreement with said Negro to emancipate him, Now therefore in pursuance of said agreement, I Armistead Harwell do hereby manumit and set absolutely free the said Negro man slave by name Jones Mitchell, as witness my hand and seal this 26th day of September 1846.[33]

Unlike Jones Mitchell, some slaves did not advance the money in the first instance. For example, Charles Herndon of Fredericksburg purchased the slave Thomas Gibbs from Reuben T. Thom and after Gibbs repaid the purchase price, granted Gibbs a deed of manumission. In this same way James B. Sublett of Richmond had bought William Marshall with the understanding that when Sublett was reimbursed, Marshall should be set free. Marshall apparently fulfilled this condition, for he later received his freedom.[34]

Some slaves passed out of the possession of the second or temporary owner immediately, by emancipation on the same day on which the purchase was made. James May, a white man, the temporary owner of Tom Bolling of Petersburg, in a deed of manumission said: "I set free my Negro man slave Tom . . . sold and delivered to me this day by George W. Bolling" (April 29, 1843). On this same day May had paid Bolling $375 for this slave. In a similar manner William A. Anderson manumitted Leander Slaughter of Petersburg "sold and delivered to me by Robert B. Bolling, [this day]

---

[33] *Ibid.*, 16, p. 21.
[34] Clerk's Office, Fredericksburg, Deed Book S, p. 384; City Hall, Richmond, Deed Book 41, p. 107.

April 30, 1846." [35] It is unreasonable to assume that in such cases the owners conferred freedom on their slaves as a gift after having just paid a large sum of money for them. In all probability Tom Bolling and Leander Slaughter paid the money themselves, either before or after the date of their manumission. Furthermore, as this discussion will later show, both of these men were persons of thrift who could buy themselves. This type of manumission was important, for in all three of the cities under consideration there were more deeds of manumission which made no statement about money advanced by a Negro than there were deeds that openly stated that the slave was purchasing himself.

The service of free Negroes in buying slaves and acting as intermediaries to freedom is significant in that the number of such cases exceeds those in which slaves purchased themselves directly. Free Negroes purchased their wives, husbands, other relatives, and friends for the express purpose of setting them free. Such efforts are well illustrated by the following Petersburg cases. Liddy Bailey, a free woman, gave freedom to "the Negro man Godfrey Goodwyn who was," said she, "sold and delivered to me by Peterson Goodwyn." Samuel V. Brown liberated his wife by saying "[I] set free my wife, Alice Brown, a woman purchased by me from Mary Ann Vizzoneau." Winnifred Bonner on February 17, 1852 gave freedom to her "Negro man slave Samuel Wilkins" whom she had bought from Thomas A. Green six months before for $600. Letty Campbell, a free woman of color, acted under similar conditions:

> In consideration of the natural love and affection which I have for my husband James Campbell who was purchased by me from G. A. Farley as appears by his bill of sale dated the 22nd day of February 1860 . . . I do . . . set free my said slave James Campbell hereby discharging him from all obligation to service and investing him with all the rights and privileges of a free person of color as far as it is in my power to do.

[35] Clerk's Office, Petersburg, Deed Book 13, p. 346; 15, p. 491.

Jesse Green, a "free man of color," set free his wife Aggy Green and her four children, all of whom he had just purchased for $665.[36]

In Richmond likewise free Negroes gave freedom to members of their own race. In the following list of some individuals of Richmond who liberated their slave relatives and others, the "grantor" is the free Negro liberator; the "grantee" is the person who received freedom. It is to be noted from the column headed "remarks" that nearly all of the persons receiving their freedom had been purchased previously by the grantor.[37]

TABLE XIV

Manumission of Slave Relatives by Free Negroes of Richmond

Grantor	Grantee	Relationship to Grantor	Date	Reference Deed Book	Page	Remarks
Reuben Morton	Clara & 4 children	Wife and children	1830	29	609	Purchased for the express purpose of liberating them.
Charlotte Smith	Jane Mercer	Granddaughter	1833	32	194	Purchased previously.
Isaac Reynolds	Isaac Reynolds	Son	1831	35	273	Had previously purchased his wife also.
Hope Butler	Maria	Daughter	1833	44	199	Purchased in 1830.
John Elson	Clemenza & Lloyd	Grandchildren	1839	40	351	Purchased from M. W. Bracket.
Harrison Swann	Maria	Wife	1840	41	411	Purchased from Colonel S. Myers.
William Marshall	Frances	Wife	1841	48	17	Purchased 1840 from John Brockenbrough.
John Logan	Maria & 4 children	Wife and children	1841	42	520	

[36] *Ibid.*, 10, pp. 52, 419; 18, p. 201; 19, p. 200; 25, p. 538.
[37] All of these grantors except Isaac Reynolds are found in the court records of Richmond at the City Hall. Like many other Richmond deeds, Reynolds' is found in the Henrico County clerk's office.

TABLE XIV (*continued*)

Grantor	Grantee	Relationship to Grantor	Date	Deed Book	Page	Remarks
Samuel Anderson	Nathan	Son	1842	44	457	Purchased 1833 for $475.00.
Richard C. Hobson	Martha Ann and child	Wife and son	1850	58	244	
Michael Brooks	Amy	Wife	1850	57	439	
William Marshall	Maria	Daughter	1851	60	641	Purchased 1849 from John Brockenbrough.
John Hopes	Walter Hopes	Son	1853	63	447	Purchased 1848 from Dr. James D. McCaw.
Maria James	Joseph Anderson	Husband	1854	67B	143	Purchased from Hiram W. Tyler.
James Johnson	Mary Cooley	Mother	1855	69B	16	Purchased from Thomas Roberts.
John Norman	Sarah and child	Wife and son	1856	70B	405	Purchased from Mrs. Mary Muse.
John Hopes	Minerva	Granddaughter	1856	70A	561	Purchased 1837 from Mary Weidsinger.
Caiberry Burton	Caiberry & Robert	Sons	1857	71A	441	Bought originally by a white man; Burton refunded the payment by working for him.
Henry Matthews	Catherine and two children	Wife and children	1859	74A	125	Purchased 1856 from John Gammel, "my wife and children."

Two of the free Negroes enumerated in this list, William Marshall and John Logan, were more than once responsible for the freeing of others. William Marshall first bought his wife in 1840 and liberated her in 1841. Ten years later he freed his daughter, whom he had recently purchased. John Logan in an interval of two years bought and liberated one daughter and then his wife and four other children. Logan's deed of emancipation in this second instance is worth quoting in full:

I, John Logan, a free man of color of the city of Richmond being now the lawful owner of Maria who I have for many years had as my wife and owning also my four children born of the said Maria to wit: Mary Ann, Virginia, John and Sarah Frances and being desirous of emancipating my said wife and children: Now therefore in consideration of the natural love and affection that I bear them I do hereby emancipate and forever set free said Maria Logan, Mary Ann Logan, Virginia Logan, John Logan, and Sarah Frances Logan and do by these presents declare them free and forever emancipated from all servitude and bondage whatever. In witness whereof I do hereby set my hand and seal this 16th day of July, A. D. 1841.[38]

This type of action was common in all of the cities and towns of Virginia. In Fredericksburg the free Negro men Anthony Bascoe, William Gibbs, William Gordon, and Fred Dawson bought their wives and liberated them; on the other hand, Jesse Miller, Betty and William Morton, Elizabeth Scott, Sarah and John Wilkins, and Colin Williams were bought and liberated by their respective fathers.[39] Carter Armistead was bought by his wife. Unlike these others, Charles Lewis of Fredericksburg obtained his own freedom by paying $410 to the free Negro James Wilkins, who had previously paid this same amount to Lewis' master.[40] Some of these purchases were costly. Peter Morton, for instance, paid the sum of $1,000 for his children, Betty and William.

It is clear that free Negroes bought slaves outright because of blood relationship or because they wished to assist

---

[38] City Hall, Richmond, Deed Book 42, p. 520.
[39] Clerk's Office, Fredericksburg, Deed Book J, pp. 83, 227; K, pp. 74, 277; N, pp. 299, 340; O, pp. 37, 491; S, p. 402; T, p. 210.
[40] *Ibid.*, I, p. 122; N, p. 300.

members of their race even if there was no blood kinship. Thus, even more than white persons, free Negroes stood as intermediaries for slaves in their journey from slavery to freedom. Certain free Negroes are celebrated for the number of times they engaged in this undertaking. On seven occasions altogether Jane Minor of Petersburg granted freedom to a total of nineteen persons. In one instance she liberated a mother and five children on the same day on which she purchased them for $1,500. On another occasion she set free a woman for whom she had recently paid $600. In another instance, however, she had owned one Mary Jane Swann for "some years since," before freeing her. In one other case she merely indicates the manumission of five slaves without showing how long she had owned them. It is probable that in some of these cases the money that Jane Minor paid for the slaves was advanced by the slaves to be liberated. Slave owners perhaps used this woman as a convenient channel for the liberation of slaves whom they did not care to set free themselves. The high regard in which Jane Minor was held by the people of the town as a nurse would support this interpretation.[41]

Any discussion of the activities of free Negroes always raises the question of the law of Virginia on that subject. In a previous chapter it has been shown that the code of Virginia hedged the free Negro with numerous restrictions. Foremost among these limitations were the laws against a further increase of the whole group of free Negroes, and the efforts made by the state and by private organizations to remove this group altogether. The famous law compelling all slaves above the age of twenty-one to leave the state within twelve months after emancipation remained on the statute books from its passage in 1806 until 1865. This

[41] Clerk's Office, Petersburg, Deed Book 10, p. 438; 11, p. 517, 518; 12, p. 200; 13, p. 57; 16, p. 206. Jane Minor, a mulatto woman, was once a slave herself. Her master in 1825 liberated her for her "most unexampled patience and attention in watching over the sick beds of several individuals of this town" in the preceding year. *Ibid.*, 7, p. 267.

measure was so well known throughout the commonwealth that every act of manumission involved the problem of either moving from Virginia in compliance with the law or getting special permission to remain.

What, then, became of the thousand or more Negroes who received their freedom in Virginia cities after 1830 when public utterances and state and local laws condemned them as a class? A mere reading of the laws and the speeches of public officials would convey the impression that the freedmen were forced to leave Virginia. One might also get the impression, from the acts of manumission performed in the state at large for the express purpose of sending manumitted slaves to Liberia, that this city group of Negroes sought freedom because of their desire to escape from the land of slavery. On the contrary, the records of the 622 Negroes manumitted in Richmond and Petersburg show that the vast majority of them applied for permission to remain in Virginia; that the local courts granted such permission; and that their desire in winning freedom was not to risk an uncertain future in distant lands, but to stay in their native cities, buy property, and generally improve their status.

These manumitted Negroes, one after another, placed themselves at the mercy of the local justices. In Petersburg, Alice, the wife of Samuel V. Brown, bought by him in 1831 and manumitted on November 1, 1838, applied in the following month for permission to remain. About three weeks later her petition was granted. Ten months after this event the local justices granted permission for the daughter, also liberated by Samuel V. Brown, to remain.[42] During the 1850 and 1851 sessions of the Petersburg court, many applications for permission to remain in Virginia were made. Upon application the twenty-four slaves freed by the will of James Dunlop were allowed to remain at the February session of

---

[42] Clerk's Office, Petersburg, Minute Book (ms.), 1838–1840, p. 5. Among other Negroes given permission to remain, at this same session of the court, was Winney Eppes, who had been owned and liberated by another Negro, Jamima Coleman.

1851; and six in November.⁴³ For some reason the Dunlop slaves were at first refused permission, but this action was rescinded three months later.

In seeking permission to remain, many of the manumitted Negroes probably followed the method of Jane Green. This woman had once been a slave in a Petersburg family by the name of Finn. In the year 1854, or some time before, Jane Green became the slave of a free Negro, John Updike, through money which either he or she advanced. In November the Negro master liberated his slave; in the following January she was duly registered as a free person by the clerk of the Hustings Court. But notwithstanding, her registration certificate carries this stipulation: "No permission has been granted her to remain in the commonwealth by the said court." Realizing her precarious position, Jane Green at this time had already begun to secure written testimonials from her former white owner and friends. One of these persons said: "The bearer of this paper, Jane, was . . . owned by my husband and lived with us about four years. During this time, and since as far as I know, she has comported herself well and has earned our good opinion as well as that of many friends." Twelve persons wrote: "I concur with [this testimony]." Still another asserted: "I have known Jane for 7 or 8 years and have always believed her to be a woman of good character and industrious habits." On the strength of these statements Jane Green was permitted to reside in Petersburg.⁴⁴

Richmond was outstanding for the number of its free Negroes permitted to stay in the commonwealth. Two classes

---

⁴³ *Ibid.*, 1848–1851, p. 352; 1851–1853, pp. 7, 51, 94.

⁴⁴ Manuscripts in possession of the writer. The Petersburg slaves who bought their freedom by direct bargaining constituted another group who fell under special dispensation. Among those listed in Table XIII, James Bolling, Coy Quivers, Hubbard Wynn, Eliza Thornton and her children, Armistead Wilson, and Doctor Walker were given permission to remain in the state. George Parker, one of the group, did not seek such permission, inasmuch as his intention was to go to Liberia. He went about Petersburg seeking funds for this purpose. *Daily Express*, Oct. 6, 1859.

of free Negroes were affected, those who incurred court action because they had continued to live in the state more than a year after manumission, and those who had forestalled such action by asking permission to stay, at some time prior to the lapse of the twelve months' period. Action concerning persons in the former group was sometimes taken after a number of cases had accumulated. Facing such a number, the court might allow all the offenders to remain in Virginia through the simple entry of *nolle prosequi*. Such, at least, was the disposition made in the cases of forty-three Negroes in the year 1834. Seven years later the commonwealth attorney with the advice of the court likewise entered *nolle prosequi* in the indictments of twelve others who had remained contrary to law.[45]

For more than fifty years, free Negroes sought permission to remain in Virginia. In the early period the effort was directed to the state legislature; in the later period it was transferred to the local units of government. In the cities the movement was pronounced, especially during the decade of 1850. Thus at the very moment when the laws of Virginia against free Negroes were increasing in number and severity, this other action which nullified all such measures was silently taking place. The number of free Negroes granted permission to remain in Virginia continued especially large in Richmond. Such permission was granted to at least fifteen applicants in 1856, twelve in 1857, thirteen in 1858, and twenty-seven in 1859.[46] In most cases the application was made within a year after manumission; in others it was delayed ten or more years. For example, Nancy Willis was

---

[45] City Hall, Richmond, Minute Book 11, pp. 565, 567; 14, p. 354.

[46] *Ibid.*, 22–27. The law of Virginia on the right of manumitted Negroes to remain in the state was changed several times. Petitions to the legislature for this privilege became so numerous as to constitute a burden. At least twice the state lawmakers authorized the local courts to take jurisdiction on the many applications. These local bodies were empowered to grant favorable decisions "on satisfactory proof that the person is of good character, peaceable, orderly, and industrious." Guild, *Black Laws of Virginia*, pp. 111, 118, citing the acts of 1837 and 1850.

manumitted in 1847 but did not receive permission to remain in the state until 1859.

All the free persons allowed to stay in Virginia were given this privilege on similar grounds—that they were persons of "good character, sober, peaceable, orderly, and industrious." In some cases the permission was granted for the further reason that the Negro in question was "not addicted to drunkenness, gaming, or any other vice." Although these records follow the verbiage of the original state law, the word that should be stressed is "industrious." An examination of the forces behind the frequent granting of privilege to remain in the Virginia cities, shows the influence of the economic revival, which made the labor of free Negroes necessary and valuable. Although the movement for manumission was slight in rural, agricultural Virginia, the labor of the free Negro in this region also was found indispensable. Here, too, arose able defenders of the right and the necessity of the free blacks to continue residence in the state.

Free Negro applications to remain were seldom refused. Perhaps not more than one in twenty was so treated in urban Virginia toward the close of the period under consideration. In some instances a rejection was later followed by permission to stay. For example, the application of Thomas Braxton of Richmond was rejected on August 16, 1855, but on February 14, 1857, after reconsideration, he was allowed to remain.[47] The Richmond cases were carried through, however, with one justice, Joseph Mayo, frequently dissenting. This man, the mayor of the city, cast his vote in opposition, on the ground that by the constitution of the state "the court have no right to grant said applications." [48]

Leniency similar to that shown to manumitted slaves was also shown toward the illegal practice which frequently led to manumission, namely, self-hire. During the decade of 1820

---

[47] City Hall, Richmond, Minute Book 22, p. 154. Some of the cases of rejection led to appeals to the legislature.
[48] *Ibid.*, 25, p. 424.

slave owners in Petersburg were frequently prosecuted for this practice, and such action was common in Richmond until as late as 1844; but in both places after this time such prosecutions rarely occurred.[49]

Not only did liberated Negroes continue to live in Virginia, but many of them also became property holders. Some of the privileged persons passed through the stages, first, of buying themselves, second, of buying members of their family, and, third, of buying real estate. Others traveled similar arduous routes that ended with property holding.

Several cases showing this progress from slavery to property ownership may be cited from Petersburg. Jesse Green, a slave, passed into the temporary possession of Robert Holloway, a freedman, who liberated Green in 1850. Eleven days after Green received his freedom from Holloway he purchased his wife and four children for $665, and about a month later he freed them. After spending several years in this process of purchasing and liberating, Green bought a house and lot in Petersburg, which in 1860 was valued at $600.[50] Phil Sewell, a drayman, was freed in January, 1854 by R. A. Martin, "on account of the high regard had for him." Six months later he was granted permission to stay in the state. Sewell, like Green, proceeded at once to purchase and liberate the members of his family. He paid $800 for his daughter alone. Strange to say, this man had bought real estate for $410 in 1852, while he was still a slave, two years before his manumission. In 1860 this property was valued at $1,250.[51] Armistead Wilson, a blacksmith, bought his freedom in 1856 with the borrowed sum of $800. One year later

---

[49] Clerk's Office, Petersburg, Minute Book, 1823–1827, April 16, 1824; *Ibid.*, 1830–1834, p. 363; City Hall, Richmond, Minute Book, 1831–1835, pp. 518, 593, 647; 14 (1840–1842), pp. 504, 524.

[50] Clerk's Office, Petersburg, Deed Book 18, p. 145; 22, p. 198; Land Book, 1860.

[51] Clerk's Office, Petersburg, Minute Book, 1853–1856, p. 103; Deed Book 20, p. 570. In this case a lawyer served as the trustee for Sewell's property until he obtained his freedom and the legal right to own it.

he bought property, valued soon afterwards at $1,500.⁵²
Eleazar White, a slave manumitted in 1850, did not acquire
real estate before 1860, but as a hack driver he soon accumulated valuable personal property. Jane Green, previously
mentioned, purchased a small lot for $100 in 1855, the same
year in which she was liberated by John Updike, the free
Negro boatman.⁵³

Some of the manumitted Negroes of Richmond who were
granted permission to stay in Virginia acquired extensive
property. Gilbert Hunt, a blacksmith manumitted in 1829,
bought in 1844 a house and lot which were valued in 1860 at
$1,376; Fields Cook, manumitted and allowed to remain in
1853, made three purchases of property at a total cost of
$2,430.⁵⁴ William B. Lyon, a barber, manumitted and allowed to stay in 1853, had within six years purchased three
pieces of property, valued in 1860 at $1,420. Ann Maria
Dean, a seamstress, who was manumitted and allowed to remain three years after Lyon, bought a house and lot on Third
Street in 1860 at a cost of $2,500.⁵⁵ Richard C. Hobson, another barber, was emancipated in 1841. Nine years later,
after having purchased his wife and son, he emancipated
them, and all were allowed by the court to remain in Virginia. As in other instances, the purchase of members of the
family was followed by the purchase of real estate. Hobson
made such purchases on two occasions in the 1850 decade.⁵⁶

The progress of these manumitted Negroes of Richmond
and Petersburg was paralleled in the other cities and towns

⁵² Clerk's Office, Petersburg, Land Book, 1860. After returning borrowed
money to his creditor, A. Donnan, Armistead Wilson bought this property
from the same creditor. Deed Book 23, p. 478.
⁵³ Clerk's Office, Petersburg, Deed Book 22, p. 432.
⁵⁴ City Hall, Richmond, Deed Book 49, p. 532; 63, p. 32; 70B, p. 728; Land
Book, 1860. It is interesting to note that Fields Cook, like Phil Sewell of
Petersburg, made his first purchase of property in 1852 while he was still
legally a slave.
⁵⁵ *Ibid.*, 75A, p. 259.
⁵⁶ *Ibid.*, 59, p. 428; 70B, p. 361. In 1870 Hobson also purchased several
lots and a "brick dwelling thereon" at a cost of $3,000. Deed Book, 91A, p. 86.

of the state. In Lynchburg, Jack Carter was emancipated in 1849 and bought property shortly afterwards. In Winchester, Edmund Kean, the livery stable operator, within ten years bought himself, members of his family, and also five or more pieces of real estate. Randle Evans, the confectioner of Winchester, experienced similar progress.[57]

A few urban Negroes, after receiving freedom, preferred to leave Virginia for other parts of the United States, and in some instances these emigrants became very prosperous. Robert Gordon, for instance, while still a slave had been allowed to operate a coal yard in Richmond and to keep for himself all the money received from the sale of slack in this business. After purchasing his manumission, Gordon went to Cincinnati, Ohio, and there operated a coal yard. Despite prejudice and the severe competition of white coal dealers in this place, Gordon managed to accumulate a small fortune in Cincinnati by the purchase of United States bonds during the Civil War and the heavy purchase of real estate later on Walnut Hill.[58]

Emanuel Quivers, one of the many hired slaves at the Tredegar Iron Works in Richmond, persuaded Joseph R. Anderson, the iron master of Tredegar and employer of hired slaves, to purchase him. Quivers' value as a worker is indicated by the fact that Anderson paid $1,100 for him. Once in the hands of his new master, this thrifty slave might become a free man, because Anderson stood ready to promote the advancement of any Negro slave who showed ambition. His opportunity to acquire freedom was improved by the fact that this iron establishment paid money to its hired slaves for extra work. Quivers eventually became a foreman at the Tredegar Iron Works and received a wage of $1.25 a day. After a period of about four years he accumulated enough to buy not only himself, but also his wife and four

---

[57] Clerk's Office, Lynchburg, Deed Book Q, p. 562; Will Book B, p. 344; Petition, Frederick, 1849; Land Books, Frederick, 1850–1860.
[58] Woodson, *The Negro in Our History* (6th ed.), p. 261.

children at the price of $750.21. This freedman went first to the North, for a short time, and afterwards to California as a mechanic to a Virginia adventurer in the gold fields of that State. His son became a foreman in the firm of agricultural manufacturers at Stockton, California.[59] The rise of this Negro family was made possible by Joseph R. Anderson, a man of the benevolent type of Virginia slaveholder.

[59] City Hall, Richmond, Deed Book 63, p. 126; Bruce, *Virginia Iron Manufacture*, pp. 239-242.

CHAPTER VII

PROPERTY IN SLAVES

AS indicated in the preceding chapter, some free Negroes became owners of slaves. In all the cases there cited, however, the slave ownership was temporary and benevolent, with a free Negro merely serving as intermediary for the eventual manumission of his friends or kin. Still other cases to be cited in this chapter show that some free Negroes held slaves as permanent property.

An analysis of free Negro ownership of slaves necessitates the consideration, in particular cases, of the motives of ownership and the method of acquiring ownership. Since slave hiring was so widely practised in Virginia, it is frequently difficult to distinguish whether a given holder was the real owner or merely the hirer of slaves. On the surface it might appear that the individual hiring slaves was the actual owner, inasmuch as he paid the tax on them, when in reality the ownership was vested in another person.[1]

Despite these difficult problems, consideration of this subject is necessary in determining the economic status of free Negroes, because slave ownership represents a form of prop-

[1] The subject of slave ownership was treated by federal census enumerators under the following instructions: "The person in whose family, or on whose plantation, the slave is found to be employed, is to be considered the owner." The principal object of this method was to obtain the total number of slaves in a community and not the number of masters or owners. U. S. Census, 1850, *Instruction to U. S. Marshals.* The same system apparently operated in the enumeration of slaves by Virginia in its taxation of slave property.

The records that treat slave ownership present another difficulty in that the federal statistics give the whole number of slaves, regardless of age, owned by an individual, whereas the state enumeration, or tax list, embraces the slaves of taxable age only: those above the age of twelve. In many instances persons cited as slaveholders by the Virginia records have no such rating under the federal census, and vice versa.

erty ownership and because the expenditures for slaves in some communities rivaled the expenditures for property in houses and lots. Slaves were subject to taxation, and payments in taxes for this kind of property likewise in some cases rivaled the tax payments for other forms of property.[2]

In Petersburg during the year 1827 free Negroes owned property in slaves exceeding in value their property in real estate. At this time sixty-nine free Negro owners held 101 slaves distributed in groups of one, two, three, and five slaves apiece.[3] Against this number of owners of slaves there were only twenty-five free Negro owners of real estate.[4] Assuming that the slaves had an average value of $250 on the market, the total value of this property was slightly in excess of $25,000, whereas the total value of the real estate was only about $17,000. The total tax for the 101 slaves at forty-seven cents each was $47.47; the total tax for the real estate, at eight cents on each hundred dollars of value, was slightly less than half this amount. All told, in the state at large the value of the real estate held by free Negroes in 1830 was less than the value of their slaves. The proportion of slaveholding free Negro families to the non-slaveholding families was relatively high in the cities. The federal enumeration shows that in Petersburg in 1830, among the 503 heads of families, 107, or practically 21 per cent, held slaves; that in Richmond, among the 589 heads of families, 155, or about 26 per cent, held slaves; and that in Norfolk and the other cities the percentage was about the same.[5]

[2] The question whether a slave was a person or property gave Virginians difficulty for a long time. If he was property, did he represent real or personal property? The state finally decided that slaves should be considered as personal property. Guild, *Black Laws of Virginia,* Introduction.

[3] Personal Property, Petersburg, 1827. This number includes only slaves of taxable age.

[4] Clerk's Office, Petersburg, Land Book, 1827.

[5] U. S. Census Bureau, Heads of Families (ms.) 1830; Carter G. Woodson, ed., *Free Negro Owners of Slaves in the United States in 1830.* Woodson's compilation, based on the original census enumeration, was the first work of its kind on this subject. In checking the lists of names of free Negro slave-holders in this volume against the city and county lists of taxable slaves

The number of slaveholding families of free Negroes in rural Virginia fell short of the number in the cities. In no county did the proportion exceed 14 per cent. In 1830 there were no free Negro slaveholders in 30 per cent of the counties. If this statement is limited to families with taxable slaves (those above the age of twelve) the proportion was smaller still. Whether the state or the federal enumeration is accepted, the total number of Negro slaveholders in all rural areas was not more than 50 per cent of the number for the entire state. Expressed otherwise, fully half of all the slaveholding among the free Negroes of Virginia was concentrated in the relatively small urban areas.

There were two types of free Negro slaveholding: benevolent and commercial. That much of the slaveholding was benevolent in purpose is indicated by the fact that most of the free Negro slaveholders in Virginia held one slave only, often a blood relative. Although in some cases purchase led to manumission, in the majority no such end was contemplated because of the legal necessity—at least until about 1840—of sending the manumitted person away from Virginia. Fraternal ownership also was frequently extended to persons outside the family.

and slaveholders in the Virginia personal property books the present writer has found a few serious errors. Many of the largest slaveholders listed in the Virginia section of *Free Negro Owners of Slaves* are not Negroes but white persons. Among these white persons are Joseph Bragg of Amelia County, William Daniel and Thomas A. Morton of Cumberland, William Brockenbrough of Hanover, Philip Haxall and Curtis Carter of the city of Richmond, Benjamin O. Taylor of King George, and Littleton Walker of York County. The number of slaves credited to each individual in this compilation varies from 18 to 71. Free Negroes in Virginia never owned slaves on so large a scale.

The error in racial identification arose from a misinterpretation of the records. The editor says: "In the South where almost all of the Negro slaveholders were . . . we find some of them competing with the large planters in the number of slaves they owned. . . . Sometimes a free Negro had charge of a plantation, but did not own the slaves himself, and the enumerator returned him as the owner." Introduction, p. viii. The truth is that in many instances the planter in charge was a white man and not a free Negro. It may be more correct to say that the white planter was the head of a "family" of slaves and free Negroes (since they were frequently employed together) without any persons of his own family or race living with him.

Slaveholding by free Negroes was chiefly concentrated in cities, for the reason that the city was the common meeting-ground of slaves and freemen, where the distinction between free and slave Negroes was not sharply drawn and where the two classes frequently intermarried.[6] Furthermore it was the place where both free Negroes and slaves had more opportunity to earn money for themselves, because both classes might readily follow their trades in cities, without serious white competition. The slave in this instance was frequently a man hired either to himself or to another individual. The close association of slaves and free Negroes in cities is further shown by the fact that they held membership together in the several large Baptist churches in Richmond, Petersburg, Norfolk, and elsewhere.

The contention that free Negro slave ownership was largely fraternal and involved the purchasing of relatives on this basis may be illustrated by reference to the early experiences of Frank Gowen of Amelia County, Henry Burch of Hanover, Mosby Shepherd of Henrico, and Samuel Johnston of Fauquier. Frank Gowen, after being emancipated by his master, purchased his wife and two children for $500. and held them as slaves permanently. Unlike Gowen, Henry

[6] In some cases slaves who were the property of a white person lived on such satisfactory terms with free Negroes that both parties had to be reminded of their actual legal status. A case in point is that of John H. Suttle of Stafford County, the white owner of the slave wife and children of the free Negro James Johnson. In a deed of loan Suttle made the following arrangement with Johnson:

Whereas a Negro woman named Maria and her children belonging to Mrs. Catherine Suttle have for some years been living with James Johnson the husband of said woman and father of some of said children and a free man of color and may continue to live with him for some time to come— To avoid misunderstanding and to give notice to the world whose property the said woman and children are, it is hereby declared by and between John H. Suttle husband and trustee of the said Catherine Suttle and the said James Johnson that the said woman and children and other children which she may have, shall remain with the said Johnson and in his possession, only during the pleasure of said Catherine Suttle or her said trustee, or her exor's, admn's or assigns. Witness the hands and seals of the parties this 23rd day of Dec. 1843.

Clerk's Office, Stafford County, Deed Book N, p. 268.

Burch purchased his two sons with the intention of holding them as slaves temporarily. Mosby Shepherd, who was emancipated by the legislature of Virginia as a reward for the information he gave concerning the Gabriel insurrection, likewise purchased his son with the intention of holding him as a slave only temporarily. Samuel Johnston bought his own freedom at a high price and then bought his son and daughter, whom he intended to hold as slaves for a limited period of time only.[7]

The benevolent buying and holding of slaves just indicated took place before 1830, but the process continued throughout the period under discussion. Some of the persons who bought their relatives during this period and held them permanently or temporarily as slaves were Stephen Bias of the town of Charlottesville, who purchased himself and held his wife and children as slaves; Arthur Lee of Alleghany, who bought himself for $500 and his wife for $1,250, and held her as a slave; Rica Stephens of Northampton, who successively purchased his daughter Sarah, his daughter Rachel, and finally his wife and another child, all of whom he held temporarily as slaves; and Frank Allen of Richmond County, who bought his wife and two children and held them as slaves until his death.[8]

---

[7] Petitions, Amelia County, Dec. 6, 1806; Hanover, Dec. 20, 1810; Henrico, Dec. 10, 1810; Fauquier, Dec. 16, 1815; Dec. 14, 1820. Other cases of similar nature may be cited. Henry Carter of Charles City County, after emancipation by his master, bought his wife in the hope that she might be allowed to remain in the state with him if he freed her. *Ibid.*, Charles City, Dec. 21, 1815. Lewis Turner of Sussex County bought his wife and held her as a slave during his life but willed her her freedom and 148 acres of land. *Ibid.*, Sussex, Dec. 10, 1818. After many difficulties Charles Cousins of Nottoway bought his wife and held her as a slave; but, like others, he looked forward to liberating her. *Ibid.*, Nottoway, Dec. 20, 1819. Cæsar Hope of Henrico bought his daughter, kept her as a slave during his life, and freed her by his will. *Ibid.*, Henrico, Dec. 21, 1819; Dec. 4, 1821. Simon Parham of Prince George County bought his wife and son and later willed them their freedom and two lots of land. *Ibid.*, Prince George.

[8] *Ibid.*, Albemarle, Dec. 11, 1835; Feb. 14, 1839; Alleghany, Dec. 28, 1835; Northampton, Feb. 15, 1843; Richmond, 1845. Other cases falling in the latter part of the period were those of Henry Smith of Henrico County, who held his wife and child as slaves but in time manumitted them (Clerk's Office.

Though benevolent slaveholding predominated in 1830 and later, there were some free Negroes at the same time whose slaveholding was commercial. Some of it involved permanent possession; much of it merely involved the temporary hiring of slaves. Among the free Negroes in counties and cities in a particular year, then, certain persons can be listed as probably holding slaves purely from the commercial or profit motive. It is to be remembered, however, that any list of slaveholders may include hirers of slaves as well as owners proper. The following table of free Negro slaveholders in counties in 1830 indicates the names of the commercial slaveholders with the number of slaves.[9]

TABLE XV

Free Negro Slaveholders in Counties in 1830

Name	County	Number of Slaves
Turner Pinn	Amherst	4
John Chavis	Charlotte	3
Archibald Batte	Chesterfield	6
Judith Lipscomb	Cumberland	2
Billy Mayo	Cumberland	4
Thomas Berry	Dinwiddie	3
Jesse Norris	Fluvanna	4
John Cousins	Fluvanna	3
John Lynch	Goochland	4
John Pearce	Goochland	10
David Watkins	Greensville	3
Nathaniel Hawkins	Isle of Wight	4
Edward Eppes	Lunenburg	4
Priscilla Ivey	Mecklenburg	5

Henrico, Deed Book 54, p. 5), Lot Higby of Henrico, who manumitted his son, once held as a slave (*Ibid.*, 55, p. 8); Richard Carter of Orange County, who by will manumitted his son Richard, whom he had previously bought and held as a slave (Clerk's Office, Orange, Will Book 12, p. 491); and Peter G. Morgan of Nottoway, who for several years held members of his family as slaves but liberated them after he removed from this county to the city of Petersburg (Clerk's Office, Petersburg, Deed Book 28, p. 125).

[9] Personal Property, 1830.

TABLE XV (continued)

Name	County	Number of Slaves
Fanny Woodford	Middlesex	4
William Woodford	Middlesex	3
David Woodford	Middlesex	4
Michael Pearman	New Kent	5
Edward Sorrel	Northumberland	2
Williams Rolls	Orange	3
Robert Campbell	Orange	3
John Lipscomb	Powhatan	2
Thomas Wright	Warwick	2
Thomas Jarvis	York	3
John Jarvis	York	3
George Morris	York	5

The commercial holding of slaves in cities may be illustrated by conditions in Petersburg. Among the sixty-nine slaveholders of this town in 1827 only about seven—John Booker, Elizabeth Elebeck, John McCrae, Jacob Page, John T. Raymond, Judith Angus, and Charles Lewis, holders of two to five slaves—can be designated as commercial slaveholders. The proportion was about the same in the other cities. Other years during the thirty under discussion would yield a list, for either counties or cities, similar in number to that just given, but with a shifting personnel. In a few instances, however, slave ownership persisted in one family throughout the entire thirty-year period, a fact that strongly suggests ownership for profit. The story of commercial slaveholding by the preceding free Negroes and others is revealed through marriage contracts, deeds of trust, wills, inventories and appraisement of estates, and occasionally deeds of bargain and sale.

Two early marriage contracts indicating the ownership of slaves are those executed by Lydia Thomas and John Booker of Petersburg. Before her marriage to John Stewart, about 1817, Lydia Thomas conveyed her personal estate in trust to other free Negroes. Among the items in this personal estate was one Negro woman slave named Joan.[10] Booker, a blacksmith, on the occasion of his marriage conveyed to certain trustees one house and lot, two other lots, and a slave, J. Lindsay.[11] During the late twenties Booker always held from three to five slaves, some of whom he probably owned, while others he hired. Booker's slaveholding is of particular interest in that he himself had formerly been a slave.

Deeds of trust, executed to pledge security for loans, were relatively common. Two such deeds were drawn in the decade of 1830 by William Rolls of Orange County and George Morris of Yorktown. Rolls, a blacksmith and owner of real estate, on several occasions offered various items of personal property and slaves as security for loans. In 1828, for example, he offered three slaves, Aggy and her two daughters, along with two sets of blacksmith tools, four beds, and other furniture.[12] Six years later Rolls offered the same slave property under like conditions. He was given until January 1, 1834, to pay a certain debt; if it was not paid by that time these slaves were to be sold to the highest bidder at public auction.[13] George Morris, in order to secure the payment of $375 to one Samuel Shield, offered him his slave property: Joe, Milly and her child, and George. Shortly after this transaction, under similar circumstances, he offered his slave Bill as security. Five years later Bill was again offered as security for the payment of $104 to another free Negro, Thomas Jarvis.[14]

[10] Clerk's Office, Petersburg, Deed Book 5, p. 288.
[11] *Ibid.*, 8, p. 188.
[12] Clerk's Office, Orange, Deed Book 32, p. 220.
[13] Clerk's Office, York, Deed Book 34, p. 312.
[14] *Ibid.*, 11, p. 107; 12, p. 216. The pledging of slaves as collateral for free Negroes' debts also occurred earlier than the decade of 1830. In 1808 Edward Eppes, a farmer of Lunenburg County, offered as security for a debt of thirty-two pounds several items of property, including one gray mare, two head of cattle, one feather bed and furniture, and one Negro woman slave named Phillis. Clerk's Office, Lunenburg, Deed Book 21, p. 177. Some time later, in this same county, Nancy Kelly, another farmer, offered to her creditors for her indebtedness of thirty-seven pounds and a bond of $194.30 one Negro

Among the wills made in the decade of 1830 disposing of slave property are those of Archibald Batte of Chesterfield and Anthony Matthews of Henrico. Batte, who owned land in two counties, designated as beneficiaries of his will made in 1830 his wife, son, and daughter-in-law. To his "beloved wife" he gave his lots, houses, furniture, tools, stock of all kinds, and nine Negro slaves; to his son Henry he gave his land in Prince George County and two slaves; to his daughter-in-law he gave two Negroes "to keep them all the days of her present life." In addition to the land and Negroes mentioned above, the son Henry was to inherit, after his mother's death, all the property except a portion allotted to the daughter-in-law.[15] After the testator's death, about 1830, his administrator's account shows that one slave, Arthur, was hired out for $20, and two, Winnie and Jim, were hired out for $18. Matthews owned slaves as members of his family and also one outside this circle. By his will made in 1836 his wife and two sons, whom he had purchased, were given their freedom; and after the payment of all his debts Betty, his wife, inherited the rest of his estate, including the slave Titus "to hold the same for her own use and comfort during her life." [16]

Inventories and appraisals of property bequeathed by will often throw light on property. The Jarvis family of York County was one of the conspicuous property-holding and slaveholding families among the free Negroes of Virginia.

man, Edmund; one woman, Julia; and one girl, Jincy. *Ibid.*, 26, p. 359. William Colson, the barber and Liberia colonizationist, held one slave in his family for at least seven years. In 1827, having borrowed $50 from a free Negro woman, Mary Ann Vizzoneau, he offered to his trustee as security one Negro woman named Rachel and various barber shop fixtures. Clerk's Office, Petersburg, Deed Book 8, p. 86.

[15] Clerk's Office, Chesterfield, Will Book 11.

[16] Clerk's Office, Henrico, Will Book 12, p. 276. Nancy Byrd of Richmond willed to her six children her house and lots and "a Negro slave named Eliza." Clerk's Office, Richmond, Hustings Will Book 8, p. 333. Lewis Turner of Sussex County owned his wife on a fraternal basis and another slave apparently on a commercial basis. Along with his plantation Turner bequeathed to his wife the services of "the boy" James Wright, who was to become free at the age of twenty-one. Clerk's Office, Sussex, Will Book H, pp. 534–537.

In certain years between 1815 and 1830 the slaveholders in this family were Charles with one slave, William with five, Thomas with three, and John with three. Some of these slaves had been inherited through the will of William Jarvis. The elder Jarvis' will, in 1824, gave to his wife, along with $500 and other valuables, one Negro girl named Maria; to his sons Thomas and John respectively a Negro boy named Major and one named Curtis.[17] The inventory and appraisal of Jarvis' estate also lists the following slaves with their valuation: Samuel, $400; George, $150; Dilcy, $125; Joe, $350; Sally, $225; Mishan, $350; Adam, $100; Allen and two children, $350.[18] Another free Negro, Robert Campbell of Orange County, a cooper, accumulated a large personal estate including five slaves. At the time of his death in 1834 these were appraised as follows: Daphine, $100; Philip, $400; William, $400; George, $300; Mary, $250. These slaves were later sold and the proceeds, $2,075, were added to the estate by the administrator. Three of these slaves brought the sum of $848; two others, Philip and William, brought $1,227.[19]

Commercial slaveholding, evidence of which has been cited for the decade of 1830, continued throughout the next two decades until the general emancipation of the race. Again, evidence of this is to be found in legal instruments. Henry Wilkerson, a farmer and the owner of 160 acres of land in Louisa County, twice borrowed funds for his operations. For the first loan, $600, he offered as security one tract of land and one Negro woman, Martha; for the second, along with one yoke of oxen, three cows, and other chattels he pledged the slave Martha again and in addition one boy, Thomas, and "one other Negro boy named William James." [20] The

---

[17] Clerk's Office, York, Will Book 10, p. 503.
[18] *Ibid.*, 11, pp. 44-48.
[19] Clerk's Office, Orange, Will Book 8, p. 58.
[20] Clerk's Office, Louisa, Deed Book C C, p. 272; D D, p. 560. It is barely possible that in some of these cases the slaves offered as security for a loan were members of the grantor's family. If so, the slave ownership in question

will of Virginia Cunningham of Richmond directed that one John D. Quarles should have immediate possession of her woman slave, China, but that her brother should have the first increase of this slave's body.[21] The inventory and appraisal of the estate of William Walker, a shoemaker of Petersburg, shows that he had possessed, besides a personal estate valued at $213, two slaves, Flora and her son Henry, valued at $1600.[22]

That some free Negroes engaged in slaveholding on a commercial or profit basis is further indicated by their practice of hiring their slaves to other masters. Catherine Harris of Richmond, for example, was the actual owner of a slave named Robert, though legal title to him rested in a trustee. In a deed of agreement she requested her trustee to "apply and appropriate the hires, profits, labor and services" of her slave as she directed. She also made provision in this agreement for the possible sale of the slave but stipulated that her trustee should not be empowered to sell Robert without her

---

was still fraternal. The free Negro may have offered such property with no expectation of failing to pay the debt and with confidence that he would not lose the member or members of his family. In the case of Henry Wilkerson, one of his descendants declared to the writer that the Martha in question was Wilkerson's wife, who he had previously bought. Interview with John L. Wilkerson, July 30, 1936.

[21] Clerk's Office, Richmond, Hustings Will Book 20, p. 499. Two other wills of this later period are those of William Pretlow of Surry County and Mildred Pearce of Goochland. Pretlow provided that his wife should inherit all of his estate, real and personal, and that at her death his land should be divided among their children but that his two slaves, Ruffin and Margaret, not members of his family, should be set free. Clerk's Office, Surry, Will Book 8, p. 241. The will of Mildred Pearce provided that her slave Franklin should have his freedom after serving her two daughters Mary and Jane for two years. She further expressed the wish that the county court of Goochland should allow Franklin to remain in Virginia after his manumission. Clerk's Office, Goochland, Deed Book 36, p. 222.

[22] Clerk's Office, Petersburg, Will Book 4, p. 226. Two other free Negroes of this city left slaves whose value was appraised at the time their wills were proved. William Jackson had a total property of $208.25, practically all of which was represented in the sixty-five-year-old slave Mathew. Mary Jackson left a personal estate including one slave Silvia and her child Robert, valued at $600. *Ibid.*, pp. 271, 272.

consent.²³ The Pearce family of Goochland owned a number of slaves, who were either hired out in Richmond or directly used by John Pearce himself, a mechanic in the city about 1850.²⁴ William Walker, the Petersburg shoemaker mentioned above, apparently hired out his slaves; certainly after his death this practice was followed in order to settle the claims of the five Walker children against the inheritance of their mother, Jane Walker. The children were to relinquish all their rights to the two slaves, Flora and Henry, after they had been hired out for a period of time. For four years, 1853–1857, the hiring of these slaves brought income to the family. In 1854, after the charges of the administrator of the estate had been deducted, each of the Walkers, six in all, received $9.31 as his share of the hire of Flora and Henry. In 1855 the hire of Flora brought to the family $65. Henry's hire in that year brought them nothing since all he could command was his "victuals and clothes and that for only a part of the year." In 1856, however, the hire of Henry was $30 and that of Flora, $70, so that in this year each of the Walker family received as his share $13.71. In 1857, the year in which all claims were satisfied among the members of the

---

²³ City Hall, Richmond, Deed Book 74A, p. 606. Another free Negro who hired out his slaves was Frank Lipscomb of Cumberland County, owner of 119 acres of land and member of a family that held slaves for a period of forty years or more. Following the established practice of white owners, Lipscomb put a female slave of his in charge of a Richmond broker to be hired out in that city. A letter written to this dealer in 1855 by a friend of Lipscomb's indicates that the dealer was not exercising due care respecting the slave's health and the amount to be paid for her hire. The free Negro owner therefore desired to find a new agent to hire out his property, take proper security for the yearly hire, and return him the bond. Virginia State Library, Pension Papers, War of 1812, Letter of the Rev. Hezekiah Hord to John K. Martin of Richmond, Dec. 18, 1855.

²⁴ Personal Property, Richmond, 1843–1855. Occasionally the writer has met older Negroes of this day who have some knowledge of free Negro slaveholding and whose testimony frequently substantiates that of the written record. George W. Lewis of Richmond, born in 1857, testified to the writer that the Pearces of Goochland and Richmond were commercial slaveholders. The Rev. Samuel A. Brown of Petersburg, on the other hand, testified that his grandfather, Samuel Brown of Charles City, held slaves purely on a fraternal basis.

family in the chancery suit of Walker vs. Walker, the amount received by each member was $15.05.[25]

Other free Negroes who had no slave property of their own made a practice of hiring slaves to work for them. Mechanics and business men who needed help turned to this available supply of labor. As hirers of slaves they sometimes, like white persons, broke the law with respect to allowing hired slaves to roam at large or to re-hire themselves. Such was the case of Minnis Hill, a free Negro of Richmond, who was fined in court for permitting his hireling Sam to hire himself out contrary to the act of the Virginia assembly.[26] James Carter, a carpenter of Petersburg, was a hirer of slaves. In May, 1860, he hired one by the name of Ledley, paying to the owner of Ledley the high price of $50 for the first quarter's hire; later in that year he paid the same amount for the third quarter.[27] A very unusual case of a free Negro hiring slaves is that of Thomas Whitico of Henry County. Throughout the decade of 1850 this man paid a tax of $3.60 on three slaves, none other than his wife and two children,

---

[25] Clerk's Office, Petersburg, Chancery Papers (mss.), "Chancery Causes Ended," 8, 9, 10. Another small slaveholder was James Sims, a cooper of Manchester (South Richmond). After his death his administrator's account, rendered to the court for the years 1853 to 1855, showed the hire of Louisa and another slave at $7.50 per quarter. As a prosperous mechanic and property holder Sims had no doubt found use for these slaves during his lifetime. Clerk's Office, Chesterfield, Will Book 21, p. 207.

[26] City Hall, Richmond, Hustings Court Minute Book 11, p. 647.

[27] Private papers in the possession of the Carter family of Petersburg, descendants of James Carter. Slave hiring by free Negroes is a subject of such importance that any list of free Negro slaveholders must be carefully scrutinized. As noted previously, federal census enumerators and state officials made no distinction between actual slave ownership and slave hiring. Another hirer of slaves in Petersburg at an earlier day, and also an owner on a fraternal basis, was the boatman John Updike. In a general bill of indebtedness to Robert Bolling for vessels and equipment, Updike lists $60 as Negro hire. In all probability he continued to hire slaves during his entire career of about thirty years as a boatman in Petersburg. Clerk's Office, Petersburg, Deed Book 8, p. 371. Richard Jarratt, a boatman of this town in a still earlier day, hired slaves and paid taxes on them. In 1819 he paid a tax of $1.40 on two slaves; in 1820 a tax of seventy cents on one. Jarratt Family Papers, in possession of William Jarratt of Petersburg, great-grandson of Richard Jarratt.

whom he hired from their owner, a man by the name of King.²⁸

Slave ownership for profit sometimes existed even within a family group. This type of ownership may be classified as a blend between fraternal ownership and ownership for profit. The will of Judith Angus of Petersburg indicates this dual type of slaveholding. Judith Angus had three sons—George, Moses, and Frank—and a grandson, Henry. By her will, made in 1832, Moses became her principal heir, as the other brothers were slaves. George was to be freed; but if Moses, who was then in Tennessee, should return to Petersburg, then George should not become free but should belong to Moses "and be at his disposal." Her grandson Henry was left in possession of this favored son until he became of age, when he should either receive his freedom and leave the state, or remain as the property of Moses. While George and Henry remained slaves they were to be hired out, and the money derived from their hire and from her real estate should be used for the purchase of her son Frank, who was then a slave in the hands of another slaveholder. Two other slaves outside the family circle, Jinney and Docey, were to work until they earned money enough to enable them to leave the state in accordance with the law. Favoring Moses again at the expense of the others, Judith Angus finally provided that in case Jinney and Docey stayed in Virginia they should belong to Moses.²⁹

The will of Samuel Smith of Chesterfield, making his daughter-in-law his heir, runs in part as follows:

I give and bequeath to my daughter-in-law Betsy Smith all my personal estate consisting of my wife Molly Smith, my son Joseph Smith, my son Harry Smith, my son Jerry Smith, my daughter Biddy Smith and her increase and their increases; my daughter Lucy Smith and her increase and their increase—to hold the above men-

---

²⁸ Personal Property, Henry County, 1860.
²⁹ Clerk's office, Petersburg, Will Book 3.

tioned slaves during her natural life, and at the death of the above named Betsy Smith, I desire that they shall be free.

The testator further provided that his daughter-in-law should inherit his eleven acres of land, his stock, furniture, and other property. When Betsy Smith died, this land was to be sold and the proceeds distributed equally among the slaves so that they might be liberated and settled in a free state.[30]

The nature of slaveholding among free Negroes can be appraised not only by examining the legal instruments just discussed but also by considering the general economic status of these slaveholders. It has been shown that some free Negroes were prosperous as the operators of large farms, as business men, or as mechanics. Such men might well have needed the services of extra laborers, and some of them supplied this need by the hiring or by the complete ownership of slaves.

In the investigation of the possible needs of free Negroes for the labor of others, it is to be recalled first of all that in 1860 in Virginia there were 173 free Negroes who operated farms of 100 acres or more. One of this number owned a plantation of 1,300 acres, two had 500 acres or more, and eight owned about 300 acres. Farms of this size would make additional labor necessary. In cities free Negroes operated livery stables and shops of various kinds—barber shops, shoe shops, and blacksmith shops. Many of these mechanics and business men owned their residences and lived in a style that might require the help of servants. In short, in the matter of income a considerable number of free Negroes were equal to

---

[30] Clerk's Office, Chesterfield, Will Book 17, p. 151. The arrangements made in this will probably represent a mere legal device, since the testator may have been prompted entirely by benevolent motives. Earlier this same man, on the occasion of incurring a debt of $102.04, offered as security one Negro boy, Sam, who may have been his son. In case of non-payment of the debt the creditor was allowed to "expose the said Negro boy for sale." *Ibid.*, Deed Book 20, p. 481. The will of John Cosby of Southampton left a sum of money to each of his free sons and made one of them responsible for taking care of his slave son Dempsey and sending him to free territory after his manumission. Clerk's Office, Southampton, Will Book 9, p. 287.

some white persons and superior to others. It is likely that such free Negroes, if listed as slaveholders in public records, maintained slaves for their labor and not because of kinship. But even if these persons are classified as slaveholders for profit, many of them may have been merely the temporary hirers of slaves. A knowledge of the length of time particular slaves served free Negroes would make clear this distinction. The holding of the same slaves by one person or one family over a period of twenty years, for example, would indicate actual possession rather than casual hiring.

The majority of the free Negro slaveholders in the early part of the period from 1830 to 1860 were farmers.[31] In 1830 Amherst County had three such slaveholders, two with one slave each and one with four. This last was Turner Pinn. In 1830 Pinn owned 100 acres of land and fifteen years later he became the owner of an additional farm of 176 acres. In all probability he needed slaves in his growing farm business. Greensville County in 1830 had four free Negro slaveholders, the chief of whom was David Watkins. As early as 1817 this free Negro was the owner of three tracts of land totaling 521 acres, all of which he had purchased.[32] During a fifteen year period he owned from three to seven slaves, who no doubt were necessary for his farming.

In the group of persons who held slaves over a long period of time, and who therefore probably owned them, were Thomas Pearman of New Kent County and Edward Sorrel of Northumberland County. Pearman owned three tracts of

[31] Notable among the non-agricultural slaveholders of the early period were Archibald Batte of Chesterfield and Prince George counties, a merchant, and Abram Howard, a contractor in the town of Falmouth. Batte, whose will is discussed earlier in this chapter, owned fifty acres of land in Prince George County, but his chief property holdings were a lot, a dwelling, and a mercantile establishment at Bermuda Hundred in Chesterfield County, property valued in 1830 at $1,250. At this port of entry on the James, he apparently had a business large enough to utilize the five to ten slaves he owned between 1810 and 1830. Abram Howard, one of the ten or more free Negro property owners of his town in 1830, owned or hired eight slaves. Land, Personal Property, Stafford, 1830.

[32] Clerk's Office, Greensville, Deed Book 4, p. 186; 5, pp. 28, 53.

land; Sorrel owned one hundred acres. Each held two or three slaves. Some farm tenants enjoyed prosperity sufficient to enable them to hold slaves for a considerable period of time. Such was the situation with John and Mack Chavous of Charlotte County and Edward Eppes of Lunenburg County, who held three or four slaves apiece.

Several free Negro families may be rated as important slave-holders both because of the long period of time they held slaves and because of the size of their business operations. Prominent among these were Jacob Sampson of Goochland County, Richard Parsons of Campbell, Priscilla Ivey of Mecklenburg, and the Lipscombs of Powhatan and Cumberland counties.

Jacob Sampson of Goochland began about 1830 with one tract of land and within thirty years built an estate consisting of eight tracts totaling more than 500 acres. With every addition of land Sampson appears to have increased his number of slaves; at any rate, he increased his holdings from one in 1840 to three in 1844; from four in 1850 to six in 1853; from six in 1853 to eight in 1855; and finally from this number to eleven in 1860.[33] Since he farmed on an extensive scale and also operated a tavern at the Goochland court house, Sampson needed this increasing number of slaves. Richard Parsons of Campbell County also followed two occupations, as farmer and boatman. Parsons was both a benevolent and a commercial slaveholder; he held slaves as members of his family and also other slaves as laborers. In a will made in 1842 he carefully provided for the manumission and rearing of his slave children. But while planning for the freedom of these "slaves" he came into possession of nine others who served him either as his direct property or as hired persons.[34]

Priscilla Ivey perhaps surpassed all other free Negro

---

[33] Land, Personal Property, Goochland, 1830–1860.
[34] Clerk's Office, Campbell, Will Book 14, p. 21; Personal Property, Campbell, 1840–1860.

slaveholders with reference to the length of time she held slaves. In each year from 1821 to 1856 this woman held five or more slaves. Her inherited estate of 1,304 acres amply warranted the use of slaves as laborers.

The Lipscombs of Powhatan and Cumberland numbered twelve or more families. In 1860 one family held 320 acres and another 119 acres. Prior to 1830 slaveholding was evenly distributed among all the Lipscombs, but by 1860 only two of the families held slaves. Frank and John held three slaves apiece at this time.[35] As noted previously, Frank hired out at least one of his slaves in Richmond, and as a hirer on one occasion he became uneasy concerning the proper returns on the hire of his slave.

Slaves were owned in largest numbers by the free Negroes of Amelia County. Most of this ownership appeared during the last fifteen years of the slavery period. The Anderson brothers and Frankey Miles outranked all others. Francis Anderson with 600 acres, Alfred with 670, and William with 278 acres necessarily had abundant use for the slaves they held. Among these brothers the number ranged from one to ten. Frankey Miles was one of the largest slaveholders among the free Negroes of Virginia during the entire period under review. In 1860 this woman, as previously noted, owned a plantation of 1,100 acres; and doubtless she had need for the nineteen slaves she owned.[36]

Commercial slaveholding was common not only among farmers but also, especially in the later part of the period under consideration, among small tradesmen and artisans. The blacksmith trade probably embraced more slaveholding than any other occupations, for about one fifth of all the free Negro blacksmiths in 1860 held slaves. The number held by each blacksmith, however, was small. It was usually one, and never more than three. In this trade in particular most of the so-called holders of slaves were probably hirers. One explana-

[35] Personal Property, Goochland and Powhatan counties, 1820–1860.
[36] Personal Property, Amelia, 1860.

tion for the slaveholding of blacksmiths lies in the fact that the method of welding iron in that day called for the assistance of another worker, who was known as a striker. But the presence of slaves in blacksmithing did not necessarily indicate general prosperity among the blacksmiths; more than half of those who maintained slaves held no real property.

Conspicuous among the Negro blacksmiths about 1830 in rural Virginia was William Rolls of Orange. This free Negro maintained three or more slaves and held them for their labor, as his deeds of trust, discussed earlier, indicate. Rolls lived in a well-furnished house, the upkeep of which may have offered further employment to his slaves.[37] In the larger towns of Virginia such as Richmond and Petersburg, blacksmithing and slaveholding were also related. Gilbert Hunt of Richmond operated a blacksmith shop for a number of years and for fifteen or more years regularly held two slaves.[38] Armistead Wilson's situation in Petersburg was similar.

The cooper trade produced a few slaveholders. If a cooper had a heavy demand for barrels and hogsheads he would need additional laborers. Such was the case of Robert Cambell of Orange, whose flourishing business involved the ownership of five slaves valued at $1,450. James W. Sims of Manchester and Jack Booker of Petersburg were also slave-owning coopers. Jack Booker has already been noted as the owner of one slave in a certain deed of trust, but as a matter of fact at one time (1827) he held five slaves.[39]

The carpenter trade made demands for slaves, especially when the carpenter became a contractor. Into this class fell the DeBaptists of Fredericksburg, the several families of

---

[37] Personal Property, Orange, 1825–1835. In the town of Tappahannock there were two free Negro blacksmiths, James Lewis and William Breedlove, one of whom owned town lots and houses and both of whom held one or two slaves. Personal Property, Essex, 1860. Two blacksmiths in Lawrenceville, Gideon Goldsberry and Thomas Coleman, held a slave apiece in the fifties, and other property. Personal Property, Brunswick, 1850–1860. William B. Howard of Warrenton was similarly situated.

[38] Personal Property, Richmond, 1840–1860.

[39] Personal Property, Petersburg, 1820–1831.

whom maintained from one to five slaves each [40] and were among the aristocracy of the free Negro group. The Beatie family of the town of Bristol were similar to the DeBaptists of Fredericksburg. Washington Beatie was a master carpenter who owned fifty-two acres of land and also one slave. Richard Hill of Dinwiddie likewise combined carpentry and farming. He was the owner of 137 acres of land, which with his carpenter trade explains his ownership of one and two slaves.[41]

Among the boatmen, Richard Parsons of Campbell County probably led all others in the volume of his business and in the need for extra help in the form of slaves. Houses and lots in Lynchburg, a 175-acre farm in the county, a number of boats, and nine slaves combined to make Parsons a man of means. Washington Logan of Powhatan County, another boatman, owned no real estate, but he did own an unusual amount of personal property. His business assumed proportions sufficient to necessitate the regular use of one or two slaves for a period of thirteen years or more.[42]

Shoemaking produced a small number of slaveowners. In this group may be mentioned Monday Robinson of Frederick County, who in the fifties held or hired four slaves; William Evans of Hanover County and Benjamin Judah of the city of Richmond, who about the same time held one slave; and Booker Jackson of Farmville, who during the late fifties held from two to four slaves. It is possible that Monday Robinson, like Booker Jackson, combined with shoemaking other activities that made slave labor necessary. Booker Jackson owned carriages and wagons, three or four horses, and other livestock; in fact, he discontinued shoe-

[40] Personal Property, Fredericksburg, 1825-1840.
[41] Personal Property, Dinwiddie, 1848-1860; Land, Dinwiddie, 1860. Mathew Hicks of Franklin County held no real estate, but his trade apparently necessitated the two slaves he held in 1860. Another carpenter, Rhyburn Bundy of Essex County, employed one slave. Personal Property, Essex, 1850-1860. Walter Jackson of Fredericksburg and Thomas Scott and Christopher Stevens of Petersburg, carpenters, held one slave each in 1860.
[42] Personal Property, Powhatan County, 1840-1860.

making to operate a livery stable. In 1859 this thrifty free Negro paid a tax of $15.15 on two slaves, three vehicles, four horses, a clock, and a watch.[43] The next year he paid a higher tax on the ownership of three slaves, four vehicles, and five horses.

Though many barbers were slaveholders, none of them held slaves on an extensive scale. The usual number was one only. Six of the Richmond barbers held one slave each and at times two slaves.[44] One of them, Richard C. Hobson, held his wife and son as slaves, but in 1850 he manumitted them. Toward the end of this decade he held one other slave, who no doubt labored for him as a servant. Slaves held by barbers served in their homes or in their shops as regular barbers. According to a conversation reported by Russell, Reuben West of Richmond during the fifties regularly held a slave as a barber in his shop.[45] The Lynchburg barbers— Armistead Pride, Claiborne Gladman, and Thomas Gladman—held one, two, and three slaves respectively. Claiborne Gladman had manumitted the slave members of his family in 1817, but after this event he held slaves apparently on a commercial basis. Pride held one slave over a period of at least twenty-five years.[46]

The free Negro draymen and teamsters employed slaves on a scale comparable to the blacksmiths. Each of the five draymen of Norfolk held from one to three slaves over long periods of time.[47] Two of these slave owners, Ned Keeling and Ackey White, had once been slaves themselves. Leander Slaughter and Eleazar White of Petersburg, who owned

---

[43] Personal Property, Prince Edward, 1850–1860; tax receipts of Booker Jackson, private documents in possession of the writer.

[44] The six barbers were Reuben West, Richard C. Hobson, John Ferguson, George P. Gray, George Ruffin, and Richard W. Henderson. Personal Property, Richmond, 1840–1860.

[45] John H. Russell, *Free Negro*, p. 151.

[46] Clerk's Office, Lynchburg, Deed Book E, p. 350; Personal Property, Lynchburg, 1823–1851. Crawley Mitchell, free Negro barber of Farmville, held one slave.

[47] Clerk's Office, Norfolk, 1830–1865. These draymen were Ned Keeling, Caleb Pitt, William Lewis, and Ackey and Edward White.

from one to three slaves, had also been draymen as hired slaves, had purchased their own freedom, and afterwards became owners of real estate and slaves. James Robinson of Richmond, another teamster, in 1860 owned ten horses, a number of wagons, and three slaves.[48] In all probability these draymen and teamster slave "owners" were actually hirers of slaves. They were no doubt similar to Luraney Butler, the operator of a dray in early Petersburg, who in 1817 paid to J. S. Gilliam $51.75 for "the hire of a Negro" the previous year.[49]

The livery stable men regularly held slaves. With the exception of certain farmers, they were the largest holders of slave property. In most cases the livery stable operator had once been a slave himself; the thrift he showed in buying his freedom carried over into his business as a free person. Edmund Kean of Winchester was such a man. Shortly after his emancipation, about 1849, his business grew so fast that, whereas in 1851 he held only three slaves, by 1860 he held ten.[50] This increase in slave ownership was of course accompanied by a steady growth in the ownership of horses, carriages, houses, and lots. Robert Clark of Petersburg had an almost identical experience. His manumission and business career began about the same time as Kean's. Clark's use of slaves, however, was less extensive than Kean's, since he advanced from owning one slave in 1860 to owning five in 1862, his highest number.[51]

Some slaveholding existed among the limited number of merchants or storekeepers. Russell Thomas of Lynchburg, a grocer, held one slave.[52] John Cooper of Port Royal held one, and Randle Evans, the confectioner of Winchester, a

---

[48] Personal Property, Richmond, 1850–1860.
[49] Butler Family Papers, in the possession of the writer.
[50] Personal Property, Winchester, 1850–1860.
[51] William Peters of Harrisonburg, another operator of a livery stable, held one slave. Personal Property, Rockingham, 1860. Booker Jackson of Farmville, as has been noted, held two and later three.
[52] Personal Property, Lynchburg, 1850–1860.

former slave, held one over a period of at least twenty years.

Certain free Negro women, concubines of white men or general prostitutes, held slaves in proportion to their affluence. Sylvia Jeffers of Petersburg regularly kept in her possession from one to three slaves for a period of twenty years of more.[53] Living in the same town and under similar conditions were Rebecca Gilliam and Sarah F. Taylor, both of whom held several slaves. The situation in Petersburg was paralleled in other towns and localities of the state.

Slaveholding by free Negroes, particularly holding of the commercial type, raises the question of the method by which they came into possession of slaves. Apparently some free Negroes who held slaves for their labor secured their slaves in the general market, as white persons did. Certainly Reuben West, the Richmond barber, bought a woman from the slave dealers on one occasion and later released her because of her rebellious nature.[54] In other instances free Negroes acquired title to slaves by will from white persons. Such bequests usually were made only in cases of illicit relationships between white men and free Negro women. They are important in this study because in many cases of the largest slaveholdings, the ownership came by bequest from a white person.

A white man of Cumberland County by the name of Henry Lipscomb willed a number of slaves to a free Negro family which also bore the name of Lipscomb. Heading the list of these legatees was Nancy Lipscomb, "a free woman of color." Along with fifty acres of land he gave this woman four Negro slaves; to Kitty Lipscomb, he gave four; to eight other members of the family he gave tracts of land and from one to eight slaves each, making a total of twenty-seven for the entire family.[55] At least two of the Lipscombs, as has

[53] Personal Property, Petersburg, 1830-1860.
[54] John H. Russell, "Colored Freemen as Slave Owners," in *Journal of Negro History*, 1:238-239 (July, 1916).
[55] The eight other Lipscombs were Billy, Sally, Frank, James, Polly, Judy, Frank, and James. Clerk's Office, Cumberland, Will Book 8, pp. 212, 365.

been noted, held these slaves or their offspring until the Civil War, and certain others kept their land; but most of the family had dissipated this property, material and human, by 1860.

Another wholesale allotment of slaves by a white man to free Negroes was made by the will of Walter Boyd Gilliam of Prince George County in 1821. The chief beneficiary in this instance was Easter Tinsley, alias Gilliam. This woman inherited twenty slaves, and her two daughters received five slaves each. With this bequest went the usual allotment of large amounts of land.[56] One provision of this will, that the slaves assigned to Easter Tinsley should descend to the two daughters upon her death, may account for the large number of slaves later held by Rebecca, the daughter who became the wife of James Z. Matthews. At the time of her death in 1849 the inventory of Rebecca Tinsley Matthews' estate shows a total of twenty-eight slaves with a value of $8,400.25 and furniture with a value of $234.25. With her real estate valued at $1,400 this woman's total estate amounted to $10,034.25.[57]

Two years prior to the making of this inventory Rebecca Matthews executed a will by which these twenty-eight slaves were given in turn to her children. Thus this unusual number of servants stayed in possession of the family, presumably until 1865. She gave her daughter Sarah Elizabeth seven slaves of the lot; her daughter Jane, six; her son John Walter, four; and she provided that her husband should enjoy the annual proceeds of the hire of the slaves Frances and George. Nine of her slaves were emancipated by her will because of the money and services she had already received from their labor.[58] The provision that the husband should merely receive the profit from the hire of Frances and George was in line with a policy Rebecca Matthews had announced nine years previously. In 1838, at the time of her marriage to

---

[56] Clerk's Office, Petersburg, Will Book 2, p. 178.
[57] Clerk's Office, 3, p. 512.   [58] Clerk's Office, 3, pp. 507–509.

James Z. Matthews, she had provided through a marriage agreement and a deed of trust that her husband was to share in no way in her slave property. Instead, with the consent of her trustee, she was to have the exclusive use and service of all of these slaves and the profits arising therefrom, either by keeping them in her own employ or by hiring them out.[59]

Priscilla Ivey of Mecklenburg County was another prominent slaveholder whose slaves came to her through a white man. Five or more slaves were in her possession for thirty-five years, from 1821 until her death in 1856. She inherited these slaves at the time when she received her plantation of 1,304 acres. Like Rebecca Gilliam, this woman willed her slave property to her children: to her son, Fred Ivey, "a Negro girl Susan and her increase" and to her grandson, James Chavous, "a Negro boy Fred and a Negro girl Betsy."[60] In 1856 Susan and her child were valued at $800; Betsy and Fred were valued at $800 and $600 respectively.

Martha Farley, Alfred Anderson, and Frank Anderson, one family of Amelia County free Negroes, were other large slaveholders whose slaves and plantations came into their possession by the will of Henry Anderson. Martha Farley was perhaps the mother of Alfred and Frank Anderson and the mistress of Henry Anderson. To Martha Farley in 1849 Henry Anderson gave a female slave named Libby and her two children. To Alfred Anderson, "free man of color," he

[59] Clerk's Office, Petersburg, Deed Book 10, p. 557. This story of Walter Boyd Gilliam and his free Negro beneficiaries is of particular importance to this study in that it illustrates how the records fail to give complete information on slave ownership. Twenty-odd slaves remained in the hands of three generations of people, but in no case do the state records assign any of them more than three slaves. In all probability the majority of these slaves were hired to other persons, who are listed as the owners.

[60] Clerk's Office, Mecklenburg, Will Book 19, pp. 16, 38. Priscilla Ivey was a woman of dark complexion. Still another instance of the transfer of slaves to free Negroes by will from white men is seen in the career of Benjamin Hoard, Fanny Woodford, and other members of her family, all of Middlesex County. Each of these persons owned about four slaves, acquired by the will of James Ross of this county in 1825. Petition, Middlesex, Dec. 7, 1826. Archibald Batte, the free mulatto of Bermuda Hundred, probably came into possession of his eight or more slaves in a similar manner.

gave Amelia and her four children, who were none other than the wife and children of the beneficiary. Along with these members of his own family Henry Anderson also gave Alfred Anderson ten other slaves. To Frank Anderson, "free man of color," Henry Anderson gave two slaves, Lemm and Washington, who had already been in the possession of Frank Anderson about seventeen years.[61]

The amount of slaveholding by free Negroes in 1860 in comparison with 1830 does not correlate with the amount of real estate holdings at the two dates. There were fewer slave owners in 1860 than in 1830, and the character of slaveholding itself had undergone change. In the earlier period the bulk of free Negro slaveholding was fraternal and fairly widespread; in the later period it had become largely commercialized, based on hiring, and confined to a few. In the cities, to which fully 50 per cent of all free Negro slaveholding was confined, this change was especially pronounced. Petersburg offers an example of these two different types of slaveholding. Whereas this city had seventy Negro owners of taxable slaves in the earlier period, the majority of whom were blood relatives of their slaves, the number had dropped to nine owners in the later period. These nine included such persons as Robert Clark, livery stable operator; Thomas Scott and Christopher Stevens, contractors; Leander Slaughter, drayman; and Armistead Wilson, blacksmith. These men, constituting a group whose occupations and stage of advancement required extra labor, found this labor in hired slaves and other free Negroes. Much of the slaveholding in the counties in 1860 was likewise confined to persons of similar occupations—blacksmiths, carpenters, and boatmen.

[61] Certified copy of the will of Henry Anderson, senior. Frankey Miles of this same county inherited nineteen or more slaves by the will of Nathaniel Harrison, and held them until the emancipation of the entire race in 1865. From the standpoint of the slaveholder employing his own slaves, this woman ranks as the largest free Negro slaveholder in Virginia. Rebecca Gilliam of Petersburg owned a greater number, but she and her descendants always hired out most of them.

The trend toward slave hiring and a smaller number of owners was perhaps accelerated by the increasing restrictions imposed on free Negro slaveholding under Virginia law. By an act passed in 1858 free Negroes on the one hand were denied the privilege of acquiring additional slaves on the fraternal basis, and on the other were forbidden to own any slaves whatever outside the fraternal circle. It is apparent that although free Negroes might not "own" slaves outside the family circle under the provisions of this act, they might still "hire" them.

In summary, the number of free Negroes who owned slaves on the profit basis commonly associated with the white ownership was very limited. Free Negro ownership was not a system of slave bondage. This discussion has revealed a "white" type of ownership because some of it did exist; yet, during the entire thirty year period, there were not more than fifteen persons who ever held more than five slaves as their own direct property. Moreover, the few who did own a fairly large number as their immediate property held them as a gift from white persons. Free Negroes in Virginia held slaves chiefly as blood relatives, secondly as hired persons, and third, or least of all, as chattel property for profit.

This chapter and two earlier chapters have discussed free Negro property in farm land, in town lots, and in slaves. At this point an appraisal and a summary of property holding in general among the free Negroes of Virginia may be desirable.

In the field of personal property, as in real estate, the majority of the free Negroes owned no possessions subject to taxation. In the list of nineteen articles levied upon by the state in 1860 the taxable possessions of these people were limited to four items, namely, slaves; horses; cattle, sheep, and hogs; and household furniture. No doubt a fairly large number owned oxen and ox carts, but these were not subject to taxation. In some counties the value of the personal property held by free Negroes exceeded the value of their real estate. For example, of a group of twenty-four selected counties, ten show the value of personal property to be in excess of the value of real estate. This difference in favor of personal property held true especially in the counties of a limited free Negro land ownership and a high degree of tenantry. Thus, the free Negroes of Caroline County held a total of personal property valued at $9,000 and a total of real estate valued at only $5,047. The amount of taxable personal property in counties naturally exceeded the amount in cities because of the equipment necessary for farming.

In the field of real estate, the number of Negro owners in both country and town increased from 875 in 1830 to 1,971 in 1860. Assuming that each owner of property was identified with a family, one family in ten was a property-holding family in 1830; one in five was in this position thirty years later.[62] During the thirty year period there was an increase of 23 per cent in the free Negro population, but the number of property owners increased 128 per cent. For all practical purposes, then, the number of owners was doubled in the thirty years; the number of acres and town lots was likewise doubled.

Still greater gains are to be noted with reference to property values. Whereas the total value of real estate owned by Negroes in country and town was $253,079 in 1830, this amount had increased to $829,911 by 1860. The valuation in the later period was thus three and a half times greater than in the earlier. The total value of the real estate in 1860 was less than one million dollars, but if the value of personal property is added, the total property holdings amounted to at least one and a half million dollars.[63] To express these

---

[62] The average free Negro family in Virginia was made up of 5.5 persons. On this basis there were approximately 9,000 such families in 1830 and 11,500 in 1860.

[63] The subject of labor and property among the free Negroes in the South as a whole is treated in five pages of Alfred H. Stone's article, "Free Contract Labor in the Ante-Bellum South," in *The South in the Building of the Nation*,

data in terms of the standing of the Negro race in a later day, the free class of the slavery period held property on a ratio equal to that of this group in Virginia in 1890 and in the entire South in 1910. The growth that came after the emancipation of the entire race is generally regarded as remarkable; if so, the advance made by the free Negroes of Virginia from 1830 to 1860 is likewise remarkable.

As free Negroes advanced in property holding they also contributed increasingly to the revenue of the state. In 1830 the state assessment on real estate stood at the very low rate of eight cents on each hundred dollars of value. In 1860 this amount had increased to forty cents on each hundred dollars. With land values much higher in the later period and with the tax rate five times greater than formerly, the contribution of all citizens to the public treasury was much greater than at the earlier period. At the rate indicated the free Negroes in 1830 were assessed for only $202.50, whereas in 1860 their real estate assessment was $3,319.64. In addition to the tax on real estate there was levied on free Negro males in 1860 the special capitation tax of $1.80. The actual collection from this source in that year amounted to $13,065.22.[64] This particular tax was not in operation at the earlier period. Altogether, then, the free Negroes paid into the state treasury in 1860 for real estate and capitation $16,384.86. State taxes on personal property would probably augment this amount to $20,000.

5: 134-139. In this short critical article the author makes an analysis of the free Negro that is unique for its interpretation and breadth of view. He estimates that this class held about twenty-five million dollars worth of property, ten to fifteen millions of which was in Louisiana. This particular phase of his argument seems to be overdrawn. On the basis of the findings presented here for Virginia, his estimate for the South as a whole is probably excessive.

As this study shows, one characteristic of free Negro property ownership in Virginia is the absence of very large holdings by any one person, in decided contrast with glowing reports given by historians for single large ownerships in Charleston, S. C., and in the state of Louisiana. Virginia is characterized by the diffusion of property holding among a relatively large number of free Negroes, the property having been acquired by purchase and not by bequest or gift from white persons.

[64] Virginia, Auditor of Public Accounts, *Annual Report*, 1861, no. 5.

Aside from state taxes there were the usual county and city taxes, which were sometimes greater than the state levy. Thus James Carter, a carpenter of Petersburg, in 1858 paid a state tax of $10.40 on his property whereas his city tax at about this time was $17.04.[65] Altogether, state and local taxes on real estate, personal property, and capitation from free Negroes amounted to more than $25,000. In taxpaying, as in land ownership, this group was thus of far greater value to the government of Virginia in 1860 than it had been in earlier years.

The greatest contribution of free Negroes to the economic life of Virginia lay not in property holding and taxpaying, however, but in the field of manual labor. Indeed with the passing of time they became all the more valuable as laborers. Labor and property holding together gave the free Negroes an established footing in the state, a place so important that all the schemes to deport the entire group met with dismal failure. Their property, though of no great economic significance to the state, was enough to throw doubt on the many statements of present-day orators that the Negro started his career in 1865 with nothing.[66] Such a statement at least does not represent the situation of the Negro in Virginia.

[65] Carter Family Papers.   [66] Cf. Wesley, *Negro Labor*, pp. 65–66.

BIBLIOGRAPHY

Manuscript Sources

The Archives of the United States, Washington, D. C.
    United States Census, Free Inhabitants.
    United States Census, Slave Inhabitants.
    Letters of the American Colonization Society, Board of Managers, Library of Congress.

The Archives of Virginia, Richmond, Virginia.
    Tax Books, Land and Personal, Counties and Cities, State Library.
    Legislative Papers, a Collection of Petitions Sent to the Legislature of Virginia, State Library.
    Letters of the Commissioners of Revenue to the State Auditor, State Library.
    Pension Papers, War of 1812, State Library.
    Records, Counties, State Library.
    United States Census, Agriculture, State Library.
    Land Patents, Land Office, State Capitol.
    Military Certificates, Land Office, State Capitol.

The Archives of Cities and Counties, Clerks' Offices.
    Annual Reports of the Overseers of the Poor.
    Accounts Current, Petersburg.
    Chancery Papers, Chancery Causes Ended.
    Birth Registers.
    Marriage Registers.
    Marriage Bonds.
    Registers of Free Negroes and Mulattoes.
    Deed Books.
    Order Books (Minute Books).
    Will Books.
    Minutes, Common Hall, Petersburg.

Diaries.
> Diary of Dr. B. H. Walker, King and Queen County, 1858–1885, Photostat, State Library.

Church Record Books.
> Gillfield Baptist Church, Petersburg.
> First African Baptist Church, Richmond.
> Bute Street Baptist Church, Norfolk.

Family Papers.
> Jones (Newby) Family, Norfolk.
> Butler Family, Petersburg.
> Carter Family, Petersburg.
> Colson Family, Petersburg.
> Jarratt Family, Petersburg.
> Thomas Family, Petersburg.

Miscellaneous.
> Leslie and Brydon Tobacco Factory Record Books, Petersburg.
> Letters, tax receipts, registration papers, original wills, etc.

Government Documents

United States.
> *Census of the United States, 1810–1860. Population and Manufactures.*
> *Census of the United States, 1850. Instruction to U. S. Marshalls.*
> *Negro Population, 1790–1915.* Bureau of the Census. (Washington, 1918.)
> *Seventh Census, 1850. Instructions to U. S. Marshalls.* (Washington, 1850.)
> *Statistical View of the United States: Being a Compendium of the Seventh Census.*

Virginia.
> *Annual Reports of the Auditor of Public Accounts, 1850–1860.*
> *Annual Reports, Board of Public Works to the General Assembly. Acts of the General Assembly, 1807–1865.*
> *Code of Virginia.* (Richmond, 1849.)
> *Code of Virginia.* (Richmond, 1860.)
> *Charter and Laws of the City of Petersburg.* (Petersburg: O. Ellyson, Printer, 1852.)

Documents of the House of Delegates, Containing the Messages of the Governors to the General Assemblies and Annual Reports of the Public Officers of the State, 1814–1865.

Documents of the Senate, Containing Bills Introduced and Passed by the Senate, Reports of Commissions and Various Other State Papers, 1831–1865.

Documents Containing Statistics of Virginia. Ordered to be Printed by the State Convention Sitting in the City of Richmond, 1850–1851. (Richmond, 1851.)

Journals of the House of Delegates of the Commonwealth of Virginia, 1776–1865. (Richmond.)

Journals of the Senate of the Commonwealth of Virginia, 1778–1865. (Richmond.)

Revised Code of Laws of Virginia. (Richmond, 1819.)

Supplement to the Revised Code of Laws. (Richmond.)

Virginia Statutes at Large. New Series, III, 1803–1808. (Richmond.)

Contemporary Writings

Andrews, Ethan A., *Slavery and the Domestic Slave-Trade in the United States, in a Series of Letters Addressed to the Executive Committee of the American Union for the Relief and Improvement of the Colored Race.* (Boston: Light & Stearns, 1836.)

Ball, Charles, *Fifty Years in Chains; or the Life of an American Slave.* (Indianapolis: Dayton and Archer, 1859.)

Claiborne, John H., *Seventy-five Years in Old Virginia, with Some Account of the Life of the Author, and Some History of the People amongst Whom His Lot Was Cast.* (New York and Washington: Neale Publishing Company, 1904.)

Clark, James F., *Present Condition of the Free Colored People of the United States.* (New York, 1859.)

Delaney, Martin R., *The Condition, Elevation, Emigration and Destiny of the Colored People of the United States.* (Philadelphia, 1852.)

Dew, Thomas R., *Review of the Debate on the Abolition of Slavery in the Virginia Legislature of 1831 and 1832.* (Richmond: T. W. White, 1832.)

Douglass, Mrs. Margaret, *Educational Laws of Virginia. The Personal Narrative of Mrs. Margaret Douglass, a Southern Woman, Who Was Imprisoned for one Month in the Common Jail of Norfolk, under the Laws of Virginia, for the Crime of Teaching Free Colored Children to Read.* (Boston: J. P. Jewett & Co., 1854.)

Fitzhugh, George, *What Shall be Done with the Free Negroes. Four Essays Written for the Fredericksburg Recorder.* (Fredericksburg, Va.: Recorder Office, 1851.)

Giles, William B., *Political Miscellanies, Compiled by William B. Giles.* (Richmond, 1829.)

Howe, Henry, *Historical Collections of Virginia.* (Charleston: Babcock & Co., 1845.)

Howison, Robert R., *A History of Virginia, from its Discovery and Settlement by Europeans to the Present Time.* (Richmond: Drinker and Morris, 1848.)

Hundley, D. R., *Social Relations in Our Southern States.* (New York: Henry B. Price, 1860.)

Lyell, Sir Charles, *Second Visit to the United States of North America,* 2 vols. (New York: Wiley and Putnam, 1849.)

Mallard, R. Q., *Plantation Life before Emancipation.* (Richmond: Whittet and Shepperson, 1892.)

Martin, Joseph, *A New and Comprehensive Gazetteer of Virginia and the District of Columbia.* (Charlottesville: W. H. Brockenbrough, 1835.)

Mordecai, Samuel, *Richmond in By-Gone Days; Being Reminiscences of an Old Citizen.* (Richmond: G. M. West, 1856.)

Olmsted, Frederick L., *A Journey in the Seaboard Slave States, with Remarks on their Economy,* Vol. I. (New York: Dix & Edwards, 1856.)

———, *The Cotton Kingdom: A Traveler's Observation on Cotton and Slavery in the American Slave States,* Vol. I. (New York: Mason Bros., 1861.)

Ruffin, Edmund, *Address to the Virginia State Agricultural Society.* (Richmond, 1853.)

———, *The Political Economy of Slavery; or, the Institution Considered in Regard to its Influence on Public Wealth and the General Welfare.* (Washington: L. Towers, 1857.)

———, *Slavery and Free Labor Described and Compared.* (No date)

Russell, Robert, *North America, Its Agriculture and Climate.* (Edinburgh, 1857.)
Russell, Sir William Howard, *My Diary, North and South,* 2 vols. (London, 1863.)
Rutherford, John C., *Speech . . . on the Removal of the Free Colored Population.* (Richmond: Ritchies and Dunnavent, 1853.)
Smith, James L., *Autobiography of James L. Smith.* (Norwich, Connecticut: Bulletin Company Press, 1881.)
Trowbridge, John T., *The South; A Tour of its Battlefields and Ruined Cities, and Talks with the People.* (Hartford, 1866.)
Views on the Internal Improvement System of Virginia. (Petersburg, 1854.)
Wealth, Resources, and Hopes of the State of Virginia. (Norfolk, 1857.)

Secondary Sources

Ambler, Charles H., *Sectionalism in Virginia from 1776 to 1861.* (Chicago: University of Chicago, 1910.)
Ballagh, James C., *A History of Slavery in Virginia.* Johns Hopkins University Studies in Historical and Political Science. (Baltimore: Johns Hopkins Press, 1902.)
———, Ed., *The South in the Building of the Nation.* Vol. V, Southern Economic History. (Richmond: Southern Historical Publication Society, 1910.)
Bancroft, Frederic, *Slave Trading in the Old South.* (Baltimore: J. H. Furst, 1931.)
Bassett, John S., *Slavery in the State of North Carolina.* (Baltimore: Johns Hopkins Press, 1899.)
Bruce, Kathleen, *Virginia Iron Manufacture in the Slave Era.* (New York: Century Co., 1930.)
Catterall, Helen H., ed., *Judicial Cases Concerning Negro Slavery,* 3 vols. (Washington: Carnegie Institution of Washington, 1926.)
Channing, Edward, *A History of the United States,* Vol. VI (New York, Macmillan Co., 1923.)
Cole, Arthur C., *The Whig Party in the South.* (Washington: American Historical Association, 1913.)
Craven, Avery O., *Soil Exhaustion as a Factor in the Agricultural*

History of Virginia and Maryland, 1606–1860. (Urbana: The University of Illinois, 1926.)

———, *Edmund Ruffin, Southerner; A Study in Secession.* (New York: D. Appleton, 1932.)

Dodd, William E., *The Cotton Kingdom; A Chronicle of the Old South.* (New Haven: Yale University Press, 1919.)

Dozier, Howard D., *History of the Atlantic Coast Line Railroad.* (New York: Houghton Mifflin Co., 1920.)

First Century of the First Baptist Church in Richmond. (Richmond, 1880.)

Fox, Early L., *The American Colonization Society, 1817–1840.* (Baltimore: The Johns Hopkins Press, 1919.)

Gewehr, Wesley M., *The Great Awakening in Virginia, 1740–1790.* (Durham: Duke University Press, 1930.)

Gray, Lewis C., *History of Agriculture in the Southern United States to 1860.* (Washington: The Carnegie Institution of Washington, 1933.)

Guild, June P., *Black Laws of Virginia: A Summary of the Legislative Acts of Virginia Concerning Negroes from Earliest Times to the Present.* (Richmond: Whittet & Shepperson, 1936.)

Jenkins, William S., *Pro-Slavery Thought in the Old South.* (Chapel Hill: University of North Carolina Press, 1935.)

Munford, Beverly B., *Virginia's Attitude Toward Slavery and Secession.* (Richmond: L. H. Jenkins, 1909.)

Phillips, Ulrich B., *American Negro Slavery.* (New York: D. Appleton & Co., 1918.) A Survey of the Supply; Employment and Control of Negro Labor as Determined by the Plantation Regime.

———, *Life and Labor in the Old South.* (Boston: Little, Brown and Co., 1929.)

Pinchbeck, Raymond B., *The Virginia Negro Artisan and Tradesman.* (Richmond: The William Byrd Press, 1926.)

Russell, John H., *The Free Negro in Virginia, 1619–1865.* (Baltimore: The Johns Hopkins Press, 1913.)

Russel, Robert R., *Economic Aspects of Southern Sectionalism, 1840–1861.* (Urbana, The University of Illinois, 1924.)

Taylor, Rosser H., *The Free Negro in North Carolina,* in the James Sprunt Historical Publications. (Chapel Hill: North Carolina Historical Society, 1920.)

Van Deusen, John G., *Economic Bases of Disunion in South Carolina.* (New York: Columbia University Press, 1928.)
Washington, Booker T., *The Negro in Business.* (Boston: Hertel, Jenkins & Co., 1907.)
Weeks, Stephen B., *Southern Quakers and Slavery; A Study in Institutional History.* (Baltimore: Johns Hopkins Press, 1896.)
Wertenbaker, Thomas J., *Norfolk, Historic Southern Port.* (Durham: Duke University Press, 1931.)
Wesley, Charles H., *Negro Labor in the United States, 1850–1925; A Study in American Economic History.* (New York: Vanguard Press, 1927.)
Whitfield, Theodore M., *Slavery Agitation in Virginia, 1829–1832.* (Baltimore: Johns Hopkins Press, 1930.)
Woodson, Carter G., *A Century of Negro Migration.* (Washington: The Association for the Study of Negro Life and History, 1918.)
————, *The Education of the Negro Prior to 1861; A History of the Education of the Colored People of the United States from the Beginning of Slavery to the Civil War.* (New York: G. P. Putnams Sons, 1915.)
————, ed., *Free Negro Heads of Families in the United States in 1830, Together with a Brief Treatment of the Free Negro.* (Washington: The Association for the Study of Negro Life and History, 1925.)
————, ed., *Free Negro Owners of Slaves in the United States in 1830, Together with Absentee Ownership of Slaves in the United States in 1830,* compiled under the direction of, and edited by, Carter G. Woodson. (Washington: The Association for the Study of Negro Life and History, 1924.)
————, ed., *The Mind of the Negro as Reflected in Letters Written during the Crisis, 1800–1860.* (Washington: The Association for the Study of Negro Life and History, 1926.)
————, *The Negro in Our History,* 6th ed. (Washington: Associated Publishers, 1932.)
Wright, James M., *The Free Negro in Maryland, 1634–1860.* (New York: Longmans, Green, & Co., 1921.)

Magazines, Periodicals, and Directories

Annual Reports of the American Society for Colonizing the Free People of Color. (Washington, 1818-1832.)

DeBow, J. D. B., ed., *Commercial Review of the South and West.* (New Orleans, 1846-1860.)

Dodge, David, "The Free Negro of North Carolina," *Atlantic Monthly,* LVII (January, 1886), 29.35.

Farmers' Register, 10 vols. (Shellbansk, Petersburg, Va., 1833-1842.)

Harpers Magazine, Vols. IV, V (1851-1852).

Hartgrove, W. B., "The Story of Maria Louise Moore and Fannie M. Richards," *Journal of Negro History,* I (January, 1916).

Minutes, Baptist Associations. Virginia Baptist Historical Society Library.

Niles Weekly Register. (Baltimore, 1811-1849.)

Norfolk City Directory, 1806, 1851-1852.

Petersburg City Directory, 1866, 1876-1877.

Railroad Advocate. (Rogersville, Tennessee.)

Richmond City Directory, 1850-1851.

Southern Planter. (Richmond, 1840-1860.)

Virginia Directory and Business Register for 1852. (Richmond, 1852.)

Newspapers

Petersburg, McKenney Free Library:
    Petersburg *Intelligencer,* the *Intelligencer and Commercial Advertiser.*
    Petersburg *Republican.*
    The American Constellation.
    Daily Republican.
    South-Side Democrat.
    Daily Express.
    The Press.

Richmond, Virginia State Library:
    Richmond *Enquirer.*
    Richmond *Whig.*

Richmond *Daily Times*.
Richmond *Daily Dispatch*.
Religious Herald.
Fredericksburg, Fredericksburg Public Library:
Fredericksburg *News*.
Fredericksburg *Weekly Advertiser*.

APPENDIX I

Free Negro Owners of Property, Petersburg, 1860

Value of $1,000 or More

				Reference	
Owner	Value 1860	Purchase Price	Date of Purchase	Deed Book	Page
Mary M. Auter	$ 400	$ 100	1848	17	141
	1,400	—	—	—	—
Nancy Ampy	1,110	190	1851	19	10
Jane Allen	—	150	1803	3	159
	1,100	350	1817	5	214
James Bolling	1,600	260	1842	12	495
Thomas Bolling	2,000	1,200	1846	16	280
Henry Brander	1,000	100	1846	15	297
Berry Bonner	1,250	250	1843	13	230
James Carter, Sr.	100	125	1856	23	86
	350	117	1855	21	603
	1,100	50	1853	20	286
James Carter, Jr.	1,803	—	1858	24	535
Letitia Campbell	1,680	330	1857	23	669
Catherine Cook	1,500	501	1832	8	396
	1,500	625	1848	17	326
Margaret Cook	1,250	1,000	1856	22	686
Sarah Dabney	1,300	100	1849	17	479
Henry Elebeck	3,000	By inheritance	—	—	—
	88	112.50	1857	24	219
	150	—	1857	24	510
	200	—	1857	25	40
Mary R. Faulkner	1,000	135	1842	19	330
Eliza Gallee	500	—	1851	—	—
	900	535	1857	24	429

FREE NEGRO PROPERTY IN VIRGINIA

				Reference	
	Value	Purchase	Date of	Deed	
Owner	1860	Price	Purchase	Book	Page
Harriet Harris	$1,250	$ 450	1845	15	38
Sylvia Jeffries	2,250	435	1821	6	317
James Z. Matthews	1,100	600	1845	15	38
Jack McRae	650	130	1841	12	174
	900	200	1844	14	337
Thomas Prichett	1,300	Certain agreement	1856	22	625
Lavinia Sampson	300	100	1842	13	89
	800	50	1849	18	151
	350	—	1855	22	110
	600	200	1858	24	588
	1,250	260	1858	24	594
Philip Sewall	1,250	410	1854	20	570
Thomas Scott	3,100	5	1845	15	55
	—	250	1846	15	687
William Stevens	1,400	375	1845	14	505
(estate)	—	100	1846	15	291
Sarah Taylor	1,000	Gift	1845	15	146
John Updike	1,000	30	1838	10	308
Armistead Wilson	1,500	5 and other payments	1857	23	478
Elizabeth Walker	1,500	100	1851	18	467

Value between $500 and $1,000

James M. Auter	800	950	1853	20	437
Jane Atkins	520	—	1843	13	207
William Atkins	960	100	1845	15	95
Rebecca Ampey	600	30	1857	23	662
John Berry	550	600	1857	23	475
Susan Berry	600	350	1840	11	364
John Brooks	650	250	1851	19	68
Elizabeth Brander	475	573.38	1857	24	221
	500	—	—	—	—

APPENDIX I

Owner	Value 1860	Purchase Price	Date of Purchase	Reference Deed Book	Page
Fleming Brown	$ 900	$ 100	1848	17	299
Samuel Bonner	720	50	1853	20	34
John Crocker	700	256.50	1859	25	42
Lucretia Coleman	800	—	—	—	—
Caroline Chappel	550	—	—	—	—
Mary Dangerfield	775	88	1858	24	577
Bryant Day	550	90	1855	22	241
Nicholas Diggs	850	120	1854	21	299
Robert Dinkins	350	77.50	1852	19	344
	175	—	—	—	—
Samuel Duncan	715	800	1847	16	110
Winney Epes	625	87	1855	23	77
Philip Evans	500	50	1858	24	388
Christina Goode	750	125	1855	22	97
Jesse Green	600	600	1855	22	198
Margaret Gibbs	650	80	1854	21	548
Elizabeth Graves	900	—	—	20	52
Mary E. Gilliam	600	350	1845	14	580
Edith Gilliam	600	400	1839	11	241
Stephen Goode	857	237	1857	23	693
Celia Hill	800	775	1857	23	730
John Hope	650	350	1854	21	63
	150	305	1856	23	3
Wesley Hill	800	1	1853	20	56
John Hill	500	70	1856	22	629
Jackey Harris	500	265	1834	9	155
Daniel Jackson	650	360	1823	7	216
Moses Joyner	730	300	1853	20	45
	—	165.75	1857	24	55
Watkins Jones	600	—	—	—	—
William King	500	—	—	—	—
Francis King	750	75	1854	21	474
Cynthia King	350	200	1855	22	76
	250	—	—	—	—
Archer Lowry	748	300	1857	24	207
William Lively	600	167	1857	23	465

FREE NEGRO PROPERTY IN VIRGINIA

				Reference	
Owner	Value 1860	Purchase Price	Date of Purchase	Deed Book	Page
Jane Lockett	$ 690	$ 250	1859	25	167
Maria Mathews	500	200	1859	24	717
Baylor Mathews	750	250	1840	11	321
Richard Malone	650	128.75	1854	21	535
Mary Northington	600	100	1843	14	84
Ary Pettiford	—	150	1852	19	452
Betsy Parham	300	—	1853	20	133
	475	5	—	21	556
Coy Quivas	600	75	1853	20	463
Harriet Roberts	550	70	1849	17	616
Virginia Sturdivant	840	175	1857	24	37
Mary A. Stevens	800	75	1850	18	473
Robert Stewart	658	—	1860	25	582
Louisa Tucker	—	350	1852	19	272
Ed. Williams	167	50	1850	18	331
	100	165.75	1858	24	227
	650	125	1859	25	54
Dennis Wallace	550	80	1854	21	550
John Warren	500	150	1854	21	573
Margaret Walthall	500	—	—	—	—
Martha Whitfield	500	75	1846	15	285
Alex Walker	900	175	1851	18	469
John Walker	575	15	1859	25	172
Thomas Walden	800	300	1839	11	128

Value less than $500

Josiah Albert	275	45	1854	21	199
Moses Anderson	330	354	1857	24	184
Alex Brander	20	62.50	1858	24	696
Collin Bland	—	330	1858	24	396
Nancy Bailey	159	36	1858	24	386
Patsey Butler	150	75	1853	24	118
William Banks	150	37.50	1853	20	15
John Butcher	300	25	1851	18	501

APPENDIX I

Owner	Value 1860	Purchase Price	Date of Purchase	Reference Deed Book	Page
Mary Butler	$ 200	$ 790	1860	26	326
Loraine Butler	—	20	1851	19	49
Mary Butler	138	Love and affection	1857	23	719
William Bonner	280	300	1853	20	308
Archer Boon	175	67.50	1855	21	590
John Bannister	100	85	1855	22	121
William Berry	25	—	1857	23	614
Emmeline Boon	225	130	1858	24	537
Ann Berry	125	—	1853	20	45
Catherine Brown	75	33	1856	22	597
Salina Bonner	350	—	1853	20	56
Robert Buck	350	50	1854	21	245
Hannah Bird	100	65	1854	21	247
Thomas Brown	150	122	1854	21	440
Anderson Brander	175	38.75	1853	20	401
James Carter	217	Exchange of property	1858	24	535
Fleming Barnett	250	Love and affection	1842	13	8
Ambrose Bonner	300	50	1848	17	303
Thomas Berry	—	75	1858	24	326
Betsy Campbell	475	75	1860	25	730
Hezekeiah Chappel	175	75	1846	15	409
Sampson Chappel	375	50	1850	18	367
James Chavers	200	—	1856	26	645
Susan Chavers	50	50	1855	22	95
Henry Claiborne	—	300	1846	15	273
Benjamin Claudy	300	100	1854	21	248
Frances Cooley	230	—	—	—	—
Susan Curl (estate)	300	350	1822	7	80
Salina Darden	150	50	1858	24	357
Martha Diggs	366	300	1857	24	20
Ann E. Durden	250	Love and affection	1859	24	729

FREE NEGRO PROPERTY IN VIRGINIA

Owner	Value 1860	Purchase Price	Date of Purchase	Reference Deed Book	Page
John Durken	$ 250	$ 60	1854	24	729
Betsy Edmunds	50	50	1859	24	42
Philip Ellis	200	40	1855	22	318
John Adkins	450	5	1845	15	134
Caroline Farley	350	50	1845	21	472
George Farley	450	60	1842	13	54
Sylvia Farley	350	60	1856	22	731
William Finney	350	Love and affection	1853	20	126
James Ford	175	—	1857	23	725
John Garnes	100	Love and affection	1855	22	293
Thomas Garnes	—	500	1854	22	724
Ann Gilliam	240	72.50	1859	25	107
Asbury Gilliam	200	270	1856	23	365
Burwell Green	50	50	1857	24	180
Jane Green	100	100	1855	22	432
James Griffin	250	50	1854	21	545
Charles Haley	250	250	1855	21	613
Agnes Hargrave	400	250	1859	24	673
Laura Hargrave	100	Love and affection	1859	26	675
Maria Harris	400	—	1860	—	—
Nancy Harris	250	Love and affection	1846	15	375
Benjamin Hargrave	—	100	1858	—	—
Wiley Harris	350	100	1851	19	18
Maria Harrison	275	50	1852	19	350
Nancy Heath	100	150	1853	20	42
Glenery Henderson	100	80	1855	21	623
Amanda Hill	200	350	1856	22	695
Augustus Hill	100	150	1819	6	106
Mary Hill	400	50	1854	21	478
Mary A. Hill	300	75	1847	16	381
Polly Hill	450	35	1847	16	85
William Hill	50	100	1854	21	477

APPENDIX I

Owner	Value 1860	Purchase Price	Date of Purchase	Reference Deed Book	Page
Harriet Holloday	$ 375	$ 150	1857	24	163
Micajah Holloway	50	55	1858	24	382
Richard Hunt	380	190	1853	19	561
John Jackson	100	—	—	—	—
Milly Jackson	350	—	1846	15	557
Thomas Jackson	225	—	1853	20	563
William Jackson	400	30	1851	19	135
Henry Jenkins	225	114	1857	23	387
Joseph Jenkins	75	360	1857	23	497
Mary A. Jenkins	200	150	1855	22	6
Moses Jenkins	200	142.50	1855	22	316
Armistead Johnson	100	110	1854	21	250
Lucy Johnson	150	60	1833	9	32
Moses Johnson	350	12	1853	20	184
Susan Johnson	300	422.50	1856	23	307
Israel Jones	400	90	1860	26	110
Peter Jones	350	300	1857	23	647
Thomas Joynes	300	Love and affection	1860	25	442
Cynthia King	250	200	1855	22	76
James King	450	460.50	1853	20	236
Nicholas Mabry	70	40	1859	25	131
Willis Mabry	346	—	1856	22	557
Martha McKenna	200	300	1855	21	629
Henry Mason	300	450	1854	21	656
Peter Mathews	250	1	1830	8	319
Robert Merritt	175	150	1857	24	92
William Mitchell	225	67.50	1854	21	476
John Nash	100	70	1853	19	558
James Newsom	450	70	—	19	343
Arthur Parham	400	50	1854	21	249
Eliza Parham	350	80	1855	22	317
Hartwell Parham	175	50	1845	15	135
Robert Pelham	275	112.50	1854	21	474
David Penn	300	75	1854	21	325
Delphia Penn	175	55	1853	20	220

Owner	Value 1860	Purchase Price	Date of Purchase	Deed Book	Page
Robert Penn	$ 250	$ 250	1859	25	35
Nancy Ricks	275	70	1855	21	602
Thomas Rosser	260	Gift	1858	24	395
George Ruffin	200	100	1832	9	5
Luch Scott	75	200	1857	23	575
Mary Scott	240	72.50	1859	24	728
John K. Shore	100	200.60	1855	22	375
Lucrecia Smith	425	125	1853	20	45
Robert Smith	75	120	1859	25	97
Christopher Stevens	—	50	1858	24	407
Sally Steward	225	—	1843	14	427
Sarah Still	100	47.50	1855	22	253
Edward Stokes	207	—	1841	12	117
Margaret Swan	150	38.75	1858	24	479
Frances Tatum	250	—	—	—	—
William Taylor	250	20	1854	21	294
Aggie Thomas	180	—	1845	14	512
Elizabeth Thomas	50	—	—	—	—
Lillie Thomas	50	—	—	—	—
Mathew Thomas	475	—	—	—	—
Robert Thomas	80	—	—	—	—
Nancy Thompson	200	62.50	1855	21	747
Hosea Valentine	100	200	1857	23	578
John Valentine	350	120	1853	20	560
Milly Valentine	250	167.50	1853	20	328
Nancy Valentine	50	190	1857	24	81
Peter Valentine	458	—	1841	11	357
Rebecca Valentine	125	80	1856	22	494
Susan Valentine	488	425	1860	26	38
William Valentine	20	62.50	1852	19	390
Elizabeth Watkins	75	33.75	1858	24	477
John White	300	77.50	1853	19	558
John White	325	95	1847	16	572
Cudjo Williams	100	—	—	—	—
Alfred Winfield	274	65	1854	21	587

APPENDIX II

Free Negro Owners of 100 or More Acres

County	Farmer	Number of Acres
Accomac	Thomas Cropper	150
Albemarle	Anthony Shelton	100
Alleghany	Arthur Lee	413
Amelia	Alfred Anderson	670
Amelia	Francis Anderson	600
Amelia	William Anderson	278
Amelia	Nancy Harris	146½
Amelia	Edwin Harrison	290
Amelia	Peggy Holland	100
Amelia	Franky Miles	1,100
Amherst	Frederick Beverly	166½
Amherst	Samuel Beverly	201
Amherst	William W. Cooper	200
Amherst	James Clark, Sr.	230
Amherst	Preston Clark	200
Amherst	Peter Curry	250
Amherst	William B. Johns	109
Amherst	Henry A. Peters	200
Amherst	Clara A. Peters	141
Bedford	Edward Moss (est.)	140
Brunswick	Benjamin Manning	235
Brunswick	Nathaniel Moss	100
Brunswick	John Steward	421
Buckingham	John Epperson	198
Campbell	Ann Garvin	150
Campbell	Richard Parsons	175
Campbell	Morton Roberts	142
Campbell	Charles Wilson	200

County	Farmer	Number of Acres
Caroline	Washington Jeter	144
Caroline	Daniel Johnson	124
Caroline	Taliaferro Parker	184
Charles City	Samuel Brown, Jr.	110
Charles City	Samuel Hampton	360
Charles City	William Turner	152
Cumberland	Frank Lipscomb	119
Dinwiddie	John Harris	105
Dinwiddie	Richard Hill	137
Dinwiddie	Theophilus Steward	100
Elizabeth City	Carey Nettles	100
Essex	John H. Fortune	100
Fairfax	William Conner	200
Fairfax	George Harris	158
Fairfax	Jesse Harris	264
Fairfax	Osmond Quander	168
Fauquier	John Phillips	148
Floyd	Lot Jefferson	107
Fluvanna	Gordon Scott	110¼
Franklin	John Green	157
Frederick	Lewis Briscoy	120
Giles	Thomas Beasley	120
Goochland	Lydia Cousins	134½
Goochland	Henry Lynch	128
Goochland	Jacob Sampson	520
Halifax	Washington Byrd	117
Halifax	William Daniel	100
Halifax	William Epps	492
Halifax	Elizabeth Sutherland	114
Hanover	Pamelia Fortune	128
Henrico	Susan Key	100
Isle of Wight	James Ash	100
Isle of Wight	Joshua Bailey	110

APPENDIX II

County	Farmer	Number of Acres
Isle of Wight	Davy Butler	131
Isle of Wight	Manning Holloway	142¾
Isle of Wight	Martha Holloway	160
Isle of Wight	Tom Holloway	160
Isle of Wight	Levy Ricks	250
Isle of Wight	Madison Red	100
Isle of Wight	Joseph Tynes	111
Isle of Wight	John Tynes	161
Isle of Wight	Cyrus Tynes	150
Isle of Wight	Henry Tynes	109
James City	James R. Crawley	102¾
James City	Edward R. Crawley	232
James City	John Jackson	112
James City	Moses Moore	150
James City	Davy Taylor	150
King & Queen	Ransom Harris	473¾
King & Queen	George Kaughman (est.)	240
King & Queen	John Robinson	149
King & Queen	Lorenzo and John Robinson	285
King William	John Anderson	170
King William	Thornton Allman	117
Louisa	Cyrus Wilkerson	517
Louisa	Henry Wilkerson	162
Madison	Thomas Arrington	104
Mecklenburg	William Hayes	106
Mecklenburg	William H. Mitchell, Sr.	244
Mecklenburg	Beverly Valentine	171
Middlesex	Elijah Dungee	169
Middlesex	Thomas Key, Sr.	113½
Nansemond	Burwell Copeland	350
Nansemond	Elvy Copeland	126
Nansemond	Lemuel Copeland	298
Nansemond	Jack Douglas	268
Nansemond	David Faulk	163

County	Farmer	Number of Acres
Nansemond	Wright Faulk	200
Nansemond	George Faulk	102½
Nansemond	Dempsey Hare	363
Nansemond	Martha Hare	285
Nansemond	William Jackson	138
Nansemond	Levy Reed	193
Nansemond	Joseph Small	108
Nansemond	Henry White	107
Nansemond	Jerry Wiggins	220
Nelson	Joseph Dunning	134
New Kent	Robert Burgoine	100
New Kent	George Fox (est.)	129¾
New Kent	Carter Lewis	108
New Kent	Thomas Pearman	178¾
Norfolk	Charles Cutherell	150
Norfolk	Samuel Cutherell	151
Norfolk	Samuel Cuffee	139
Norfolk	Edward Sanford	180
Norfolk	Jesse Watts	165
Norfolk	Stephen Watts	120
Northampton	John T. Collins	115
Northampton	John Collins	137
Pittsylvania	Jesse Booker	185
Pittsylvania	James Davis	147¼
Pittsylvania	James H. Goin	246
Powhatan	Elizabeth Lipscomb	320
Prince George	William Gilchrist, Sr.	139
Prince George	Charles A. Gilliam	125
Princess Anne	Jacob Boush	200
Princess Anne	Johnsey Harrison	108
Princess Anne	Tatt Owens	112
Prince William	Henry Cole	155
Prince William	Hampton Gaskins	107
Prince William	Enoch Grayson	205
Prince William	Thomas McKey	116
Prince William	Howson Pinn	127
Prince William	James Robinson	150½

APPENDIX II

County	Farmer	Number of Acres
Prince William	William Thomas	195
Prince William	Olley Williams	113½
Richmond	Lavinia Fawcett	123
Richmond	Joseph Sisson	100
Richmond	Henry Thompson	100
Rockbridge	Isaiah Clark	100
Rockbridge	William A. Clark	200
Rockbridge	Sara W. Lyra	116
Rockbridge	Carey Scott	200
Rockingham	Samuel Madden	100
Southampton	William Brown	125
Southampton	Amos Copeland	239½
Southampton	James Hunt	130
Southampton	Arrena Jackson	762½
Southampton	Peter Jackson	190
Southampton	Nancy Turner	242
Stafford	Sally Johnson	155
Surry	Benjamin Brown	120
Surry	Champion Clayton	110½
Surry	Ned Holmes	350
Surry	Indiana Pretlow	100
Surry	William Pool	100
Surry	Gilbert Wooten	100
Sussex	Dudley Graves	123
Sussex	Cheesman Hargrave	114½
Sussex	Johnson Hargrave	100
Sussex	Abraham Hill	105
Sussex	Frederick Hill	116½
Sussex	Edwin Sampson	100
Sussex	John Sampson	167
Warwick	Thomas Wright	119
Washington	Margaret Beatie	255
Westmoreland	James Lewis	120
Westmoreland	Rhodam McCoy	144½
Westmoreland	John Roane	164½
Westmoreland	Jordan Tate	138½

INDEX

Abolitionists, Northern, 28, 48, 173
Accomac County, 70, 102, 108, 111, 178; citizens petition legislature, 18, 84-85; expel free Negroes, 24; restrict free Negroes' selling of products, 29
Actor, James, liberated slave, 174n
Adams, John, contractor, 151n, 157, 161
Agriculture, decline of, 34; improvement of, 38; notable advancement of, 40-41; small demand for slave labor in, 50; free Negroes divided into classes in, 102
Ailsworth, John B., slave owner, 178
Albemarle County, 123
Alexandria, 70, 96, 137, 153, 156, 161, 162; free Negroes leave, 25; industrial advance of, 46; advance in property ownership in, 155
Alleghany County, 116, 132n, 204; citizens petition legislature, 84-85
Allen, Edmund, slave owner, 178
Allen, Frank, 204
Allen, Stephen, storekeeper, 81
Allergue, Betsy, storekeeper, 144n, 167
Amelia County, 111, 116, 127, 128, 136, 174n, 202n, 203, 217, 224, 225
American Colonization Society, 3, 10, 11, 12, 15n, 30, 32; in Virginia promotes petition campaign, 12; petitions of local branches, Nansemond and Elizabeth counties, 15n; Northumberland, Lancaster, and Dinwiddie counties, 16; utterances of leaders, 16; opposed by some Virginians, 27-28; influence lost, 28; in Virginia, loses state appropriation, 30
Amherst County, 101, 111, 116, 123, 124n, 128, 132, 215; citizens petition legislature, 83n
Ampey, Backy, farmer, 129n
Anderson, Alfred, land owner, 122, 128, 215; free Negro slaveholder, 224, 225
Anderson, Benjamin, 118
Anderson, Francis and William, 127n, 128, 217; free Negro slaveholders, 224
Anderson, Henry, slaveholder, 127n, 128, 223, 224
Anderson, Joseph, iron master, Tredegar Iron Works, 54, 59, 178, 199
Anderson, Nathaniel, livery-stable operator, 142, 143
Anderson, William A., slave owner, 186
Angus, George, Moses, and Frank, sons of Judith, 213
Angus, Henry, grandson of Judith, 206, 213
Angus, Judith, free Negro slaveholder, 213
Antislavery sentiment, 7
Armistead, Carter, slave, 190
Armistead, Lewis, livery-stable operator, 141n, 143
Arrington, Thomas, 118
Artis, Dinks, apprentice, 73
Artis, O., apprentice, 75
Ashlock, John, teamster, 134
Ashton family, Westmoreland County, 104
Ashton, land owner, James City County, 106n
Atkins, Isaac, 83
Augusta County, citizens petition legislature, 8

Augusta, Georgia, 53
Auter, James, barber, 157

Bailey, Ben, 106
Bailey, James, 153
Bailey, Liddy, 187
Bailey, Samuel, barber, 141
Bailey family, 115
Baltimore, 47
Bancroft, Frederic, author, 176, 176n
Baptists, manumission by, 182-183n
Barber, James, 105
Barber trade, important in leading to property ownership, 156-157
Barbers, 101; a free Negro aristocracy, 97-98; advertise business, 97n; as slaveholders, 220
Barnes, Jacob, slaveholder, 75
Bartlett, Joseph, 142
Bascoe, Anthony, 190
Bath County, 109
Batte, Archibald, farmer, property holder, slaveholder, 208, 215, 224
Beasley, Thomas, 22
Beatie, Washington, master carpenter, 219
Beatty, Elizabeth, seamstress, 158n
Bedford County, 38, 125, 129, 132n
Bell, Graham, shoemaker, 144n, 167
Beneficial Society of Free Men of Color, constitution of, 163n
Bermuda Hundred, 224n
Berry, John, barber, 157
Berry, Thomas, 158n
Beverly, Fred, farmer, 128, 132
Beverly, Sam, farmer, 128
Beverly, slave, 177
Bias, Stephen, 204
Bird, H. D., railroad president, 74
Birkley family, 155n
Blacksmiths, numerous class of workers, 80; occupy a leading place, 95; rural, frequently successful, 134-135; ownership of property by, 157; ownership of slaves highly prevalent among, 217-218

Bland, Collin, 158n
Bledsoe, Alfred, proslavery advocate, 9
Blye, John, 141n
Boatmen, 101, 134; numerous class of workers, 77-79, 79n; as slaveholders, 219
Bolling, George, Petersburg slaveholder, 186, 212n
Bolling, Peter B., Virginia Negro in Ohio, 113n
Bolling, Robert, Petersburg slaveholder, 186, 212n
Bolling, Tom, slave, 186, 187
Bonner, Ambrose, 158n
Bonner, Berry, blacksmith, 157
Bonner, Winifred, 187
Booker, Jack, blacksmith, 144, 144n, 205n, 218
Booker, Jesse, farmer, 81, 132n
Bowles, Lucy T., 174n
Boyd, Henry, doctor, 165n
Brander, Moses Cook, 165n
Brander, Shadrack, cooper, 144, 144n
Brandum family, 82
Braxton, Thomas, 195
Bray, James, manumits slaves, 123
Breedlove, William, blacksmith, 218n
Brick masons, limited number in rural sections, 80; in cities, 96; farm owning by, 134
Brick yards, few operated by free Negroes, 81
Briggs, Robert M., Ohio slaveholder, 174n
Bristol, 219
Broadnax, General, 23
Brooks, Albert, livery-stable operator, 77n, 179n
Brooks, Patsey, 158
Brooks, Walter, minister, 77n
Brown, Abraham, blacksmith, 157
Brown, Alice, slave, 187, 192
Brown family, Charles City County, 119n, 121, 160, 160n
Brown family, Surry County, 120n
Brown, Hannah, 166

Brown, John, 99n
Brown, Samuel V., 187, 192
Brown, Samuel, Virginia-born Negro in Ohio, 113n
Brown, William, 140
Brunswick County, 107, 119, 133; citizens petition legislature, 83n
Bryant, William, 75
Buckingham County, 107n, 132n, 134; citizens petition legislature, 85-86
Bundy family, 114
Bundy, Rhyburn, carpenter, 219
Burch, Henry, 203, 204
Business enterprise, 81-82, 96-97. See also Merchants.
Butler family, 115
Butler, James, 99n
Butler, Luraney, drayman, 221
Byrd, Nancy, 208n
Byrd, William, 142

California, 199
Campbell County, 77, 111, 121, 132, 216, 219; citizens petition the legislature, 86
Campbell, James, Petersburg, 187
Campbell, James, Staunton, encounters the toils of the law, 21n
Campbell, Letty, 187
Campbell, Robert, barber, 156
Campbell, Robert, cooper, slaveholder, 209, 218
Carey, Archer, hackman, 26, 99, 143
Carey, Loudon and Judith, boatman and wife, 164
Carey, Lott, minister and missionary, 143, 146, 149
Carey, Sarah, 139, 166n
Carey, Thomas, 140, 166n
Caroline County, 108, 129, 227; citizens petition legislature, 8
Carpenters, numerous class of workers, 80, 95; in Mecklenburg County, 82; ownership of slaves by, 218-219
Carter, free Negro, 106
Carter, Jack, slave, 198

Carter, James, carpenter, hirer of slaves, 212, 212n, 229
Carter, Richard, 205n
Carter, slave, 64
Chandler, Phillip T., slaveholder, 73
Chandler, Richard, 85n
Channing, Edward, author, 43
Chappell, Howell, manumits slaves, 175
Charity family, 120n
Charity, Samuel, blacksmith, 134
Charles, free Negro, 83
Charles City County, 119n, 121, 132n, 134, 160, 204n, 211n; citizens petition legislature, 18
Charles, slave, 64
Charleston, John, 83n
Charleston, S.C., 119n, 228n
Charlotte County, 216
Charlottesville, 91n, 204
Chavous, John and Mack, Charlotte County, 216
Chavous, John, Mecklenburg County, 108, 224
Chesterfield County, 58, 75, 123, 208, 213, 215n; decline in free Negro population, 24
China, slave, 210
Chisman, Samuel, 105
Church life, 180n; interfered with, 21-22; deacons and trustees in, 96n; independent, 163
Church property, ownership of, in cities, 159-163
Clark, James A. L., Virginia-born Negro in Ohio, 113n
Clark, Robert, livery-stable operator, 97n, 156; slaveholder, 221, 225
Cocke, William, 142
Coleman, Jamima, 192n
Coleman, Thomas, blacksmith, slaveholder, 218n
Coles, Edward, manumits many of his slaves, 123
Colliers, in town of Manchester, 75
Collins, John T., farmer, 131
Colonization, to Liberia, watchword

INDEX

Colonization (*continued*)
of the day, 19, 31; from cities, 146-148
Colonization Society, American. *See* American Colonization Society.
Colson, James M., barber, 144n, 145n, 163n, 169
Colson, James M., shoemaker, 96n
Colson, William N., barber, business adventurer in Liberia, 144n, 145n, 147, 148, 149, 169, 208n. *See also* Roberts, Colson, and Company.
Combs, Beverly, shoemaker, 134
Comer, Dennis, blacksmith, 84n
Concubinage, a common practice, 93
Confectionaries, a few operators of, 81; property ownership by operators of, 156
Contractors, 95-96; extensive property owners, 157-158
Conveyance of property. *See* Wills.
Cook, Catherine, 149
Cook, Fields, 151n, 197, 197n
Cook, Harriet, 86
Cook, Jane, operator of boats, 164
Cooks, number of, comparatively small, 94
Cooler, Phil, 83n
Cooper, John, storekeeper, 81; slaveholder, 221
Coopers, 80, 95; a few slaveholders among, 218
Copeland, Charles, liberates slaves, 172
Cosby, John, 214n
Cousins, Charles, 83n, 107, 204n
Cousins, Phillip, boatman, 132n
Craghall, Elijah, hires out a slave, 177
Cuffee, William Miles, 24n
Culpeper County, 58, 73; citizens petition legislature, 60, 67
Cumberland County, 77, 80, 111, 118, 119n, 125, 126, 129, 202n, 211n, 216, 217, 222n
Cunningham, Virginia, seamstress, 151n, 158n; as slaveholder, 210

Cunningham, William, Virginia-born Negro in Ohio, 113n
Curry, Peter, farmer, 128, 132n

Dailey, Joseph, fisherman, 142
Daniel, Charles, 121n
Daniel, William, and family, 121
Davis, Gresset, liberates slaves, 172
Davis, James City County land owner, 106
Davis, Merit, apprentice, 73
Dawson, Fred, 140, 190
Dean, Ann Maria, seamstress, 197
Dean family, mechanics, 83n
DeBaptist family, contractors, 140, 154, 157; as slaveholders, 218
Debrix, John, 120
Deed, making of debts by trust, 104-105, 104n-105n; purchase of property by bargain and sale, 117-118, 138-139; bequest of property by gift from free Negroes to relatives, 167, 167n; slaves liberated by manumission, 174n, 175n; slaves offered as security for loans by trust, 207, 207-208n
Dentists, "tooth drawers," 142
Depp, Abraham, blacksmith, 84, 123
Dew, Thomas R., proslavery advocate, 9, 10, 27
Dinwiddie County, Colonization Society of, 16, 58, 81, 107, 111, 115, 124n, 129, 132n; acts of manumission in, 175, 219
District of Columbia, 98; receives Alexandria free Negroes, 26, 155
Ditchers, free Negroes fitted for, 66; numerous, 80-81; ownership of property by, 157
Docey, slave, 213
Donnan, A., creditor to free Negro, 197n
Douglas, Jack, 152, 153
Douglass, Mrs. Margaret, illegal school teacher, 20n
Downing family, 108

INDEX

Drake, Francis, barber, 141
Draymen, 97; slaveholders, 220-221
Driver, Samuel, oysterer, 134
Drummond, Braxton, oysterer, 134
Dungee, waterman, 83n
Dunlop, Alexander, blacksmith, 153, 153n
Dunlop, James, 165n, 192
Dunnaway, Robert, 175
Dunstan family, musicians, 83
Dunston, James City County land owner, 106

Eastern Shore, seat of hostility to free Negroes, 13, 24; 111-112, 130
Edmund, slave, 177
Education, unlawful to obtain, 19-21, 21n; common among barbers, 98; provision for in wills, 165
Elebeck, Elizabeth, slaveholder, 206
Elebeck, Henry, barber, 157
Elebeck, Major, father of Henry, 96n, 99n, 144n, 145n, 163n
Elick, carpenter, 83n
Elizabeth City County, declines in free Negro population, 24; free Negro farm tenantry in, 105, 124
Ellis, James, Virginia-born Negro in Ohio, 113n
Elson, John, groceryman, 143
Emancipation, gradual, 8, 9
Emigration, 35; competition of free Negro causes white, 68
Employment, free Negro, conditions of, 70-71; systems of, 71-74; apprenticeship contract for, 72-73; with slaves, 74-75; in gangs, 75; greater opportunity for, in cities, 91-92; preponderance of women in, 92-93; demand for women as servants in, 94. *See also* Labor, Wages.
Epperson, John, wheelwright and farmer, 107n, 132n
Eppes, Edward, farmer, 207n, 216
Eppes, Winney, manumitted slave, 192

Epps, William, farmer, 107, 129, 129n
Essex County, 114, 116, 219n; citizens petition legislature, 85
Evans, Margaret, 139
Evans, Phillip, 158n
Evans, Randle, confectioner, 97, 156, 198; slaveholder, 221
Evans, William, shoemaker, 219

Fairfax County, 58, 176; agricultural improvement in, 41
Falmouth, gains in property ownership, 141, 215n
Family relations, 167-168, 171, 181, 187-188, 204. *See also* Wills.
Farley, G. A., sells slave, 187
Farley, Martha, mistress, slaveholder, 224
Farmers, in Mecklenburg County, 82; owners of slaves, 215-217
Farming, types of, subsistence, 110, 134; commercial, 128-134; truck, 130; general, 130-132
Farm home, the typical farm, 110
Farm laborers, 77; preponderance of, 102-103, 134-135
Farm land, ownership of, 102, 109-112. *See also* Farm owners.
Farm owners, 102; process of becoming, 106-107; number of, 109-110; areas of most rapid progress of, 110-111; areas of limited number of, 111, 114; Virginia-born, in Ohio, 112-113, 113n; effect of color on number of, 115-116, 116n; land of, acquired by purchase, 117-118; land of, acquired by will, 118-121, 120n; land of, held by successive generations, 119, 119n; land of, acquired by gift from white persons of, limited, 121-127; land of, acquired by gift dissipated, 125-126, 126n; land of, acquired by miscegenation, 126-127, 127n; percentage of, 134; number acres held by, in 1860, 136

Farm products, 107-108, 128-132
Farm property, chattel, 104-109, 128-133, 133n
Farm tenants, process of becoming, 104-106; valuable to communities, 107-108; number of, 109
Farmville, 95, 96, 137, 156, 219, 220n
Farrow, Joseph, carpenter, 91n
Fauquier County, 63, 72, 80, 111, 116, 124n, 176, 203
Fentress, Emanuel, 124
Ferguson, James, 139
Ferguson, John, 151n, 166n; as slaveholder, 220n
Finney, William, 158n
Fishermen, 79, 142; numerous class of workers, 77. See also Boatmen.
Fishmongers, 97
Fitzhugh, George, proslavery advocate, 9, 27, 66, 90
Flora, slave, 210, 211
Florida, 89
Floyd family, mechanics, 83n
Floyd, Governor, of Virginia, 8, 21, 28
Fluvanna County, 134, 135n
Ford, James, barber, 157
Fort Monroe, 81
Foster, John T., 174n
Francis and George, slaves
Francis, Robert, slave hirer, 177
Franklin County, 219n
Fraternal societies, ownership of property by, 162-163
Fred, Betsy, and Susan, slaves, 224
Frederick County, 63, 103, 134, 219
Fredericksburg, 96, 122n, 137, 139, 145, 157, 161, 162, 166, 218, 219; free Negroes petition legislature, 20; manufactures of, 45-46; advances in property ownership in, 139-141; declines in property ownership in, 153-154; manumission in, 174, 184-191
"Free Contract Labor in the Ante-Bellum South," by Alfred H. Stone, 227-228n

Free Negro Heads of Families in the United States, Carter G. Woodson, editor, 71n
Free Negro Owners of Slaves, Carter G. Woodson, editor, 201n-202n
Free papers, free Negroes punished for loss of, 19
Friends. See Quakers.
Fruit vendors, 97

Gallee, Eliza, 149
Gallego, Humbro, 143
Gardner, Dawson, drayman, 157
Garnes, Thomas, bricklayer, 96n, 158n
George, slave, 64
Gibbs, Thomas, receives deed of manumission, 186
Gibbs, William, 190
Gift of property, uncommon from whites to free Negroes, 117, 121-122, 126, 138; by miscegenation, 126-127, 127n. See also Deed.
Giles County, free Negroes petition legislature, 22
Giles, Governor, of Virginia, 27, 28, 89
Gilliam, J. S., hires slave to free Negro, 221
Gilliam, Rebecca, bequest of slaves to, 222, 225n
Gilliam, Walter B., wills allotment of slaves to free Negro, 223, 224n, 225n
Gilly, manumitted slave, 172
Gist, Samuel, liberator of many slaves, 123
Gladman, Claiborne, barber, 143
Gladman, Thomas, barber, 220
Gloucester County, 79, 81, 119n, 126n, 134; citizens petition legislature, 14, 83n
Godfree, subject of petition to legislature, 83n
Godwin, Benjamin, subject of petition to legislature, 99n

Goldsberry, Gideon, blacksmith and slaveholder, 218n
Goochland County, 30, 81, 89, 106, 116, 118, 121, 123, 130, 132, 134, 136, 177, 210n, 211, 216; revokes license of free Negro, 29
Goodman, Ben, carpenter, shoemaker, 85
Goodwyn, Godfrey, slave, 187
Goodwyn, Peterson, 187
Gordon, Robert, slave, buys himself, 198
Gordon, William, 190
Grant & Stone, merchants, Philadelphia, 148
Graves, Elizabeth, daughter of Richmond Graves, 165n
Graves, Richmond, livery-stable operator, 144, 144n, 148
Graves, Susannah, widow of Richmond Graves, 165
Gray, George, barber, 151n; as slaveholder, 220n
Gray, Isaac, storekeeper, 156
Gray, Lewis C., author, 173
Gray, William, butcher, 156
Green, Aggy, slave, 188
Green, Burwell, 106
Green, Jane, manumitted slave, 193, 197
Green, Jesse, 188, 196
Green, Thomas A., sells slave, 187
Greenhow, Solomon, bricklayer, 134
Greensville County, 81, 215
Griffin, Thomas, 165
Grimes, Susan, farmer, 129n
Grocers, 81; numerous in Richmond, 97, 143; property ownership of, 156

Hack drivers, 97; property holders, 157
Halifax County, 82, 107, 129
Haines, R., farmer, 129n
Hall, Thomas, 151n
Hamilton family, 155n
Hampton, Samuel, farmer, 132n
Hampton, town of, advance in property ownership, 152-153
Hanover County, 49n, 123, 134, 174n, 202n, 203, 219; types of farm population, 105-106
Harding, Joseph, liberator of slaves, 172
Hardships of free Negroes, public opinion hostile, 3; laws, state and local, restrain, 3-5; numbers kept as small as possible, 5-6; proslavery sentiment increases, 6-10; efforts made to remove, 8-11; laws to restrain increase in number after 1830, 11, 19-23; citizens petition to remove, 11-16; citizens petition to restrict, 17-19; communities resort to physical violence, 23-24, 112; literature denounces, 26-27; governors attack, 28; undesirable in a land wedded to slavery, 31; public sentiment hostile in Ohio, 113-114
Hare, Dempsey, farmer, 130
Hare, Elijah, 112n
Harris, Catherine, 210
Harris, Ransome, farmer, 116, 130
Harris, Sterling, manumitted slave, 174n
Harrison, Edwin, tobacco farmer, 128
Harrison, Nathaniel, 127, 223
Harrisonburg, town of, 156
Harwell, Armistead, 186
Hawkins, Peter, dentist, 142, 165
Haxall mill, oldest flour mill in Richmond, 43
Hayes, William H., wagoner, farmer, 80, 83, 132n
Haynes, Thomas, 125
Henderson, Richard W., barber, slaveholder, 220n
Henrico County, 125, 130, 150, 203, 204n, 205n, 208; Quakers defend free Negroes, 19; Quakers manumit slaves, 150; citizens petition legislature, 67
Henry County, 103n, 212
Henry, slave, 210, 211

Herndon, Charles, liberates slave, 186
Hicks, Mathew, carpenter, slaveholder, 219n
Higby, Lot, 205n
Hill, Mathew, 107n
Hill, Minnis, hires out slave, 212
Hill, Richard, carpenter, 132n; as slaveholder, 219
Hill, Robert, blacksmith, 157
Hoard, Benjamin, 83n; wills slaves to free Negro, 224n
Hobson, Richard C., barber, 161, 197; as slaveholder, 220
Holloway family, 115
Holloway, Robert, 196
Hope, Caesar, liberates slave daughter by will, 204n
Hope, Mary, seamstress, 158n
Household furnishings, 144, 168-170
Howard, Abram, 141, 215
Howard, William B., blacksmith, slaveholder, 218n
Hungerford, P. C., 104n
Hunt, Gilbert, blacksmith, 157, 197, 218

Illinois, 59, 123
Indiana, 68
Insurrection, slave, Nat Turner in, 7, 13, 21
Internal improvements, backwardness of, 36-37; building of railroads and canals as, 38-39; rapid advancement in, 46-47
Isaac, farm manager, 84
Isaacs, Tucker, painter, 113n
Ishmael, liberated slave, 172
Isle of Wight County, 14n, 70, 71, 106, 111, 115, 119n, 124, 126, 129, 132, 135; citizens petition legislature, 83
Ivey, Fred, inherits slaves from mother, Priscilla, 224
Ivey, Frederick, wills large estate to Priscilla Ivey, 127

Ivey, Priscilla, large land owner, 122, 127; as slaveholder, 216, 224

Jackson, Booker, shoemaker, 96, 156, 166n; as slaveholder, 219
Jackson, Daniel, preacher, 144, 144n
Jackson, Edward, 166
Jackson, Henry, pilot, 141, 142
Jackson, James, 127n
Jackson, Mary, 210n
Jackson, Patty and Arrena, 127n
Jackson, Robert, Virginia-born Negro in Ohio, 113n
Jackson, Walter, carpenter, 219n
James City County, 14n, 70, 106, 111, 116, 134
James, slave, 64
James, William, slave, 209
Jarratt, Alexander, writes letter to wife Nancy, 167
Jarratt, Richard, boatman, 77, 96n, 144, 144n, 167; hirer of slaves, 212n
Jarvis family, will property to one another, 119; slaveholders, 208
Jarvis, Thomas, 207
Jeffers, Sylvia, 222
Jenkins, Joseph, 158n
Jenkins, Peter, 118, 129n
Jenkins, Sarah, 124
Jenkins, William, hires slaves, 177
Jeter, Washington, farmer, 129n
Jimmerson, William, oysterer, 134
Jinney, slave, 213
Joan, slave, 206
John, sawyer, 84
Johns, Tarleton, farmer, 128
Johnson, G. G., manumits slave, 184
Johnson, George, shoemaker, 141n
Johnson, Governor, of Virginia, 28
Johnson, James, 203n
Johnson, Jesse, 73
Johnson, Levi, shopkeeper, 141, 141n
Johnson, Richard, Virginia-born Negro in Ohio, 113n
Johnston, Samuel, slave, buys himself and members of his family, 203, 204

Jones, Elvira, 99n
Jones, Israel, 158n
Jones, William, 125
Jones, William, pensioner from the Revolutionary War, 140
Jordan, Fleming, 85
Judah, Benjamin, shoemaker, 151n, 157
Judkins family, 115

Kean, Edmund, livery-stable operator, 86, 97, 152, 155, 198; as slaveholder, 221
Keeling, Ned, drayman, 141n, 154, 157; hires slaves, 220
Kelley, John, farmer, 120
Kelly, Nancy, 207n
Kennard, Richard, 97
King, Rhoda, seamstress, 158n
King and Queen County, 38, 116, 130, 131n, 134, 136, 177
King George County, 104, 108, 111, 116, 202n
King William County, 124n, 126n, 134; citizens petition legislature, 83n
Knight, Thomas, barber, 141, 142

Labor, reorganization in the system of, 48; by white men, 58-59, 63; conflict of white and black, 59; by white women, 60-61; free Negro, 61; great demand for free Negro, in manufacturing, 64, 68-69; demand for white, in factories, 64-65; advantages of free Negro, 65-67; disadvantages of white, 67; competition of free Negro and white, 67-68, 153-154; free Negro, indispensable in certain areas, 70-71; free Negro, indispensable to the state, 87-90, 101; free Negro, valuable in estimation of governors, 89; free Negro, valuable in estimation of critics, 89; competition of free Negro and slave, 90-91; by free Negro women, 93-94; free Negro, skilled, 95-97; free Negro, valuable in urban areas, 99; free Negro, increasing in value, 229. *See also* Employment, Occupations, Wages.
Lancaster County, 16, 118, 135
Land, decline in value of, 26; rise in value of, 41, 158
Land ownership. *See* Farm owners.
Langley, Elizabeth, 93n
Langston, John M., Virginia-born Negro in Ohio, 114n
Langston, Lot, farmer, 131n
Langston, William, Virginia-born Negro in Ohio, 113n
Law of 1806, 6; inoperative, 12-13, 83; effect of, on manumitted slaves remaining in the state, 191-192
Lawrenceville, town of, 81, 218n
Ledley, hired slave, 212
Lee, Arthur, blacksmith, 84, 116, 132n, 134, 204
Lee, George, farm owner, 134
Leftwich, William, blacksmith, 132n
Legal disabilities, free Negroes, denied governmental rights and privileges, 3-4; must establish or prove free status, 4; municipalities impose restrictive ordinances on, 4; forbidden to move from place to place, 4-5, 5n; forbidden to move entirely, 5; forbidden to come into Virginia, 6; compelled to leave state after manumission by law of 1806, 6; increase in number in the period following 1830, 6; forbidden to learn to read and write, 19-20, 20n; forbidden to return to Virginia if educated outside the state, 20, 21n; unlawful for free person to bring into Virginia, 21; forbidden to preach, 21; denied right of trial by jury, 22; forbidden to keep firearms, 22; forbidden to acquire property in slaves, 23; forbidden to sell products without written certif-

Legal disabilities (*continued*)
icate, 28-29, 29n; forbidden to operate ordinaries or retail ardent spirits, 29; subject to removal from state, 29-30; discriminated against in taxation, 30; reduced to voluntary enslavement, 31. *See also* Law of 1806, Petitions to legislature.

Legal rights, of free Negroes to acquire, own, and sell property, 31

Lemm and Washington, slaves, 225

Leslie and Brydon, tobacco manufacturers, 74

Lewis, Charles, boatman, 164, 190; as slaveholder, 206

Lewis, Daniel, 141

Lewis, James, blacksmith, slaveholder, 218n

Lewis, John, 140

Lewis, Turner, 204n

Lewis, William, drayman, 220n

Liberia, 25, 30, 192; migration of Richmond and Petersburg free Negroes to, 146-149

Lindsay, slave, 207

Lipscomb, Billy and Nancy, 126, 222

Lipscomb, Frank, farmer, 129n; hires out slave, 211n

Lipscomb, Henry, wills property to free Negroes, 126; wills slaves, 222

Lipscomb, John, wagoner, 80, 217

Lipscomb, Kitty, 222

Literford, Pleasant, 113n

Liverymen, 77n, 97n, 141n, 143, 144n; slaveholders, 221

Livery stable, business of, greatest property-producing occupation, 155

Logan, John, liberates members of his family, 189-190

Logan, Washington, boatman, slaveholder, 219

Loudon County, 57, 63, 75, 132; citizens petition legislature, 8, 17, 85, 86-87; free Negroes leave, 25

Louisa County, 29n, 57, 121, 124, 129, 209

Louisiana, 116n, 228n

Lucas, John, 105n

Lunenburg County, 79, 120, 132n, 207n, 216

Lyles family, 155n

Lynchburg, 26, 47, 74, 93n, 95, 137, 139, 156, 157, 161, 162, 176, 219, 220, 221

Lyon, David, 74

Lyons, William B., barber, 151n, 197

McCowen, George, blacksmith, 134

McCoy, Fleet, 118

McCrae, Jack, restaurant owner, 97, 156, 206

McFarland, William, 73

McKenna, Martha, 158n

McPherson, Christopher, bookkeeper, 165

Madison County, 118

Manchester, town of, 137n, 218

Mann, Burwell, slave seeking freedom, 182, 182n

Manufacturing, Virginian, dependent upon North, 36; growth of, 38; great awakening of, 42-46

Manumission, slave, doctrine of rights of man leads to, 5, 171-172, 182; law of 1806 attempts to check, 6; affected by slave hiring, 52, 176-181; frequent during Revolutionary period, 171-172; frequency of, from 1830 to 1860, 173-175; confined largely to cities after 1830, 173-176; affected by presence of free Negroes, 181; promoted by owners during the Revolutionary period, 182; promoted by slaves themselves after 1830, 182-183; by self-purchase, 183-187; by purchase and act of free Negro relatives, 187-190; by purchase and act of free Negro friends, 191. *See also* Law of 1806, Permission to remain, Slaves.

Margaret, slave, 210n

Marshall, William, receives freedom, liberates others, 186, 189, 190
Martin, James A., 134
Martin, Joseph, author, 38
Martin, R. A., 196
Maryland, 59, 62, 72, 80
Mason, Henry, bricklayer, 5
Mathews, Anthony, liberates members of his family, 208
Mathews County, 57
Mathews, James Z., 223, 224
Mathews, Peter, boatman, 96n, 164
Mathews, Sarah, Jane, John, Walter, children of Rebecca, 223
May, David, 165n
May family, frequent liberators of slaves, 185n
May, James, 186
Mayo, Joseph, mayor of Richmond, 195
Mayo, William, farmer, 82
Mecklenburg County, 80, 81, 108, 127, 132n, 216, 224; occupations of free Negroes in, 82
Merchants, 81; in Liberia, 147-148; as slaveholders, 221
Methodists, manumission by, 116n, 182-183n
Michigan, receives free Negro migrants, 25, 154
Middlesex County, 119n, 124, 224n; citizens petition legislature, 83n
Migration, free Negro, forbidden to Virginia, 6, 21; to North and Northwest, 25; to District of Columbia, 26, 155; to North Carolina, 26; intrastate, from country to town, 91-92; to Ohio, 112-113, 123, 124n, 198; to Michigan, 154
Miles, Frankey, large land owner, 122, 127, 128; as a slaveholder, 217, 225n
Miller, Edward, caulker, 166n
Miller, Jesse, slave, 190
Millers, 99n
Minor, Jane, nurse, 191, 191n
Minor, John, 139, 166n

Miscegenation, acquiring land by, 126-127, 127n, 182n
Missouri Compromise, 7
Mitchell, Crawley, barber, 220n
Mitchell, Jones, 166, 186
Mitchell, William H., farmer, 82
Moore, James City County land owner, 106
Moore, Louisa, 154
Morgan, Peter G., liberates members of his family, 205n
Morris, George, 207
Morris, James, oysterer, 134
Morris, Jordan, liberated slave, 174n
Morton, Betty and William, slaves, 190
Morton, Peter, purchaser of his children, 190
Mulattoes, ownership of land by, 115-116; number less than blacks, 116n; manumission of slave, by white relatives, 182n
Munford, Beverly, author, 173
Musicians, in Mecklenburg County, 82-83

Nansemond County, 70, 112n, 115, 119n, 124n, 129, 130, 131n, 152; great increase in farm ownership, 110-111
New Kent County, 116, 136, 215; citizens petition legislature, 18, 106
New York, 147, 148, 167; foreign trade compared with Virginia, 35-36
Nooks, Noah B., Virginia-born Negro in Ohio, 113n
Norfolk, 37, 57-58, 70, 93, 98, 137, 139, 145, 146, 157, 160, 161, 162, 163, 167, 203, 220; industrial advance of, 44; fails to become great seaport, 47; citizens petition legislature, 62-63, 99-100; growth of property ownership in, 141-142; decline in property ownership in, 153-154
Norfolk County, 24n, 115, 119n, 129,

Norfolk County (*continued*) 130; citizens petition legislature, 15
Northampton County, 111, 131, 204; citizens petition legislature, 13-14; expel free Negroes, 24
North Carolina, 45, 101; migration of Virginia Negroes to, 26
Northumberland County, 16, 80, 119n, 215; citizens petition legislature, 18; declines in free Negro population, 25
Nottoway County, 107, 204n, 205n; citizens petition legislature, 83n
Nurses, services valuable, 94

Occupations, free Negro, list of, 75-76, 76n; employers and employees in certain kinds of, 76-77; skilled and unskilled, 77; competition of slaves and whites in, 77; in Mecklenburg County, 82; washerwomen and tobacco factory hands lead all others among women in, 93; barber one of leading, 95-96; list of, in Petersburg, 98-99; have good representation in certain fields in the state, 101. *See also* Employment, Free Negroes, Labor.
Ohio, 68, 123, 174n; receives Negro exiles, 25, 112; property acquired in, 112-114; bounty land in, 152n
Olmsted, F. L., author, 52, 69, 103
Orange County, 57, 205n, 207, 209, 218
Orr, James, factory owner, 74
Owen family, 119
Oysterers, numerous class of workers, 77, 79; farm owning, 134

Page, Jacob, 96n, 206
Painters, in Mecklenburg County, 82
Parham, Simon, 204n
Parham, Stith, liberates slaves, 172
Parker, Henry, 85
Parsons, Richard, boatman, farmer, 132, 216, 219

Patty, Accomac County, 85
Pearman, Thomas, 215
Penn, Robert, 158n
Pennsylvania, 59
Permission to remain in Virginia, 5, 5n, 6, 127n, 192-195; numerous requests for, 83-87; land given by whites on condition of obtaining, 124-125
Personal property, holdings of city real estate owners, 140-145, 148, 153, 156, 164-167. *See also* Household furnishings.
Peters, Henry, farmer, 132n
Peters, William, livery-stable operator, 155
Petersburg, 5n, 20n, 37, 53, 58, 64, 65, 70, 74, 78, 79, 91, 93, 94, 95, 96n, 97, 118n, 122n, 137, 138, 146, 147, 148, 154, 156, 157, 158, 160, 161, 162, 163, 164, 166, 167, 168, 172, 175n, 176, 182, 203, 205n, 210, 211, 212n, 218, 219n, 221, 222, 225, 229; enacts ordinances, 4; citizens petition legislature, 21, 99-100; manufactures of, 38-39, 44-45, 68; as slave-hiring center, 52, 177-181; increases in free Negro population in, 91-92; occupations of free Negro heads of families in, 98; property owners of, listed, 139; advances in property ownership in, 144-145, 149-152; manumissions in, 174, 183-191; manumitted Negroes seek permission to remain in, 192-196; manumitted Negroes acquire property in, 196-197; free Negro ownership of slaves in, 201, 206-207
Petersburg Daily Express, 68
Petersburg South Side Democrat, extols slavery, 26-27
Peterson, William, apprentice, 72
Petitions to legislature from white citizens, to abolish slavery, 8-9; to remove free Negro, 11-12; to condemn free Negro, 12, 13, 14, 15, 16, 17, 18, 19, 62, 67, 74, 114; to protect

INDEX

free Negro, 62-63, 83, 83n, 84, 84n, 85, 86, 99n, 100, 101
Philadelphia, 21n, 147, 148; receives free Negro exiles, 24
Phillips, Ulrich B., author, 96, 164n, 173, 178
Piedmont section, Virginia, 8
Pierce family, Goochland County, 118, 211
Pierce, John, 121, 211
Pierce, Mildred, slaveholder, 220n
Pilots, 141-142, 152n
Pinn, Turner, farmer, 215
Pitts, Caleb, drayman, 157, 220n
Pittsylvania County, 81, 123, 132n
Pleasants, John, farmer, 128, 150
Pleasants, Samuel, Quaker antislavery leader, 150
Poll tax (capitation), 228-229
Population, Virginia, distribution of free Negro, 15, 70; relative decline in, 24, 34-35; increase in, 41
Port Royal, town of, 81, 221
Portsmouth, 137, 153; citizens petition legislature, 67
Powell, E., 75
Powhatan County, 14n, 77, 116, 123, 126, 136, 216, 217, 219; citizens petition legislature, 18, 84; acts of manumission in, 175
Preachers, 143, 144n
Pretlow family, Isle of Wight County, 115
Pretlow family, Surry County, 120n
Pretlow, William, 210n
Pride, Armistead, barber, 157, 220
Prince Edward County, 77; occupations of free Negroes in, 78, 125
Prince George County, 40, 49n, 115, 124n, 129, 136, 204n, 208, 215n, 223; suffers decline in Negro population, 24
Prince William County, 103
Princess Anne County, 124, 129; suffers decline in free Negro population, 24
Pritchett family, Alexandria, 155n

Proslavery sentiment, in the South, 6-7; Virginia swings to, 7-8, 50; campaign of education to promote, 9-10
Purdie, Eliza, nurse, 85
Purdie, Thomas, 124

Quakers, 8n; befriend free Negroes, 19; manumission by, 116n, 150-151
Quarles, John D., 210
Quarles, Ralph, 114n
Quinitchett family, painters, 82
Quivas, Coy, bricklayer, 158n
Quivers, Emanuel, hired slave, 198

Ragland, Reuben, 97
Randolph, John, statesman, 37, 124
Randolph, Richard, liberates slaves, 125
Raymond, John T., school teacher, 20n
Real estate under free Negro ownership, summary of, 227; value of, 227. *See also* Farm land, Farm owners, Town lots.
Removal, of free Negroes, 10-13; bill in legislature, 14, 29-30. *See also* Colonization, American Colonization Society.
Restaurants, few operators of, 81; property ownership by operators of, 156
Review of the Debate in the Virginia Legislature of 1831 and 1832, stimulates proslavery sentiment, 10
Rich, Charles, 118
Rich family, Richmond County, 114
Rich family, Westmoreland County, 104
Richard, slave, 64
Richards, Maria, migrant to Detroit, Michigan, 154
Richmond, 37, 39, 47, 58, 59, 60, 64, 65, 70, 74, 78, 79, 91, 92, 93, 94, 95, 96, 97, 98, 122n, 123, 130, 137, 138, 139, 145, 146, 154, 156, 157, 158, 159, 161, 162, 165, 172, 176, 202n, 203, 208n,

Richmond (*continued*)
210, 211, 212n, 213, 217, 218, 219, 220, 221, 222; free Negroes of, petition legislature, 21, 99-100; manufactures of, 43-44, 46, 68-69; as slave-hiring center, 52, 177-181; slaves in factories of, 55; gains in property ownership in, 142-143, 150-152; manumission in, 174, 183-191; manumitted Negroes seek permission to remain in, 192-196; manumitted Negroes acquire property in, 197-199

Richmond County, 114; citizens petition legislature, 18; restrict free Negroes' selling of goods, 29; acts of manumission in, 175

Richmond Dispatch, opposes expulsion bill, 88-89

Richmond Enquirer, 44, 56; extols slavery, 26; opposes expulsion bill, 87

Richmond Examiner, extols slavery, 26

Richmond Times, opposes expulsion bill, 88-89

Richmond Whig, opposes expulsion bill, 88-89

Ricks family, 116

Rights of man, doctrine of, 5

Roanoke County, 109

Robert, slave, 210

Roberts, Amelia and Joseph J., Liberia colonizationists, 146

Roberts, Colson, and Company, merchant adventurers in Liberia, 146

Roberts, George, 118

Roberts, James, boatman, 167

Roberts, Joseph Jenkins, boatman, president of Liberia, 147, 148

Robinson, James, drayman, 157, 221

Robinson, Lorenzo, farmer, 131n

Robinson, Monday, shoemaker, 219

Rockbridge County, 111, 136

Rockingham County, citizens petition legislature, 17

Rogers, Aaron, shoemaker, 141n

Rolls, William, blacksmith, slaveholder, 207, 218

Ryland, Reverend Robert, pastor of Negro church, 161

Saloon keepers, 97; property ownership of, 156

Sampson, Ben, and family, 120

Sampson, Jacob, farmer, tavern keeper, slaveholder, 29, 81, 130, 131n

Sandridge, Richard, 124

Savoy, Mary, storekeeper, 156

Sawyers, numerous, 80

Schools, 20n

School teachers, 20n, 144n

Scott, Elizabeth, slave, 190

Scott, George, carpenter, 141n

Scott, Judge John, 180

Scott, Mary, 158n

Scott, Sally, farmer, 132

Scott, Thomas, contractor, slaveholder, 96n, 157, 219n, 225

Scott, William, farmer, 130

Seaman, Cora, 165n

Seamstresses, numerous, 94; rank high as property owners, 158

Seaton, George, contractor, 157

Sewell, Phil, drayman, 157, 196, 196n

Sexual vice, 93n. *See also* Concubinage.

Shanklin, William, 104

Shenandoah County, 109

Shepherd, Joseph, school teacher, 144n, 146, 167

Shepherd, Mosby, 203, 204

Shepherd, Moses, 203

Shoemakers, numerous class of workers, 80, 96; advertise business, 96n; farm owning among, 134; few slaveholders among, 219-220

Shopkeepers, majority own real estate, 156

Shore, John K., barber, 97n, 157

Sims, James, hirer of slaves, cooper, 212n, 218

Slave hiring, 62; assumes large proportions, 51-52; centered in cities, 52, 176-178; cost of, 64, 158; in tobacco factories, 94n; leads to manumission, 176-181; to one's self, 195-196

Slaveholding, free Negro, motives and methods of acquiring, 200; in Petersburg, 201, 206-207; amount of, greater in cities, 202-203; benevolent, 202-204; commercial, 205-213, 217; non-agricultural, 215n; size of farms a factor in, 214-216; size of business operation a factor in, 216-217; largest amount in Amelia County, 217; influenced by certain trades, 217-222; possession by purchase on the market, 222; possession by will from white persons, 222-225; records incomplete for full information concerning, 224n; change in character of, 225

Slave labor, 48-49; superior to Northern labor system, 49; unfitted to new Virginia agriculture, 50; in great demand in iron and tobacco manufacture, 54-56; in internal improvements, 55-56; dearth of, 62-63; high cost of, 63-64; increase of, in tobacco factories, 65

Slavery, agitation concerning, 7; attacked in legislature of 1831–1832, 9; natural lot of Negro, 12; free Negroes a menace to, 15; extolled by Virginia press, 26; extolled by writers, 27; made open to free Negroes, 31; an economic evil, 37; modification of, 39, 171, 179

Slaves, 3, 8, 13, 21, 24, 32, 170; free Negroes corrupt, 16, 18-19; free Negro right to own, curtailed, 22-23; high prices of, 51, 158; introduced into capitalistic manufacturing, 53; sale of, 64; hired, 65; earn extra money, 159, 179-180; purchase themselves, 183-187; bought by free Negroes and manumitted, 187-191; purchase of property by manumitted, 196-198; migration of manumitted, 198-199; legal status of, necessary to be shown, if living with free Negro, 203n; pledging, as collateral for free Negroes' debts, 207, 207-208n, 209-210; as property of free Negroes hired to other masters, 210-212; hiring of, to work for free Negroes, 212-213. *See also* Manumission.

Slave trade, 56; rise of domestic, 52; assumes extensive proportions, 53

Slaughter, Leander, slave, slaveholder, 186, 187, 220, 225

Smith, Betsy, 214

Smith, Governor, of Virginia, 28, 66, 68, 89

Smith, Henry, 204n

Smith, James L., 80, 83n

Smith, Laura Anna, 113n

Smith, Lomax, 151n

Smith, Robert, 158n

Smith, Samuel, 213

Smith, W. S., 105

Smyth County, 109

Snead, Peter, 85n

Solomon, gardener, 84

Sorrel, Edward, 215

South, industrial development in, 43; defends institutions against Northern attack, 48-49

Southampton County, 7, 12, 39, 70, 72, 75, 108, 112, 115, 127n, 129, 130, 214n. *See also* Insurrection, Slaves, Turner, Nat.

Staunton, town of, 21n, 156, 162

Staunton, Schuyler, boatman, 134

Stephens, Rica, 204

Stevens, Christopher B., contractor, 96n, 160, 219n, 225

Stewart, Anderson, a wagoner, 79, 132n

Stewart, John, 163n, 206

Stewart, Theophilus, 107

Stewart, Thomas, William, John, Dempsey, farmers, 107, 133, 133n

INDEX

Stockdell, John Y., cotton mill owner, 38
Stone masons, numerous in Fauquier County, 80
Stone, Samuel, farmer, laborer, 134
Stringfellow, Thornton, proslavery advocate, 9
Sublett, James B., 186
Suffolk, town of, 137; gains in property ownership in, 152
Sullivan, Mary J., seamstress, 158n
Surry County, 14n, 70, 111, 115, 119n, 120, 124n, 129, 210n
Susannah, liberated slave, 172
Sussex County, 57, 71, 73n, 74, 115, 116, 118, 119, 120, 129, 131, 135, 136, 204n, 208n; citizens petition legislature, 83; acquisition of property in, 117; acts of manumission in, 175
Suttle, John, 203n
Swann, Mary Jane, slave, 191

Tanneries, few operated by free Negroes, 81
Tappahannock, town of, 218n
Tarrant, Caesar, pilot during Revolution, 152n
Tarrant, Nancy, owner of bounty land, 152n
Tate family, 104
Tavern keepers, 81, 131
Taxation, on slaves owned by free Negroes, 200-201; on property of free Negroes, 226-229; capitation, 228
Tayburn, Luke, 96n
Taylor, F., colonizationist to Liberia, 148
Taylor, Sarah F., 222
Tazewell County, 109
Teague, Colin, colonizationist to Liberia, 146
Teamsters, ownership of farms by, 134; ownership of property by, 157
Thom, Reuben T., 186
Thomas, Chaney, and children, 103n
Thomas, Fortune, shopkeeper, 81
Thomas, Lydia, 206
Thomas, Russell, grocer, 156, 221
Thompson family, 114
Thompson, Samuel, farmer, 132
Tidewater section, 8
Tinsley, church deacon, 96n
Tinsley, Easter, slaveholder by inheritance, 223
Tinsley, Rebecca, slaveholder by inheritance, 223
Tobacco factory hands, most numerous class of workers, 94-95; few property holders among, 158
Town lots, ownership of, 102; advance in, 137-138; acquired by purchase, 138-139; Fredericksburg, 139-141, 154-155; Falmouth, 141; Norfolk, 141-142, 153-154; Richmond, 142-143, 150-152; Lynchburg, 143-144; Petersburg, 144-145, 149-150, 152; proportion of, low in 1830, 145-149; Winchester, 152; Suffolk, 152; Hampton, 152-153; Williamsburg, 153; Portsmouth, 153; Alexandria, 155
Trade, Virginia cities tributary in, to New York, 35; unadvanced in Virginia, 47
Transportation. *See* Internal improvements.
Traylor, Richard, 166n
Tredegar Iron Works, 43; as employer of hired slaves, 178, 198-199
Trent, Thomas, shoemaker, 134
Tucker, Samuel, farmer, 130
Turner, Lewis, 119, 208n
Turner, Nat, 7, 13, 21
Tyler, Carrington, ditcher, 134
Tyner, Uriah, blacksmith, 99n, 144, 144n, 162n
Tynes family, liberated slaves, 116, 125
Tynes, Joseph and John, farmers, 130n
Tynes, Timothy, farmer, 116n, 125

INDEX

Updike, John, boatman, 79, 193, 197, 212n

Valentine, Beverly, farmer, 82
Valentine, James, 4n
Valley of Virginia, 8
Vandervall, Nelson, plasterer, 158n
Vaughan, George, factory owner, 74
Venie family, 114
Vick, Osborn, storekeeper, 81
Viney, James and Joseph, farmers, 22
Virginia, hostility to free Negro in, 3, 17; swings to proslavery ranks, 7, 49-50; free Negro doomed to adversity in, 11; migration of free Negroes from, 25-26; position of, dubious in the field of economic endeavor, 34-37; economic progress of, 37-48, 158; economic revival affects labor system in, 48-61; free Negro labor finds a place in, 61-68, 101; freedmen struggle for permission to remain in, 124; free Negro farmer a reality in, 136; heyday of free Negro economic prosperity in, 164; manumission of slaves in, by periods, 173-174; slave hiring in, 179-181
Vizzoneau, Mary Ann, 187

Wages, free Negro, apprenticeship, 72-73; no money payment for, 73, 103; cash payment for, 103, 103n; upward trend of, 158-159
Wagoners, valuable to communities, 79; in Mecklenburg County, 83
Walker, Dr. B. H., hires out slaves, 177
Walker, Jane, 211
Walker, William, shoemaker, 149, 210, 211
Wallace, Ann, seamstress, 158n
Wallis, James, 106
Ward, John, manumits slaves, 123

Waring, Colson, missionary to Liberia, 144n, 146, 148, 149
Warner, David, 84n
Warren, Charlotte, 165n
Warren County, 109
Warren, John, bricklayer, 158n
Warrenton, town of, 218n
Warwick County, 130
Washerwomen, important bread winners, 93, 101
Washington, D.C. *See* District of Columbia.
Watkins, David, 215
Watts family, 119n
Welborne, Madison, farmer, 131, 131n, 132
Well diggers, numerous, 80-81
West, James, blacksmith, 140
West, Reuben, barber, slaveholder, 151, 151n, 156, 220
Westmoreland County, 70, 73, 108, 111, 118; citizens petition legislature, 14, 62; farm tenantry in, 104
What Shall Be Done with the Free Negroes?, anti-free Negro pamphlet, 27
Wheelwrights, 95; comparatively few in number, 80
Wheely, William, shoemaker, 134
White, Ackey, drayman, 62, 63, 154, 157, 220
White, Anthony and Milly, 166n
White, Edward, drayman, 154, 157, 220n
White, Eleazar, hack driver, 220
Whitehead, Colgate, 108, 130
Whitico, Thomas, hirer of slaves, 212
Wiles, John, shoemaker, 141n
Wilkerson, Cyrus and Ned, farmers, 129, 129n
Wilkerson, Henry, farmer, slaveholder, 209, 210n
Wilkins, James, 140, 141n, 190
Wilkins, Samuel, slave, 187
Wilkins, Sarah, slave, 190
William, apprentice, 73
William, slave, 64

Williams, Colin, slave, 190
Williamsburg, gains in property ownership in, 153, 162
Williamson, Billy, 86
Willis, Nancy, slave, 194
Wills, bequest of property by free Negroes to relatives in, 118-121, 140-143, 151, 164-166; bequest of property by white persons to free Negroes in, 121-127; bequest of property by free Negroes to organizations in, 166; bequest of slave property by free Negroes to free Negroes in, 208-209, 213-214, 223-225; bequest of slave property by white persons to free Negroes in, 222-225
Wilson, Armistead, blacksmith, 157, 196, 218, 225
Wilson, James and Charles, 121
Wilson, Robert, 175
Winchester, 97, 137, 155, 156; citizens petition legislature, 86, 99-100; gains in property ownership in, 152; manumitted Negroes acquire property in, 198, 221
Winn, Hubbard, slave, 184
Wisconsin, 59
Wise, Governor, of Virginia, 28, 89
Wise, Henry A., 85
Woodchoppers, numerous, 80
Wythe County, 109

York County, 70, 79, 119, 202n, 208; farm tenantry in, 105
Yorktown, 207

(1)

www.ingramcontent.com/pod-product-compliance
Lightning Source LLC
LaVergne TN
LVHW091532060526
838200LV00036B/583